Catholic Beginnings in Oceania

Marist Missionary Perspectives

Edited by Alois Greiler SM

The Marist Series
Through the Marist Series the Society of Mary (Marists) shares projects by Marists in the field of theology and history and works about the role of the Marists in the church, in particular in the Pacific.

Series Editor: Alois Greiler SM

ISBN: 978 1 921511 547

Cover design by Astrid Sengkey

Original photographs:
Front cover
L. Verguet, New Zealand Maori: General Archives of the Society of Mary (Marist Fathers), Rome, Italy and photo of the desk by Bernd Kordes SM, France.
Back cover
'The True Vine': Diocesan Archives of the Catholic Diocese of Auckland, New Zealand; photo taken by Mervyn Duffy SM, Auckland.

ATF Press

An imprint of the Australasian Theological Forum Ltd
PO BOX 504
Hindmarsh
SA 5007
ABN 90 116 359 963
www.atfpress.com

Contents

Preface

New editions of sources enable us to revisit the origins of the Catholic Church in Oceania and to discover who was behind the foundations of the Catholic Church in the emerging Pacific.

Considering the geography is important. We are looking at a third of the world, a region of 180 million square kilometres. The huge distances created immense problems of communication and logistics.

The many Pacific islands have many founding stories. We look at the islands within a triangle of thousands of kilometres originally called the Vicariate apostolic (forerunner of a diocese) of Western Oceania: from New Zealand to Samoa to Papua New Guinea. For Catholics, these stories go back to members of the Society of Mary and the man who sent them out as religious: Jean-Claude Colin. Colin accepted to staff this mission on 10 February 1836. This is the second triangle presented in this book—the Catholic Church, Marists, and Colin. A third triangle links the mission to the world church—Jean-Baptiste Pompallier as the first Catholic bishop, the Pope in Rome, and again Colin who negotiated with both in the interest of his men and the mission. And that had not been easy.

We go back in time to the first half of the Nineteenth century.[1] From the Eighteenth century on, James Cook and French explorers created a certain image of the Pacific in Europe. From 1800 on, Europeans and Americans gradually infiltrated the Pacific Islands as traders, adventurers, whalers, and immigrants. This caused various nations to establish colonies or zones of influence.

The Christian churches saw the newly discovered islands as places to begin Christian life and at the same time to bring what they saw as their unique message of eternal salvation. At the beginning, French Catholics, however, were still missionaries in their own country because of the French Revolution of 1789, the Napoleonic wars (1799–1815) and the 1830 revolution.

Before and after 1800, we find various missionary revivals in Anglican, Protestant, and Evangelical circles resulting in missionary societies. In 1797,

---

1.   See Charles W Forman, *The Island Churches of the South Pacific. Emergence in the Twentieth Century* (Maryknoll: Orbis Books, 1982), 1–13; John Garrett, *To Live among the Stars. Christian Origins in Oceania* (Geneva – Suva: World Council of Churches and Institute of Pacific Studies, 1982); Ralph M Wiltgen, *The Founding of the Roman Catholic Church in Oceania, 1825 to 1850* (Canberra, 1979); Claire Laux, 'Introduction historique', in Charles Girard (editor), *Lettres des missionnaires maristes en Océanie 1836 – 1854* (mémoire d'églises) (Paris: Editions Karthala, 2008), 19–70.

the London Missionary Society reached Tahiti. In 1820, the American Board of Commissioners for Foreign Missions (Boston) reached Hawaii. The Church Missionary Society came to Australia in 1820 and New Zealand in 1825. Methodists began in Tonga in 1826. Missionary activity spread from East to West with the Protestants as well as with the Catholics. Far away from the ecumenical age we live in, this caused rivalries and damage to the Christian message. However, it also created a Christian plurality.

The arrival of Catholic missionaries, first in Eastern Oceania (Picpus in 1827)[2] and then Western Oceania (Marists in 1837–38), added to the complicated situation. Catholics were ultimately directed by the centre in Rome, where the Pope acted through his missionary agency, Propaganda Fide (today Congregation for the Evangelization of Peoples).

The original vicariate of 'Western Oceania' has developed with a growing Church into other vicariates and—after 1966—dioceses. Once strongly French, the Catholic Church has become Pacifican.

This book offers the context to 8,000 pages of missionary letters now edited, material that will influence Pacific studies.[3] It is the fruit of the international symposium in Suva, Fiji, 5–10 August 2007[4] and focuses on the French presence, the Catholic beginnings, and the missionaries who were mostly Marists. Their contribution to the origins in Oceania is sometimes undervalued. Outside the Pacific this story is little known. These contributions offer a summary of research and explore some critical issues involved.

The book is organized into four sections. The opening section gives stories and an overview of the main actor and events. The second section highlights Colin's role in Rome and the foundations in the Pacific. A third section presents to us the men and women - some famous, some 'invisible' in their ministry. We look at the Marists, the priests, the religious brothers and sisters who came from France as missionaries. The first community of brothers was founded in 1817, of sisters in 1823, of priests in 1824.[5] They came as the Marist family—all

---

2. The Picpus or Congregation of the Sacred Hearts of Jesus and Mary and of the Perpetual Adoration of the Blessed Sacrament of the Altar (SS.CC): founded in 1800, approved in 1817. In 1833 they arrived on the Gambier Islands.

3. See the presentation by the editor, Charles Girard, in this volume. Complementary to his work are the letters of the Marist Brothers (Edward Clisby) and the Marist documents concerning France, edited by Gaston Lessard as *'Colin sup'*.

4. A similar symposium was held in Auckland, New Zealand, 27-29 July. The short papers presented at both symposia are published in the Marist journal *Forum Novum*, 8-9 (2008).

5. Marist Fathers (with non ordained members, the brothers), Marist Sisters (SM),

belonging to a new project planned in 1816 in Lyon which originally wanted men and women in one congregation for which Rome refused approval. Today they are independent congregations with the additional branch of the Marist Missionary Sisters (SMSM). They present a model of collaboration between lay and religious, men and women. A fourth section confronts us with underlying issues: the personality of Colin, the man behind the missionaries, their concepts of Church, contact with non Catholics, mission, and culture. A summary gathers the research done and points out where the 'Letters from Oceania' can yield even more fruit.

Reading each contribution is like moving from island to island—each distinct, each with its own founding story. Thus, the diversity of the presentations recalls the richness of the 'Church of the Thousand Islands'.

Various archivists contributed to the research. We thank Carlo-Maria Schianchi SM, Rome, for providing the illustrations. The copyright for the 'True vine' image was given by Bruce Bolland, Auckland, Diocesan archives, June 2008.

A heartfelt thanks goes to the authors and translators. *The Australasian Theological Forum*, Adelaide, has enabled us to share the results with a wider public.

Rome, 10 February 2009, Alois Greiler SM

Marist Teaching Brothers (FMS), and Missionary Sisters of the Society of Mary (SMSM, origins with Françoise Perroton in 1845, papal approval in 1931).

Abbreviations

Much of the Marist material was published by the general house in Rome of the respective congregation of the priests, teaching brothers, sisters, or missionary sisters.

APM = Archivio Padri Maristi, General archives of the Society of Mary, Rome, Italy

Colin sup = Gaston Lessard (editor), *'Colin sup'. Documents concernant le généralat du père Colin*, volume 1, *De l'élection au voyage à Rome (1836–1842)*, Rome, 2007.

FS = Jean Coste (editor), *A Founder Speaks. Spiritual Talks of Jean-Claude Colin (1790–1875)*, Rome, 1975.

FA = Jean Coste (editor), *A Founder Acts. Reminiscences of Jean-Claude Colin by Gabriel-Claude Mayet*, Rome, 1983.

FN = *Forum Novum* (1990ff). Journal of the Society of Mary with studies on Marist history, spirituality and the life of the congregation.

LRO = Charles Girard (editor), *Lettres reçues d'Océanie par l'administration générale des pères maristes pendant le généralat de Jean-Claude Colin*. A provisional edition of three volumes documents and one volume indices was printed in a limited number in 1999 (Rome, APM). Researchers could use a later provisional electronic version of the full edition (10 volumes). The final edition will be published in 2009.

Mayet = Gabriel-Claude Mayet sm (1809–1894), *Mémoires*, 11 notebooks, c 1837 – 1854, quoted with volume and page number, APM, Rome.

OM = Jean Coste - Gaston Lessard (editors), *Origines Maristes (1786 – 1836)*, 4 volumes, Rome, 1960 – 1967.

LO = Edward Clisby (editor and translator), *Letters from Oceania. Letters of the First Marist Brothers in Oceania 1836–1875*, ten parts, Auckland, FMS, 1993–2005.

Beyond the Horizon! Suva Colloquium 2007

Rafaele Qalovi SM

Oceania covers a third of the globe. The Marists were the Catholic pioneers in New Zealand, Polynesia and Melanesia. This colloquium discusses the experiences of the first missionaries, their relationship with other churches, the political context, and the reception of the Gospel in local cultures. All the studies are expected to relate their topics to the life of the Church of today.

The contributors and participants come from New Zealand, the Pacific, America, Africa and Europe.

Where do we meet to talk about the Catholic Church in Oceania? In Oceania itself! This reflects the importance of this local church for the Society of Mary and the Church in general.

Indeed, from the very beginning of its existence, the Society of Mary is inevitably linked to Oceania. Why was Colin willing to sacrifice from the very start many of his best men? Why did he accept to direct worldwide logistics in a century when this was an immense task? Why did he accept so many difficulties, deaths, criticism? Because the Church had asked him. And he responded.

God does not privilege one region to be the centre of Christianity. History shows that centres shifted: from Nazareth to Jerusalem and to Rome. Today the Pacific has a lively Christian community. It faces its own challenges in ecology, justice, ecumenism and sects. Will this keep us from reaching out? Do we see our island only—is our horizon the end? Islanders have a long tradition of traversing a sheer endless sea in big canoes. They followed the stars and found new places to live and dwell. Do you sense the biblical image which easily can be associated with this Pacific tradition? All local churches have members serving the local church and members accepting a call beyond. We look back on a tradition fully human—enough human failings existed. In faith we see a tradition reflecting the mystery of Christ, fully human and fully divine. The inspirations of the origins may sustain fidelity to our mission today in this local Church of the thousand islands.[1]

---

1.   Excerpt of the speeches by Father Qalovi at the *sevusevu* or formal welcome and at the closure.

The Early Marist Missionaries in Fiji and in the Pacific

Ratu Filimone Ralogaivau, Fiji

I am present not only as representative of the indigenous of the Vanua o Viti but also, in a sense, I am representing all the indigenous communities of the Pacific.

I am delighted that the topic of the early contacts between indigenous communities and the early Marists is the subject of scholarly papers being presented in the colloquium and I am delighted that this colloquium is taking place in the Pacific. This is the first time that such a colloquium has been held outside of Rome.

It is hard to realize, much less to describe, the struggles and trials so bravely borne and the victories so nobly won by the heroic band of French Marist missionaries, who have been the pioneers of spreading Christianity in the Pacific and in particular the Fiji Islands.

Their sufferings and struggle were great, in some cases they were rewarded with the crown of holy martyrdom.

The Fiji group consists of over three hundred islands of which two hundred islands are inhabited by indigenous Fijians. Missions were therefore spread across a wide area. The isolation caused these missionaries to be very much separated from each other and, as such, all communications had necessarily to be carried on by sea.

My ancestral tribal clan in Solevu on the island of Vanua Levu had witnessed a vision consisting in a bright light which resembled the cross in the middle of a dark night. A tribal priest by the name of Vodivodi was summoned by the chief to explain the phenomena which had appeared the previous night. Vodivodi advised the chief and his clan that the sign indicated a new type of religion which would arrive some years later. They were to do away with the old tribal religion of worshipping their ancestors and to adopt the new religion.

The priests of the new Christian religion had settled in Levuka on the island of Ovalau. Vodivodi advised the chief that some men travel to Levuka to bring back the priest of the new Christian religion.

After travelling by sea in a dugout canoe for three days and three nights, the men arrived in Levuka and immediately arranged an audience with the Tui Levuka, the paramount chief of Ovalau.

During this period the Tui Levuka was well liked by the white settlers and was often referred to as the friend of the white people.

Tui Levuka introduced the men from Solevu to Father Jean-Victor Favier (1816–87) who was the younger priest of the two French missionaries who arrived in Fiji in the early 1850s.

The men from Solevu narrated the vision resembling the cross which they saw during a dark night in Solevu to Father Favier.

Father Jean-Baptiste Bréhéret (1815–98), the priest in charge of the mission in Levuka, was absent. When he heard the request of the men from Solevu to take back with them Father Favier, he feared for the life of the young priest and refused to entertain their request. Father Favier insisted that he must spread the Good News to the remote island of Vanua Levu as he believed the story told by the natives.

Our ancestors were living through a violent period of bloodshed and cannibalism, and they took a leading part in all its horrors. They raised themselves to be the champions of its savagery against the newly introduced Christian religion and culture of the western world.

That they emerged in later years as refined people, courtly and dignified, and trusted friends of colonial administrators would be testimony both to their native qualities and to the power of the Christian religion.

The indigenous Fijians could be most ferocious. However, Father Favier gave such a strong example, coupled with untiring energy and patience, that gradually the chief and the people of Solevu adapted themselves to Christianity.

A commander of a gunboat before commencing to fire upon the villages sent one of his boats to convey Father Favier on board, who was the only white mean in the place. The answer the heroic priest sent back was as follows:

> I decline to go on board and desert my post. These men, whom in the ill-used name of justice, you would ruthlessly destroy, are my converts—my children before Almighty God! I have cast in my lot for many years with them; I have lived with them, have attended to them in health and in sickness and must be present to attend and minister to them when dying as you may shoot down. If needs be, I must die with them!

Words such as these show the spirit that animated and sustained these holy men.

Cannibalism is a thing of the past, and instead of the savage war dance and festivals when all those captured in civil wars were slain and eaten, we have today processions of the Most Blessed Sacrament and the Stations of the Cross in beautiful churches, attended by crowds of converts, eager in the pursuits of the new faith imparted to us and our ancestors by those zealous and untiring 'men of God'.

In conclusion, we are thankful to the Marist missionaries for establishing schools in rural areas in an effort of improving the welfare of the indigenous community. This includes the promotion of higher standards of living through the building and upkeep of schools, better sanitation, better housing, water supply and even the planting of food crops. This also functioned as a system empowered by law to organize some of the activities of the Fijian people for their own social, economic and political development, as well as for the preservation of their traditional way of life.

Studying Colin, the Marists, the Catholic Church and Western Oceania

Alois Greiler SM

I shall go myself

Jean-Claude Colin (1790–1875), superior general of the Society of Mary, never went to the Pacific. In 1843 he said he would go if things were to get precarious: 'I am ill, I have no strength, I need a year of complete rest but if I see things flagging I shall go myself. Were I half-dead, in such a situation I would rise again.'[1]

In the event it was good that he did not go. He felt Oceania was strong enough to solve its own problems. His main concern was its future. In 1842 he said that if only for the work in Oceania—this would be reason enough to justify the existence of this little Society:

> Now the two islands of Wallis and Futuna have been converted
> . . . I am not thinking of the number of islanders they have won
> over, but the succession of generation upon generation to whom
> the faith will be communicated, generations of whom they are
> the first apostles. Messieurs, if the Society had achieved no other
> good but that, we should count ourselves blessed and sing from
> dawn till dusk, and from dusk through the night till dawn: 'I
> shall bless the Lord at all times'. Ah yes, if we had not come to
> be, this good would not have come to pass.[2]

A colloquium in 2007: too late or too early?

About 170 years ago these apostles, the first Marists had arrived in the Pacific. The approbation of the Society of Mary and the foundation of the Catholic Church in Western Oceania went hand in hand. How exactly the two events were linked is still an open question.[3]

---

1. Jean Coste (editor), *A Founder Speaks* (Rome, 1975; FS), Doc. 73, 2 (1843). See Gaston Lessard (editor), *Colin sup*, Rome, 2007 (= *Colin sup*), Doc 255, for his thought to do pastoral work in Oceania. But he was too old to go.
2. FS, Doc 73.2 (1843).
3. We have two approbations: the wider Marist family—the branch of the priests. Did Rome approve the priests only because of Oceania? Did Colin opportunistically accept the offer or was he forced into it (by Cholleton and Pompallier, see Jan Snijders, *A Piety to Cope*, private paper, 2007)?

About fifty years ago, a new effort was launched towards the beatification of Colin.[4] Questions were raised about Colin and the Oceania mission, his relationship with Bishop Jean-Baptiste Pompallier (1801–71), the first apostolic vicar.

About forty years ago, New Zealand Marist Kevin Roach produced a good thesis on Colin and New Zealand.[5] He continued a great Marist tradition of men like Mangeret, Monfat, Dubois, O'Reilly and Rozier. Roach had no successor in Rome and Marist research focused on origins in France.[6] The edition of Charles Girard answers this desideratum. Now the question is: Will we read these texts? Who will translate them—from French to other languages, from the past to the present?

About four years ago, the Society of Mary leadership team decided to focus on Colin's generalate and to organize a colloquium on Oceania.[7] Already Colin had organized study conferences. Now we meet for the first time in Oceania.[8] We pay our respects to a Marist region which is of great significance for the Society. Today Oceania is sending out missionaries! The Society has grown in internationality.[9]

The 2007 colloquium has as its theme for reflection: *Colin and Oceania: The Superior General of the Marist Fathers and his Role in the History of the Roman Catholic Church in Western Oceania*

---

4.   Marists from the various branches working on the causes of Chanel, Colin, Champagnat, and Chavoin initiated the new era in Marist studies. *Origines Maristes* (= OM), *Colin sup*, *Lettres reçues d'Océanie* (= LRO) and so on are presented according to the criteria of the required historical-critical presentation of sources for the Vatican. The article by Jean Coste, 'Brief History of the Cause of Father Colin', in *Forum Novum*, (FN) 5/3 (2000): 308–314, and the decisions of the chapters since 1985 show how undecided the Society is about a possible beatification. Some of the obstacles have to do with 'Colin and Oceania'.

5.   Kevin Roach, *Venerable Jean-Claude Colin and the Mission in New Zealand, 1838 – 1848* (thesis, Rome, 1963); see Coste, 'Cause of Father Colin', 311.

6.   Alois Greiler, 'From Jeantin to Coste: A Survey on Marist Studies in the 20th Century', in FN 7/1 (2005): 38–71, here 51.

7.   Presentations published in *Forum Novum* 7/1 (2005).

8.   Alois Greiler, 'Between History and Spiritual Renewal: A Survey of Recent Marist Studies', in FN 5/3 (2000): 315–41, here 332-4; Jan Hulshof, 'Marist Studies and the Future of the Society', in FN 7/1 (2005): 5–20, here 19.

9.   The Society of Mary was dominantly French until about 1926, especially in Oceania. See Philip Graystone, *A Short History of the Society of Mary. 1854 to 1993* (Rome, 1998), 75.

Let me outline the elements to point to some hermeneutical criteria which I regard important for a study of our topic.

Jean-Claude Colin (1790–1875)

Colin: His life and generalate

Jean-Claude Colin was born in 1790, in the era of the French Revolution and the restoration—events significant for the founder. Donal Kerr summarized the story up to 1836.[10] During this period Colin was re-acting. In the following period he was a main actor.

In 1836, after twenty years, the Marist group won papal approval. At the same time the Pope entrusted to them the new mission of Western Oceania. The Pope's request met with Colin's acceptance. He sent out many of his best men — those excellent in virtue and spiritual life. Yet, he did not send administrators. A good administrator present from the start could have helped. Later, Father Poupinel (1815–84) came and did much good work.

The years of his generalate may be summarized in two periods of roughly the same length: 1836 to 1845 and 1845 to 1854.[11]

From 1836 to 1845 foundations were laid in France and in Oceania. Colin was involved in the beginnings of the priests, brothers, sisters, laity and missions. There was no established structure for recruiting, finance, formation, or ministries. Only twenty priests made profession in 1836. By 1840 there were about ninety Marists in France and thirty-three in Oceania—a big percentage for a small group. Yet, within these small numbers, it is quite astonishing what they achieved on both sides of the world. In 1845 the Marists had a name. In Oceania, Wallis and Futuna had become Christian. In New Zealand the Catholic community was established, even if struggling. Those were the years of the pioneers.

From 1845 to 1854 Colin tried to solidify the foundations. We have the first general chapters, his work on the constitutions, formation programmes, and new ministries. In formation they learned some English in preparation for the missions. He tried to safeguard the spiritual dimension already overshadowed by much activity. This is why we have the Marist retreat house at La Neylière

---

10. Donal Kerr, *Jean-Claude Colin, Marist: A Founder in an Era of Revolution and Restoration: The Early Years 1790 – 1836* (Dublin: Columba Press, 2000); Jean Coste, *Lectures on Society of Mary History (Marist Fathers), 1836 – 1854* (Rome, 1965).
11. See FS, 6f, for a general outline.

and the rule that a Marist community is not to have fewer than four priests and brothers.

To name but one external influence: France saw a revolution in 1789, in 1830 and again in 1848. Each time this had serious consequences for the nascent Society. Moreover the political situation in Oceania at that time was not at all clear either.

In 1854 Colin resigned as superior general. He had achieved much but had not achieved everything. The structural problem of the men in Oceania was left to his successor. Colin died in November 1875. On the desk of his room in La Neylière, where he spent his last years, you will find a map of Oceania with his glasses on it. I find this a telling image.

He had to wear many hats, as it were: founder, superior general, pro-vicar for Pompallier, contact person for the donations of the Propagation of the Faith, contact person for Propaganda Fide in Rome,[12] administrator, spiritual guide responsible for the Marists before God and Mary, author of constitutions, formation programmes, Marist liturgy, house rules, director of a school, contact person for home missions and retreats, visitor for convents, collaborator with the Marist Brothers, Marist Sisters and the Third Order,[13] and many more.

Colin was a man of poor health.[14] We find in him times of extreme activity and times of rest. Before ordination he had received the last sacraments twice. In 1842 he caught malaria—in Rome. His stomach was so sensitive, because of many penances, that he could not eat the lovely Italian food. Yet, it seems that challenges brought out in him hidden talents.

Intensive model of mission: religious life
What guided the main founders of the Church in Oceania?[15] David Bosch[16] and others speak of 'models of mission'. Pompallier followed an extensive model, 'cover as many islands as possible'. Colin followed an intensive model: form a

---

12.   See presentation by Carlo-Maria Schianchi.
13.   See presentations by Edward Clisby, Catherine Jones.
14.   OM 4, 523–5; Alois Greiler, 'Krankheit und Entscheidung', in *Id, Inspiriertes Leben: Sechs Hinführungen zu Jean-Claude Colin* (Dessau, 2002).
15.   Roach, *Colin and New Zealand*, 451.452.473: Colin and Pompallier agreed on the aim of personal salvation in principle. See the presentation of Jessie Munro on Pompallier, another key actor.
16.   David J Bosch, *Dynamique de la mission chrétienne. Histoire et avenir des modèles missionnaires* (Lomé, Paris, Genève, 1995). LRO, Doc 304, and *Colin sup*, Docs 268, 274, reflect Douarre's early idea of the diocese of Clermont-Ferrand, the Auvergne, as patronat for New Caledonia like the traditional model of Spain and Portugal.

spiritual centre.[17] He propagated this one generation before Charles de Foucauld (1858–1916).

The first Marist chapter ever, the gathering in New Zealand in July 1841, discussed the daily routine and details on fasting and prayers for the sick.[18] They did not discuss mission policies. By their prayers, sacrifice, witness and actions they testified to the faith. A modern version of this would be the example of Charles de Foucauld,[19] more than the example of Francis Xavier. Colin would ask Saint Francis for his intercession yet he would not follow his method. His background was France, where he could position a religious group, experts in the interior life and *communio* within an active Church body. One mission of the Marists in France has been to pray for the success of the Oceania Marists.[20]

---

17. See the summaries on Marist missionary life in Hugh Laracy, *Marists and Melanesians: A History of Catholic Missions in the Solomon Islands* (Canberra and Honolulu, 1976), 13–9; John Garrett, *To Live among the Stars: Church Origins in Oceania* (Geneva: World Council of Churches, 1982), 97. They can be read as critical commentary about little missionary work—if they are read from the perspective of an active model. They are evident if read along a missionary model of presence, witness and religious life. For Colin, however, the religious community was the *sine qua non*: Roach, *Colin and New Zealand*, 145 (1842); Claude Otto, 'Plutôt trois que deux, seuls jamais! Le Père Colin et l'isolement des missionnaires', in FN 1/3 (1989): 274–294.

18. Jean Coste and Gaston Lessard (editors), *Autour de la Règle*, volume 1 (Rome, 1991), Doc 6 (1841).

19. Jacques Gadille, 'La «transversale» contemplative des modèles missionnaires', in J Gadille (editor), *La mutation des modèles missionnaires au XXe siècle* (Les Cahiers de l'Institut Catholique de Lyon, 12, 1983), 29–38, with the contemplative model (Thérèse of Lisieux, Charles de Foucauld) at the end of the 19th century. This would make Colin a forerunner by one generation. Claude Prudhomme, 'Libermann témoin et acteur des mutations de la conscience missionnaire au XIXe siècle', mentions Libermann and Colin for the latter model in Paul Coulon and Paule Brasseur (editors), *Libermann 1802–1852. Une Pensée et Une Mystique Missionnaires* (Paris: Cerf, 1988), 333–53, about another change of models: Pompallier and Bataillon followed the 1830 romantic model of the spiritual conquest by France. Libermann and Colin represent for Prudhomme a different model: commission by the pope, building of Christianities, global vision of mission, rooted in a profound and personal spirituality.

20. Colin often asked the members of the Marist branches in France to pray for the conversion of the unbelievers in Oceania. This influenced Marist daily prayer, as the invocations added to the prayer after the midday meal show. See *Autour de la Règle* and *Colin sup*.

The New Evangelisation is a modern catchphrase. It seems to focus on action and methods. Little mention is made of religious, of presence, and evangelisation by prayer—Colin's model. And yet, we can see the relevance of authentic example over words. The early Dominicans preached as much by example as by word. Saint Francis told his companions to preach by example using as few words as possible.[21] In other words, the charismatic element contributes to the mission of the Church.

In Oceania the religious were the only priests. Maybe only today we can fully appreciate the Marist vocation now that Oceania too has the triple structure: lay, diocesan and religious. The various missionary groups of the other Christian denominations also experienced the dispute about which method or model to follow.[22]

Colin did not work in the foreign missions like other founders. He did not start a missionary congregation. He founded a religious congregation for personal sanctification and salvation of neighbour—in that order. He contributed on various levels: internal affairs, missionaries and logistics, Marists and the Catholic Church. Pressures were high from all sides in France, Rome and the Pacific. Going slowly, he tried his best. His concept of Marist religious life was his guide more than an interest in a numerical growth of Catholics. Is he a controversial figure or a holy founder? He would not be human and he would not be unique, a man with a specific mission, if he were not both. We encounter his strengths and his weaknesses, and the fruits of this man God chose to make use of.

The Marists and the foundation of the Roman Catholic Church in Western Oceania

Missionary revival in the second half of 19th century France
We know of early Catholic missionary attempts in the Pacific. The post-synodal document *Ecclesia in Oceania* says:

> 7. As early as the sixteenth century, when foreign missionaries first reached Oceania, island peoples heard and accepted the Gospel of Jesus Christ. Among those who began and carried on the missionary work were saints and martyrs; and they are not

---

21.   Brian Lucas, 'Mission and Identity of Faith-Based Organisations—The Role of the Bishops', in *The Australasian Catholic Record*, 84/1 (2007): 45–55.
22.   Examples in Garrett, *To Live Among the Stars*.

only the greatest glory of the Church's past in Oceania but also its surest source of hope for the future. [23]

A lasting start came only in the nineteenth entury. By 1814–15, various (missionary) congregations were re-established: Jesuits, Lazarists, or newly founded like the Picpus, Oblates of Mary Immaculate, and the Marists. After 1817 organisations for the missions are in operation. We have the re-organisation of Propaganda in Rome (1817), Jaricot's Propagation of the Faith (Lyon and Paris, 1822), Zoé Du Chesne's[24] Oeuvre Apostolique (Bordeaux, 1838) and the Papal work of the Holy Infancy of Jesus (1843). The years after 1850 saw more new missionary congregations again: Milan missionaries, Lyon seminary for Africa, Scheut (Belgium), Mill Hill (England), Steyl (Netherlands, Germany), and many others.

Europeans 'discover' Oceania
The sheer size of Oceania alone—one fifth of the globe—explains many of the difficulties of the origins. Christianity came as part of the European expansion. Different missionary societies of the churches of the Reformation arrived at the beginning of the nineteenth century. The Missionaries of the Sacred Hearts of Jesus and Mary ('Picpus') worked in Eastern Oceania (east of Tonga) since 1822. The Marists were sent to Western Oceania: New Zealand, Polynesia, Melanesia, Micronesia, and Papua-New Guinea.

Europeans discovered Oceania slowly on board their ships and on their desks. England and France liked reading the books about world voyages, adventures, and discoveries.[25] From the 1840s onwards, Europeans and Americans established an ever stronger presence in the various islands, changing political and economic structures.

Colin never went there. Did he know about it? The first Marists had a general knowledge of Oceania: the other side of the world, new mission territory, the Picpus were there, Protestants were established on many islands, there was a variety of local religions, islands were isolated with little regular shipping, it

---

23. *Ecclesia in Oceania* (2001): All references are to the text on the website of the Holy See (consulted 3/2007).

24. Georges Goyau, 'Les origines de l'œuvre Apostolique, Zoé Du Chesne', in *Revue d'Histoire des Missions*, 15 (1938): 161–184; Jean Coste (editor), *A Founder Acts* (Rome, 1983) (=FA), Doc 305.

25. John Dunmore (editor), *New Zealand and the French. Two Centuries of Contact* (Waikane: The Heritage Press Ltd, 1990), on the importance of explorers and their books for knowledge of Oceania in Europe.

was expensive to go or live there, cannibalism existed and poverty. Some books dealt with Oceania. The Marist had oral information from Propaganda Fide in Rome, the Foreign Mission Society in Paris, the Picpus Fathers, and from Peter Dillon who had sailed the seas. Returning missionaries, archbishop Polding in Lyon in 1841, returning lay men and the letters of missionaries gave ample data.[26] What did they know about New Zealand? Already in 1839 Colin gave a report to the French government.[27] The report reflects his sources: the letters of the missionaries and the national Catholic journal, *L'ami de la religion*. The report is a plea for support—Colin continuously tried to gather money and material and men. It was written for a purpose. The whole mission was about a goal: conversion to Christianity.

Colin knew little about the Pacific. Still, it made him an expert in the eyes of many others, the French, the Romans and the Irish. When three Oceanians arrived in France in 1840, the journal *l'Univers* addressed the public and the government in naming Colin and the Lyon Marists as the centre for this French mission.[28] We have a series of letters discussing how to bring those Oceanians to Lyon for welcome and training as future catechists of their own people.[29] Only four years after election, Colin was offered to found All Hallows College in Dublin.[30] He had to reject this excellent offer because of lack of men. Still the

---

26.   Knowledge of Oceania in 1836: Leslie Newbigin, *The Relevance of Trinitarian Doctrine for Today's Mission* (CWME Study Pamphlets, 2) (London: Edinburgh House Press, 1963); *Mission Life in the Islands of the Pacific being a Narrative of the Life and Labours of The Rev A Buzacott* (London: John Snow and Co, 1866, reprint Suva, 1985); Peter Dillon, *Voyage aux îles de la Mer du Sud en 1827 et 1828 et Relation de la Couverte du Sort de la Pérouse*, 2 volumes (Paris, 1830); Jules Sebastian César Dumont D'Urville, *Voyage de la Corvette L'Astrolabe, Exécuté par Ordre du Roi, Pendant les Années 1826–1829. Histoire du Voyage*, 5 volumes (Paris, 1830–34); Philippe Vandermaelen, *Atlas universel de géographie physique, politique, statistique et minéralogique* (Brussells, 1827); *Colin sup*, 345, footnote 3, for second hand knowledge about New Zealand in 1840. See Edward Clisby, *Marist Brothers and Maori, 1838–1988* (Auckland, 2001). The brothers also went out with very general knowledge and preparation. In 1841, Colin guessed that by now Wallis and Futuna are catholic, *Colin sup*, Doc 260, 8. Three Sisters of Saint Joseph 'heard that he is sending missionaries to Oceania' and offer to go; *Colin sup*, Doc 250 (1841).

27.   *Colin sup*, doc 100.

28.   *Colin sup*, doc 161, 3 (1840).

29.   *Colin sup*, docs 165–172.

30.   *Colin sup*, docs 187; 189. New Zealand had an expressed need for Anglophone priests (Forest). Pompallier may have heard something from the Irish priest with

offer shows the appreciation he had gained in Europe as part of an international network on missions.

He was aware of his role in the foundation of the Church in Oceania and was grateful for it—in spite of all the difficulties.[31] From 1836 to 1854 he worked hard for it. He made sure to keep source materials.[32] Above all he wanted its success. We should not look only at isolated moments of frustration.

Speaking from the point of view of Church history, or so-called mission history, we can name Colin as one of the many who 'constructed' Oceania.[33] Together with the Roman offices he drafted the outline for apostolic vicariates. He discussed mission policy. So he is something akin to one of the founders of the Roman Catholic Church. The Marists had contributed to the final major chapter of Catholic mission history.

Phases of Marist engagement in Western Oceania
The contribution of the Marists to the foundation of the Roman Catholic Church can be divided into consecutive periods:
- 1837–42: arrival, the pioneers, first success (Wallis, Futuna, New Zealand)
- 1842–62: major crisis and first solutions (two dioceses in New Zealand; new apostolic vicariates); failures like Melanesia (Marists, Milan missionaries); other new initiatives had a very difficult start but led to a Catholic foundation (New Caledonia; Fiji, Tonga, Samoa)
- 1862–96: the second generation tried to stabilise what had been achieved
- 1897: a second attempt to start in Melanesia; mission stations became Church regions or apostolic vicariates; Marist province Germany founded from Oceania
- Since 1966: Apostolic Vicariates became dioceses; Vatican II changed our

---

him, Father O'Reilly. He thought priests from the 'Seminary for Oceania' near Dublin would come to New Zealand; LRO, Doc 313 (3 February 1844), Forest and Colin; Doc 327 (3 May 1844), Pompallier–Epalle.

31. *Colin sup*, Doc 268, 2 (June 1841): Words of Colin to the Marists at Belley: 'Ah! Messieurs, que je serais heureux si avant ma mort je pouvais voir quatre ou cinq vicaires apostoliques dans l'Océanie occidentale! Quel bonheur pour moi si je contribuais un peu à les lui procurer!'

32. See FA, Doc 341 (1846), and Doc 367 (1848). Colin refused an entry in Matthieu RA Henrion, *Histoire Générale des Missions Catholiques Depuis le XIIIe Siècle Jusqu'à nos Jours*, 4 volumes (Paris, 1844–47).

33. Oscar HK Spate, 'The Pacific as an Artefact', in Neil Gunson (editor), *The Changing Pacific: Essays in Honour of HE Maude* (Melbourne: Oxford University Press, 1978), 32–45.

concept of mission and Church; Oceania sends missionaries out; Oceania is the biggest Marist province.

Colin's generalate lasted eighteen years. Four apostolic vicariates had been founded, 117 missionaries sent out, seventy-four priests and forty-three brothers (most of them teaching brothers), three diocesan priests and three laymen.[34] About fifteen of the missionaries died and ten returned to France. Some left the Society, others returned for health reasons or for other appointments (Chaurain and Bernin, having learned English in Oceania, founded the house in London in 1850. This house served Oceania and started the Anglo-Irish province). During this time, Françoise Perroton left for Wallis—the first woman to go.

The Marists evangelised first of all in France. In the second half of the century, a new wave of evangelisation outside France began. Oceania—that is a chapter in the history of all Marist congregations, a family work along the original vision of the one Society. The different branches made their specific contributions.

In 1848, Colin asked Rome to find other, more established congregations, with more members and funds, to work in Oceania. Others hesitated to accept, knowing the difficulties the Marists faced. The Society of Mary was 'hardly established'.[35] This was even more so in 1836. Much was being done in hope: vocations will come, money will come, the missionaries are still alive, the second group will find the first group, and so on. This was expressed frequently in letters and is a significant factor in understanding the slow approach Colin had chosen—in fact, had to choose.

Oceania: advantage or disadvantage for the congregation?
Was Oceania to the disadvantage of the congregation? Would the Marists have grown stronger in Europe without Western Oceania? Colin often wrote 'we are still young and we do not have many subjects. We cannot take on other works because of the missions'.[36]

---

34.   For the layman Louis Perret see the essential biography in OM 4, 326–8.
35.   See *Colin sup* about the 'Société naissante' and the 'église naissante' in Oceania: Doc 260 (1841), and others.
36.   Examples: *Colin sup*, Doc 170 (1840); In 1840, there were about ninety Marists in France and thirty-three in Oceania. However, the figure for France includes leadership, formation staff, novices and students, brothers, and those who left during the year. In 1842, the figures are c ninety-two to forty-one—not much of an increase! (Figures: cf Appendix *Colin sup* on Marist personnel); see Léon L Dubois, 'Requests Made to Father Colin for Foundations Outside of Europe', in

It is true that the growth of the Society in Europe was slow. It is also true that this little group, newcomers in a country full of new religious foundations, in fact profited from its foreign mission. French journals like the *L'ami de la religion*[37] and *l'Univers*[38] and, of course, the mission magazines reported on Colin, the Marists and Oceania. This helped to give publicity, vocations and money to the Lyon missionaries. France supported its new missions. The ordinary faithful gave their pennies to the Propagation of the Faith, religious convents assisted, priests and parishioners left their parishes to join, and the government gave grants, free travel and protection. The approval of the Society of Mary coincided with the acceptance of the Oceania Mission. The Marists in France profited in many respects from their engagement in the Pacific. It is quite clear that many priests and later young men in general joined the Marists because they wanted to become missionaries. The death of Pierre Chanel touched many hearts. The letter by the women of Wallis brought Françoise Perroton and others to join the Third Order and later the Sisters. Marist spirituality strengthened its missionary dimension.

Ever since its beginnings Oceania proved decisive for the development and identity of the Society. Pre-1836 abstract phrases in documents about going 'to whatever shore of the world' took on a new reality. 'Oceania' prefaces the Marist constitutions in the papal brief *Omnium gentium salus*. Oceania made known the Marists in Europe. And the Marists in Europe made known Oceania!

Give back or pass on the gospel?
The Marists brought the gospel to Oceania. So did other Christian denominations. What has the gospel given to the peoples? Liberation or oppression, pain or bread, sadness or joy? The Marists were not the only missionaries and not the only ones to have internal and external difficulties. This nuances some of our problems and the part Colin played. Still, for the Catholic Church in Western Oceania, he was the one responsible.

Walbert Bühlmann, missiologist, pointed to the Pacific as a new centre of the world church.[39] So it is very topical to reflect on the foundations and the future. The same author quotes the English bishop Stephen Neill (1900–84),

---

Acta Societas Mariae, 2/9 (1952/53): 15–21, for other requests Colin turned down.

37. Alois Greiler, 'L'ami de la Religion and the Society of Mary, 1836 – 1842' (research paper, 2004).

38. *Colin sup*, Doc 161 (1840), for the *Journal du Hâvre* on the three Oceanians arriving in France, and *l'Univers* referring to Colin and the Marists.

39. Walbert Bühlmann OFMCap, *Wo der Glaube lebt. Einblicke in die Lage der Weltkirche* (Freiburg/Basel/Wien: Herder, 1978/1974), here 73.

a missionary who wrote on the history of missions: 'If all are missionaries nobody is a missionary, if mission is everywhere mission is nowhere.'[40] Our understanding of 'mission' has changed—both in the sending and receiving churches. The Society of Mary has to review its position.

In 1992 Pope John Paul II was present at a memorial service in memory of 500 years of Christianity in Latin America. This event became famous for its double character: 500 years of Christianity—500 years of colonialism. The story goes that the Indios handed back the gospel to the Pope. They said: You Christians gave us this book. It brought us a lot of pain. We want to give it back!

We are not in Latin America. Still, we face similar challenges. Do we want to give back the gospel? Do we want to give back the Marist charism? Or do we want to pass on the gospel to other people—like Christians did through history?[41] Do we see the Marist charism as genuine expression of a relationship with the divine? We may need reconciliation and a better understanding of each other before we can move forward together in peace and for the good of all peoples. To consider our own tradition, Christian and Marist, Oceanian and European, is a specific challenge.[42] There are two temptations: to see only the good sides, or to see only the bad sides.

The burden of mission history could prevent us from mission today. We do not want to bring Christendom but the gospel. Each culture has to find its own way of doing it.[43]

The colloquium as forum of encounter and exchange

Tapping more sources than one
An old saying has it, fear the man who has read one book only. Hugh Laracy wrote about 'An untapped source—the Marist archives'. Yes, we have a treasure in the Marist tradition and it is time to share this treasure with others. Should I

---

40.   Bühlmann, 315. D Daughrity, Stephen Neill, 'Missions, and the Ecumenical Movement', in *International Review of Mission* 94/375 (2005): 576–584.

41.   For a positive celebration of the anniversary of the gospel in the Pacific: 'Bicentenary of the Arrival of the Gospel in Tahiti: 200 Years of Mission 1797–1997', in *The Pacific Journal of Theology*, 2/17 (1997): 107–110.

42.   Presentation by Mika Paunga.

43.   Markus Büker, 'Europa - ohne Grenzen und ohne Mission? Zur Notwendigkeit und Chance Inkulturierter Mission im Deutschsprachigen Raum', in *Neue Zeitschrift für Missionswissenschaft – Nouvelle Revue de science missionnaire*, 56/3 (2000; Sonderheft zusamme mit 'Zeitschrift für Mission'): 230–42.

add: 'Pacific studies—an untapped source for Marist studies'? In Europe much work has been done on Colin, the Marists and Oceania.[44] The Marists have a great tradition of Pacific studies. Can we bring both together?

The bold facts were followed by a period of interpretation. The complex nature of the nineteenth century Pacific requires comparative studies in various directions. Some of the presentations open this line of thought.[45]

Certain difficulties were not uniquely Marist. The vicar apostolic and religious priests also had difficulties in Manduras, the Manchurai and Oregon in the States.[46] Pompallier himself stated that this was a universal problem. The Marist case together with other cases caused Propaganda to react. The Roman reaction would be in favor of the bishops. Placed in the wider context, the achievements and difficulties of the Marist story would become clearer.

No 'Oceania' but many different case studies

The term 'Oceania' is an artificial term and its usage presupposes some form of uniformity of the region. Of course this is erroneous. There are many islands and all have their own history. The variety of cultures deserves separate studies.

Which role did the missionaries play in the coming of the European culture to the local cultures? The missionaries, at least the Catholic ones, acted on a side stage. Koskinen, who wrote a very important book on politics and missions, speaks of the 'Protestant missions and the Catholic aggression'. The Catholics, that is the French Marists, arrived after the Protestants and this complicated the situation. He also says that at the end, missionaries played a secondary role.[47] Some presentations confront us with individual regions or issues of our topic, such as politics.[48] It is true that Epalle came on a French man-of-war, it is also true that he was offered armed company and that the group was rescued by the soldiers. Still he went without a weapon and prevented any pay back.[49] This is also true and, to me, is a fine illustration of tragedy and at the same time Christian idealism in the best sense of the word.

---

44. Greiler, 'Between History and Spiritual Renewal', 329–30, for indications. There are extensive bibliographies on Pacific studies, many related to Marist issues.

45. Presentations by Broadbent and M Duffy.

46. Roach, *Colin and New Zealand* (around 1845), 426. 541.452.465.498.

47. Aarne Koskinen, *Missionary Influence as a Political Factor in the Pacific Islands* (Helsinki, 1953).

48. Presentations by Broadbent, Laracy and M Duffy.

49. Letter Colin to the missionaries on Woodlark, 24 August 1848, quoted in B Bourtot, *En l'an 1848, la Société de Marie (Pères Maristes)* (Document SM, 72) (Paris: Centre Documentation Mariste, 2007).

A colloquium in the service of the whole Church
There has been an earlier colloquium on Oceania—the Episcopal Synod of
1998. Marist history links the Synod and our meeting. Let me recall a few points
of the Roman meeting. The post-Synod Document *Ecclesia in Oceania* points
to the importance by size:

> 6. The Synod gave recognition not only to a unique area spanning
> almost one-third of the earth's surface, but also to a large number
> of indigenous peoples, whose joyful acceptance of the Gospel
> of Jesus Christ is evident in their enthusiastic celebration of
> the message of salvation. These peoples form a unique part of
> humanity in a unique region of the world.

It fittingly reminds us that religious were the first missionaries:

> 51. The history of the founding of the Church in Oceania is
> largely the history of the missionary apostolate of countless
> men and women religious, who proclaimed the gospel with
> selfless dedication in a wide range of situations and cultures.
> Their enduring commitment to the work of evangelization
> remains vitally important and continues to enrich the life of the
> Church in unique ways. Their vocation makes them experts in
> the *communio* of the Church.

The final paragraph on Mary is more than formal. It reflects the Marist
charism:

> 53. To conclude this Apostolic Exhortation, I invite you to join
> me in turning to the Virgin Mary, Mother of Jesus and Mother of
> the Church, who is so revered throughout Oceania. Missionaries
> and immigrants alike brought with them a deep devotion to her
> as an integral part of their Catholic faith; and since that time, the
> faithful of Oceania have not ceased to show their great love for
> Mary.

In 2001, Cardinal Williams of New Zealand presented the post-Synod document
Ecclesia in Oceania: Evangelisation, media, social work, a Church along the
model of the *communio*-ecclesiology. There is mention of the 'interior life':
'Evangelisation cannot take place without prayer and the interior life in union

with Christ.' Colin would have reversed the order of presentation. First, we live with God. From there all good things come.

With my own glasses . . .

Everybody has his or her own way of looking at things. Recently an Armenian lady told me with great anger about people digging up antique Armenian tombs in the search for gold. She said: 'Oh yes, I saw it with my own glasses!' She meant to say 'my own eyes'. Yet she was even more correct putting it the way she did. Yes, we wear 'our own glasses'.[50]

Our starting point is history, the experience of real people who acted within their limitations. This may help us to accept our limitations, to learn from their stories, and to enrich our life story today. Even more concretely, we refer to Jean-Claude Colin, his role, his contribution and the difficulties he had. Many of the issues discussed around Colin are not exclusively his. Other founders, superior generals and missionaries faced similar challenges. In difficulties— which instruments did he have to fall back on? Letters, silence, withholding from action to avoid accumulating tension, a few visitors from the Pacific . . . He accepted mediators willingly. This is a very modern strategy, to find a non-violent solution to a problem. The colloquium helped to do justice to a man who worked within his limits, the limits of other people and the limitations of a simply very real, very human situation.

History, as a starting point, calls us to avoid the trap of restricting events to the past or copying history directly as model for the present. We also have to be careful of evaluations made in retrospect. We know more than the people at the time could know. An anachronistic reading of the events does not do justice to them and does not help us. Before any study we would have to learn the language of the past, their language first: not only French, but even more, their world of symbols, culture and beliefs. Our study is a translation: the letters of the first missionaries from French to my language; the events of the time to our experience today. Learn languages! Learn to translate in this double sense of the word!

'Col-loquium–communication and insight

A key to understand Colin in leadership is the importance he gave to council

---

50. JC Stobart, *The Grandeur That Was Rome* (London, 1978), 3: 'This is one of the cases which prove that History is made not so much by heroes or natural forces as by historians.'

meetings. Let me call this colloquium an extended council of the Society of
Mary. It is not about administration but understanding.

The scientific community, the dialogue between partners, is one way to
exclude a too narrow perspective. Col-loquium means literally 'speaking with
each other'. For me, this word proposes a methodology. To communicate is the
process to achieve understanding.

At first sight, the colloquium is about history. Well, history is not a thing of
the past! It touches very much our present day life! For Delbos,[51] Colin was the
man before the mission. He was also the man behind and with the mission in all
those years. He may be a man for the future because of his model of spiritual
presence in a pluralist world.

51.   Georges Delbos, *L'Église Catholique en Nouvelle-Calédonie. Un Siècle et Demi
       d'histoire*, with a Preface by Cardinal B Gantin (Paris: Éditions Desclée, 1993),
       21f.

Presentation of *Lettres reçues d'Océanie*

Charles Girard SM

The *Lettres reçues d'Océanie par l'administration générale des pères maristes pendant le généralat de Jean-Claude Colin*—in English, *Letters Received from Oceania by the General Administration of the Marist Fathers during the Generalate of Jean-Claude Colin* cover nine volumes. A tenth volume contains indexes, bibliography, a list of all the missionaries, and other information.[1]

The work is intended as raw material for all who wish to study the activities, experiences and thoughts of the first Marist missionaries outside of Europe. It may also serve for the study of the history of the era, for the ethnology of early (or even first) contacts of Oceanians with people from outside. It is also intended to be of use in the study of particular questions, such as the relationship between Colin and the Oceania missions (namely the Marist personnel and vicars apostolic), as well as the study of the religious life as lived in the missions. The letters also give evidence of the conflict and competition of Protestants and Catholics in the Pacific, in an era before the advent of ecumenism.

Included are all the letters from the Oceania missions sent to (or through) the general headquarters in Lyon—at least, all those which could be found in the archives of the Marist general house in Rome. Obviously, this means the letters sent directly to Colin or the mission procurator, Victor Poupinel (1815–84), but includes letters sent to other Marists as well as to family and friends. The missionaries understood that they were to send all letters to the general house in Lyon, where they were usually read; and, if there was something of particular interest, a copy was written before they were sent on to the addressees. Some are very short, one or two pages; a few are very long, between fifty and one hundred twenty pages in the printed form. The only illustrations are the twenty-four line-drawings which some authors drew in their letters.

---

1. The final edition will be published by Karthala in 2009. On its foundational importance see Hugh Laracy, 'Une Nouvelle Source Documentaire', in *Société d'Etudes Historiques de la Nouvelle-Calédonie*. Bulletin Nr 154 (2008) 87, and 'Girard Joins Beaglehole: A Note on Some New Source Material', in *Journal of the Polynesian Society* 116 (2007): 384. Also Charles Girard, 'Un Important Projet éditorial: Une Collection de Textes Pour l'étude des Peuples d'Océanie « Maudits Européens » ou « Amis qu'on Suivra Partout » ?', in *Histoire & Missions Chrétienne*, no 6 (2008): 191–4. See also the anthology: Charles Girard (editor), *Lettres des missionnaires maristes en Océanie 1836 – 1854* (mémoire d'églises) (Paris: Editions Karthala, 2008).

This is a critical edition; that is, it intends to reproduce faithfully what is written in the manuscript, including the authors' spelling and spelling mistakes. Critical apparatus notes give the variant forms arising from the writer's additions or crossing out of words or phrases. Explanatory footnotes written by your humble servant seek to identify persons named, to explain some items which appear to be obscure in the letters, to note links with other letters in the work, and the like.

All are in the original languages. In ninety-nine percent of the letters, this means in French; there are two in Latin, and about five in English. A few are written in the various languages of Oceania, but with a French translation supplied by the letter's writer. Publication is in the hands of the Society of Mary. It is intended that there be published an anthology of selected texts in French and in English translation.

And finally, a paper edition of the whole work. The letters are given in strict chronological order. This means that letters from different parts of Oceania are mixed together according to the dates when they were written. Volume 10 will provide lists which will enable the reader to find all the letters from a particular island group, from New Zealand, or from the Procure in Sydney, Australia, or to find those letters written by a particular author. The indexes and cross references will facilitate the task of readers who wish to study a particular person or one of the places where the Marists were active at the time.

Most of the letters are quite interesting. Some go into great detail in describing the peoples, languages, and customs of Oceania. Some might even be truly edifying or uplifting. Not a few can be boring to many, unless, for example, one is studying the tools and type-fonts which a printer on Wallis or in New Zealand needs to do his work, or the way financial resources were used in various places. Some offer harrowing details of storms at sea; these letters are from those who survived such perils, but other letters give evidence of the loss of missionaries' lives, notably of Father Michel Borjon (1811–42) and Bother Déodat Villlemagne (1816–42) in waters near New Zealand, and of the three missionaries to Tikopia, Fathers Gilbert Roudaire (1813–52) and Jean-Baptiste Anliard (1814–52) and Brother Michel Anliard (1819–52), who vanished without a trace, most likely lost at sea.

Some are charged with emotion, such as Forest's recounting of the sufferings of the early New Zealand missionaries, or the agonizing declaration by Étienne Chaurain (1819–87), who had witnessed the fatal attack on Bishop Jean-Baptiste Épalle (1808–45), that he was incapable of pardoning the people who had killed the bishop. Again, when in 1854 many of the men noted that Colin had not written to them for over two years and they felt abandoned, we have the petition to leave the Society by Xavier Montrouzier (1820–97), as well as the touching affirmation of fidelity to the Society of Mary by Laurent Dezest (1822–72).

Some of the French missionaries suffered from culture shock when they encountered the peoples of Oceania; these men express revulsion and disgust with the indigenous people. It is different with Father Gilbert Roudaire who extols the Samoans who recognise rights, who obey laws and customs, who have perfect tolerance, hospitality, civil and honest forms of language; they are noted for their devotion to family, relatives, and friends; they have a low crime rate and don't even know about many of the crimes committed in Europe. It is also different with Bishop Guillaume Douarre (1810–53) and Father Pierre Rougeyron (1817–1902), who simply loved the people of New Caledonia, even though these were savage cannibals who caused the Marists to retreat three times from the island to save their lives (Brother Blaise Marmoiton [1812–47] was killed in an attack on the mission station). But three times they came back. While away from New Caledonia, both Douarre and Rougeyron wrote of their longing to return to 'my dear cannibals,' *mes chers cannibales, mes chers anthropophages*. There are many other stories, to be sure, but I can hardly begin to tell them all.

Colin and the Congregation of Propaganda Fide in Rome

Carlo-Maria Schianchi SM

Introduction

In 1835 the apostolic horizon of the little Society of Mary was very limited. Until then it had been happy to remain within France. It is true that in the Fourvière promise of 23 July 1816, the signatories had not excluded the possibility of missionary engagement *apud infideles* (among unbelievers), even if that were implicit rather than explicit. Actually they had written: 'We solemnly promise to spend ourselves and all our possessions for the salvation of souls by every means'.[1] Now such a missionary horizon had suddenly been opened up. By the intervention of several people and institutions, the offer of distant lands in Oceania had arrived on Father Colin's table in Lyon.

Everything had begun in Rome some months earlier in a palatial fifteenth century building on the Piazza di Spagna, the seat of the Congregation of Propaganda Fide, which was entrusted with the task of the evangelisation of peoples who had not yet been in contact with the gospel. This powerful congregation had jurisdiction over a great part of the world, including several countries in Europe. Its power was so extensive roman people would call the Prefect of Propaganda the 'Red Pope', referring to the colour of a cardinal's cassock.

Founded by Popes Pius V (1566–72) and Gregory XIII (1572–85) in the middle of the fifteenth century, in the heyday of geographical discovery, it had since then known ups and downs. It ceased to exist a number of times, and from its inception never had a definitive structure. It was Pius VII, pope from 1800 to 1823, who gave the congregation of Propaganda Fide a solid structure, financial means, and confided to it the task of guiding the new missionary epoch just beginning. The Company of Jesus, dissolved in 1773, was re-established in 1814 and the work for the Propagation of the Faith, founded in Lyon by Pauline Jaricot (1799–1862), was supported by the sovereign pontiff, thus preparing for a new missionary spring. The Camaldulese monk, Cardinal Mauro Cappellari had been Prefect of the Congregation of Holy Propaganda from 1826 until his election as pope on 2 February 1831. Although little prepared for taking charge of the dicastery of Propaganda, he had been able with extraordinary rapidity, to

---

1.   Jean Coste and Gaston Lessard (editors), *Origines Maristes (1786–1836)*(= OM), volume 1 (Rome, 1960), Doc 50.

take over in depth the administration of the aforesaid congregation. In particular he attended to:

1. improving the organisation of the missions
2. setting up new ecclesiastical jurisdictions
3. creating local hierarchies
4. promoting missionary colleges.

The Propaganda Congregation was also engaged in the training of missionaries. It taught them how to approach new cultures: a sort of inculturisation, before that term had been invented and even if its counsels were not always accepted in practice.

For example in a document dated 1659, Propaganda Fide told missionaries expressly:

> Make no effort, employ no means of persuasion to induce these people to change their rites, habits and customs unless these are evidently contrary to religion and good morals. Is it not simply absurd to want to transplant France, Spain, Italy or any other European country into China? This is not what you should introduce, but Faith, which does not reject or injure the rites and customs of any people, but rather tends to safeguard and consolidate them, provided these rites and customs are not evil.

After his election on 2 February 1831 and enthronement on 6 February, Cardinal Cappellari now Gregory XVI was very much in touch with the missionary situation. He made it a priority to communicate to the western Church the tasks and duties of spreading the faith, which until then had been maintained by patronage. The institution of patronage in the missions was exercised by the great colonial powers, Spain and Portugal for example, which in their expansion and conquests asked for the presence of the Church and protected it. This was not for innocent reasons, and had created numerous problems, including sometimes forced imposition of Christianity.

When new colonial powers saw the light of day this patronage ended, and with it the political dependence of the Church on political powers. Propaganda then created the *Commissio Missionum* or *Jus Commissionis*, whereby a mission territory was placed in the care of a single religious order or congregation. In virtue of this juridical instrument, the Society of Mary found itself in charge of the vicariate of Western Oceania.

This new juridical entity had been strongly supported, first of all by the publication of the encyclical letter *Probe Nostris* of Gregory XVI, dated 15 August 1840, concerning the missions; then by the approbation of several new religious congregations, and also by the support of the work of the Propagation of the Faith, Lyon. All that built up massive support for the missionary enterprise.

When Colin commenced contact with the Propaganda Fide in Rome, Cardinal Giacomo Filippo Fransoni (1775–1856)[2] had been prefect of the pontifical dicastery since 1834 and so became the person with whom Colin would liaise. In 1833, Cardinal Fransoni was already a member of the Congregation of Bishops and Regulars. As such, he had no doubt taken part in the session of 31 January 1834 of that Congregation, which had rejected Colin's projected foundation. Although we have no documentary evidence of their meeting on that occasion, it was Fransoni himself who initiated the discussions with Lyon in view of setting up a mission in Oceania. Thus Colin and the Society of Mary in Lyon on the one hand, Fransoni and Propaganda Fide in Rome on the other, became the main players in the missionary adventure in Oceania.

Colin and the Oceania missions

The idea of mission *apud infideles* (to the unbelievers), still less Oceania, does not come from Colin. In 1836 the idea came to him via Fathers Pastre (Lyon), Cholleton (vicar general of the diocese of Lyon), and Jean-Baptiste François Pompallier (1801–71). However, once the mission was launched Colin took over responsibility for developing it. He showed great capacity for understanding the situation, and consequently the people at Propaganda lent an attentive ear to him. Colin was not only a strategist, but above all a spiritual leader.

The great generosity of Colin towards the missions is shown by the fact that he sent his best sons out there. During his generalate he sent out fifteen groups, including seventy-four priests, seventeen lay-brothers, and twenty-six Little Brothers of Mary (FMS). Colin and his missionaries took risks and suffered grievous losses: Chanel in 1841, Epalle on Isabella Island in 1845, Brother Blaise at Balade, New Caledonia in 1847, three members sent to the New Hebrides were lost at sea, and in 1848 Bishop Collomb died of privation in the Solomons.

Colin lived through this difficult situation interiorly. When something happened he would spend nights writing to the missionaries. He would even send a photograph of himself with his letters, so as to reassure them of his

---

2.   See OM, volume 4 (Rome, 1967), 283.

closeness and sharing in their efforts. When bad news arrived he would feel deeply moved, taking upon himself responsibility for what had happened.

Colin not only cared for the spiritual needs of his sons, he made himself above all defender of their spiritual and religious interests. His letters to departing missionaries show most clearly his sense of spiritual fatherhood for them. Here are some of the principles expressed in the letters:

1. missionaries are members of a religious family
2. they are called to life in community
3. living in isolation may not be considered as normal.

On this point Colin constantly fought, not only with the vicars apostolic, Pompallier and Bataillon (1810–77), but also with Propaganda, which was often more interested in opposing advances being made by Protestants in the islands than by guaranteeing the very essence of the religious life for the missionaries. Colin was maintaining:

1. the essence of the Society of Mary as such
2. the conditions permitting religious life, as well as the material and spiritual safeguarding of his missionaries.

The missionaries themselves demanded this much of Colin. In a letter of 22 January 1847, Father Rougeyron (1817–1902) wrote to Colin: 'For the sake of peace, I would remind you also to distinguish clearly the powers of the provincial and the bishop, and in addition to send us a copy of the Rule. Without that we shall loose our religious spirit.'[3]

In chapter VI, article III of the Constitutions of 1872, Colin will seek to address these matters again, without however reaching a very satisfactory conclusion. By then Colin was old and tired and had little reference material at hand, because he had burnt practically all of it.

Faced with the impossibility of getting the vicars apostolic to establish conditions permitting Marists to live an authentic religious life in the Oceania missions . . . they were rather treated like merchandise . . . Colin believed in soul and conscience that he must not send any more Marists out to these missions. After 1847 he will not send any missionary to Pompallier. Even more drastic, between 1849 and 1854, no Marist would be sent to anywhere in Oceania. To be

---

3.   Charles Girard (editor), *Lettres Reçues d'Océanie par l'administration Générale des Pères Maristes Pendant le Généralat de Jean-Claude Colin*, provisional electronic version 2006 (= LRO), 1847, Doc 594.3.

precise, however, several other factors entered into Colin's decision: the political situation in Europe, his exhaustion and frequently repeated announcement of his imminent retirement.

This refusal to send new missionaries aroused among the fathers already in the islands a sad feeling of being abandoned. Father Dezest (1822–72) was in Futuna and on 28 November 1854 wrote to Colin, news of his resignation not having yet reached the islands:[4]

> Dear reverend Father, with deep grief of heart I am undertaking to write this letter to you. This distress is shared by my confreres in Futuna, Wallis, etc. We are constantly asking ourselves where we are in respect to our dear Society of Mary? Has she rejected us from her bosom, as unworthy, harmful members? For what can be the meaning of this abandonment in which she is leaving us?

After his resignation, Colin made a last journey to Rome in the summer of 1854 to deal once again with questions arising from the mission in Oceania. The good order obtained in 1857 for those in the missions will be the fruit of his efforts and struggles.

The Society of Mary had lived through the beginnings of the mission in Oceania with enthusiasm and confidence, as witness this extract from a letter from Bataillon to Colin:[5] 'God knows the feelings this last of your children has for you and how much I deem myself happy to be enrolled in a special manner under the standard of the august Queen of heaven and earth.'

How did they get from this enthusiasm of the beginnings to having the impression of being abandoned? Let us go back a bit and try to understand what happened.

On 10 January 1838, Bishop Pompallier disembarked at Hokianga (New Zealand) with Father Servant (1808–60) and Brother Michael (1812–80). That same year they begin to penetrate to the very centre of the North Island, then to the South at Akaroa, where a French company was installed. In a report to Propaganda, at the beginning of 1841 Bishop Pompallier announced figures of 164 tribes who converted to the Catholic faith: 45,000 catechumens and 1,000 neophytes.

---

4.   LRO, 1854, Doc 1363.
5.   LRO, 1836, Doc 28.

In reality, these apparent successes disguised serious difficulties, because of the too hasty and sometimes imprudent methods by which they had been obtained.

Disquieted by the situation, Father Colin sent Father Jean Forest (1804–84) to New Zealand at the end of 1841 as a visitor. At about the same time he received a long letter from Bishop Pompallier, written on 17 May 1841, and full of invectives. The bishop reproached the Superior General with causing difficulties for the mission by his delays in sending money to the missionaries and by the instructions Colin has given his men. In 1838 and 1841, Cardinal Fransoni himself suggested to Colin that he send more missionaries:

> . . . great care is to be taken to respond to the desires of the excellent bishop (Pompallier). I think it my duty nevertheless to unite my prayer to his so that within the measure of the possible you may respond promptly to the request of the prelate by sending some more zealous missionaries, for whom as he writes, a very abundant harvest has been prepared. I pray then to the Lord that he may grant you a greater joy in everything . . . very attached . . . [6]
>
> . . . recommending urgently to you the request of the prelate to send him as quickly as possible a good number of well experienced missionaries, who will find a vast and fertile land to cultivate, with a most flattering hope for abundant crops. [7]

Given these difficulties, Colin suggests to Propaganda the possibility of subdividing the vicariate. This is how Cardinal Fransoni replies:

> The plan you have suggested, namely, to erect a central vicariate apostolic in the islands of Wallis, Futuna and the neighbouring islands, with a view to lightening the burden for Bishop Pompallier and facilitating the conversion of so many souls seems very opportune to me . . . I would like to have his consent. To this end I should like you to forward the enclosed letter to him, in which I am asking him for his opinion on the proposal. [8]

---

6.   Letter Fransoni-Colin, 10 November 1838, General Archives, Society of Mary, Rome (=APM) 2213/9894.
7.   Letter Fransoni-Colin, 10 April 1841. APM 2213/9905.
8.   Letter Fransoni-Colin, 12 June 1841. APM 2213/9906.

As Colin is waiting for a reply from Pompallier and suspects it will be negative, he comes up with another proposal:[9] 'If My Lord Cardinal will permit me, we will send the next batch of missionaries to New Caledonia, from where the missionaries will quietly penetrate the neighbouring islands.'

Here is the reply from Propaganda:

> Most willingly and with great pleasure supportive of your admirable zeal, the sacred congregation approves the plan of your Lordship to forestall the sowers of darnel in as yet uncultivated regions of New Caledonia, New Britain and numerous neighbouring islands . . . [10]

In face of these evident difficulties ahead, Colin confides to Father Mayet (1809–94): 'Anyway gentlemen, let that not surprise you. In Rome I heard say that all the missions in the world, all the societies occupying themselves with the Missions have also difficulties pending in the Roman court, and much greater than ours. That is how good is always done.' [11]

Letter from Jean-Claude Colin to Giacomo Fransoni, 18 March 1842

Differences of opinion with Pompallier continue to accumulate, as also complaints from the missionaries in New Zealand. So Colin takes up his pen and writes to Fransoni from Lyon on 18 March 1842. It is worth reading some extracts from this letter which show the balance of Colin, and also his straight forwardness and the clarity with which he describes the situation:[12]

> My Lord,
> [1] It is only after long examination that we venture to tell Your Eminence of the petty human troubles which appear to exist between our confreres and the Vicar Apostolic in New Zealand. These troubles have not yet been exactly harmful to the mission. But they could become so if they are not promptly remedied.

---

9.   Letter Colin-Fransoni, 28 December 1841. APM microfilm.
10.   Letter Fransoni-Colin, 29 January 1842. APM 2213/9911.
11.   Mayet, *Mémoires*, volume 4 (= Mayet, number of volume and page), 554. 'Paroles du Père en Novembre 1846.'
12.   Letter Colin-Fransoni, 18 March 1842. APM 2213/9912.

[2] For almost three years our confreres have been complaining in their letters about the harshness of Bishop Pompallier towards them, his threats to suspend them for simple inattentions, about the inspection and censure tribunal to which he wanted to submit their letters, even those they address to the superior of the Society. They do recognize nevertheless his zeal and courage, but they would like to see in that zeal something less extravagant; a better coordinated outlook, a firmer step, less subject to variations and much greater economy in the use of the mission's money.

[3] Recognising over a long time the sensitive character of Bishop Pompallier, the difficulty other confreres have had in fully sympathizing with him, we were not at all surprised at the complaints of the New Zealand confreres, and in our replies we have constantly encouraged them in obedience and patience . . .

[5] In that letter, written no doubt in a troubled moment, after several bitter reproaches which we believe to be quite undeserved, especially our alleged delays over sending him men and money, he finds us at serious fault for authorising our confreres to write to us without submitting their letters for inspection, as is our practice, and he declares in formal terms that in virtue of the Holy See's letter appointing him Vicar Apostolic of Western Oceania, he does not recognize any other superior of his clergy than himself alone; in consequence of this, he forbids us and any other to give advices to priests and brothers of the Society at present, he tells us, exclusively under his authority.

[7] My Lord, we should have adored the will of God with humble and peaceful submission, without complaining, if Bishop Pompallier had only made known his decision to us. But his Excellency [f 103r] threatens to inform all the priests and brothers of the Society of Mary within his vicariate. Thus it is much to be feared that this declaration will upset the whole mission. This is what one of our confreres in New Zealand writes to us, dated 21st May 1841 . . .

[10] After long patience, we have thought it our duty, My Lord, to inform you of these human troubles, and to ask what we have to do in these painful circumstances. The mission in New

Caledonia and to the Kaffirs[13] in Africa will soon require us to have recourse to your Eminence.

[11] I dare to declare myself with profound respect to you, My Lord Cardinal, your very humble and very obedient servant, Colin sup(erior).

In reply, Fransoni underlines among other things:

> I cannot sufficiently praise the moderation of your Lordship and the modesty with which you speak in your letter of 18th March. Recognising the need to counter the ill with a prompt remedy, I am sending the Vicar Apostolic a leaflet exhorting him, which I enclose herewith. When you have taken note of it you will seal it and have it sent to him, in the hope he will change his manner of acting towards you as well as towards the missionaries.[14]

It is interesting to notice the address on this reply from Fransoni to Colin. It helps us to understand how badly the people in Rome knew the name of the congregation founded by Colin: 'Sig Colin Superiore della Società dei sacerdoti sotto il titolo dell'Immacolata Concezione di Maria Vergine detta Maristi, Lione' that is 'M Colin Superior of the Society of priests under the title of the Immaculate Conception of the Virgin Mary called Marists. Lyon.'

Mayet notes what Colin priorities are when he is endeavoring to straighten out the problem with Pompallier: '... and even if he could come to an agreement with Bishop Pompallier, he never had any intention of sacrificing what concerned the salvation of his children and their spiritual interests to Bishop Pompallier.'[15]

Letter Colin to Fransoni of 21 June 1842

What Colin has most at heart is the principle that these missionaries are not secular priests, but religious, maintained by their congregation and a superior general. To affirm this principle, Colin writes again to Fransoni. It is not a long letter, but contains in a clear way the requests to be asked of Rome, requests which at the end of the letter, Colin presents as precautions to be taken for the good conduct of the mission rather than privileges properly so-called:

---

13. Yvan Carré, *Le Projet de Mission Mariste en Cafrerie*, in *Forum Novum*, 8/9 (2008): 20–36.
14. Letter Fransoni-Colin, 2 April 1842. APM 2213/9913.
15. Mayet 4, 557. 'Parole du Père en Novembre 1846'.

My Lord (Fransoni),

Despite privations, dangers and difficulties of all kinds that the Mission of Western Oceania present, the Priests of the Society of Mary placing their confidence in God alone, and relying on the powerful protection of the Queen of heaven, are disposed to devote themselves to the salvation of the unfortunate peoples of this part of the world. But to dissipate some worries in the minds of the missionaries of New Zealand, and to reassure those of our confreres in France who are destined to this Mission, we venture My Lord, humbly to beseech your Eminence to authorize us in the general interest of the Mission:

1 to establish a Provincial in New Zealand to represent the Superior General of the Society, who without prejudice to the jurisdiction of the Vicar Apostolic, may watch over each of the Missionaries in concert with him.

2 to withdraw when necessary a Missionary and replace him with another, having forewarned your Eminence beforehand. Clearly we should not make use of this faculty except for major causes.

3 to require that Missionaries should not normally be stationed in isolation, as they have been in the past for whole years. Charity and prudence strongly demand that they be granted to be at least two or three together.[16]

4 to recall every four years or five years at the most, at least one of the Missionaries to inform Your Eminence and the Superior of the Society concerning everything of interest for the welfare of the Mission and each Missionary.

We think, My Lord, that these precautions are necessary to prevent serious obstacles to ensuring unity of spirit, the apostolic spirit among the Missionaries, and thus to favor the work of God.[17]

---

16.   Claude Otto, *Plutôt trois que deux, seuls jamais! Le Père Colin et l'isolement des missionnaires*, in *Forum Novum*, 1/3 (1989): 274– 294. A letter of Colin to Father. Petit in New Zealand, 18 July 1840, reads: 'I strongly desire that people are not to be isolated. Let there be at least two priests together.'

17.   Letter Colin-Fransoni, 21 June 1842. APM 2213/9911.

In Mayet's *Mémoires*, we find Colin's thoughts expressed with lively determination. We find the image of the Founder staking his all, not for his personal profit but for the good of the Society of Mary:

> It is time to act. They would think us idiots. Propaganda says: it is only Father Colin who acts like that. We must not be looked on as if we were children.[18]
>
> So then gentlemen, if Propaganda does not wish that I bring our subjects back from New Zealand while allowing to continue what can be harmful to their salvation and to the free administration of the Society, I will tell them: Gentlemen, it is not possible that the priests of New Zealand because they have made vows should be in a worse situation than secular priests, who could return from there, and that our Marist priests, because of their vows be obliged to expose their salvation much more than if they had simply not taken vows. So I will release them all from their vows: and they will do what they want![19]

In his letter of 27 June 1842 to Cardinal Fransoni, Colin again insists on the principle of the missionaries belonging to a religious congregation:

> Finally My Lord, I think the missionaries belong to a religious body and cannot completely do good in foreign countries without remaining in dependence on their immediate superior, despite the juridical rights of the vicar apostolic . . . Several superiors of orders share this way of seeing things.[20]

In the decree of the Sacred Congregation of Propaganda Fide of 16 September 1842, the essential points of this letter are accepted and approved:

> *II. Ut Superior Generalis Societatis, cuius Missionis cura commendata est, eum ex missionariis, quem in domino idoneum judicaverit, seligat, atque constituat Societatis ipsius in iis locis Provincialem, cum facultate alios vices suas gerentes pro locorum opportunite subdelegandi, qui concorditer eum Vicario Apostolico* . . .

---

18. Mayet 4, 562. 'Parole du père en Novembre 1846.'
19. Mayet 4, 563. 'Parole du père en Novembre 1846.'
20. Letter Colin-Fransoni, 27 June 1842. APM 2213/9911.

III. Ut idem Superior Generalis gracibus de causis . . .revocare queat unum vel alterum ex Operariis . . .

IV. Ut quolibet Missionarius nun sejunctus ab aliis, nisi in casu necessitatis, et ad tempus, verum cum altero saltem socio, ac si fieri poterit etiam cum duobus aliis Operariis . . .

V. Ut quolibet quadriennio, vel quinquennio . . . unum ex Missionariis advocare queat . . .[21]

(II. That the Superior General of the Society to whom the mission is entrusted may choose among the missionaries whom he judges capable, and appoint him as Provincial in those regions, giving him power to sub-delegate others to replace him as local circumstances may require. This provincial, in agreement with the Vicar Apostolic . . .

III. That the same Superior General may, for serious reasons, recall one or another of the workers . . .

IV. That no missionary be separated from others, unless in case of temporary necessity, but that he be at least with one other labourer and even, if possible with two others . . .

V. That every four or five years, he may call one of the missionaries . . .)

At the level of principles, the problem of relations between Vicar Apostolic and Superior General is the subject of three successive decrees of Propaganda, dating 30 June, 31 August and 16 September 1843. Father Roothaan (1785–1852), general of the Jesuits joined in the elaboration of the last two, which enjoined upon the Vicar Apostolic to direct his correspondence with Propaganda via the Superior General. Father Colin saw in this a source of difficulties and tried in vain to suspend the effects of the text. In fact, this decree did aggravate the unease which will be reported on 9 December 1845.

Concerning the three decrees sent out from Propaganda in rapid succession, Colin comments with humour: 'At Rome they told me that if you put all the contradictory decrees issued by the same Roman congregation on the back of a donkey, it would collapse under the burden.'[22]

When he got back to France, Colin told his confreres the significance of this decree and explained its principles:

---

21.   Decree 16 September 1842. APM, 2214/9911.
22.   Mayet 4, 564. 'Parole du père en Novembre 1846.'

[3] In Rome I asked for a decree in which it was laid down that the vicar apostolic could not post Marists to where they would be alone; they must be three together or at least two.[23]

[4] I want Rome to accept a principle, said Father, that I am superior of the Marists in Oceania (I am certainly not saying that for myself personally). If Rome does not want to recognise this principle, I will say: In that case it seems to me I must examine whether providence is not asking us to abandon the foreign missions. Basically, gentlemen, I know very well how Rome will reply; Rome knows very well that the missions which are prospering are those where there are religious bodies; look at the bishop of the Cape of Good Hope, look at such and such another bishop; for a number of years they have had only three or four priests.[24]

Colin's journey to Rome between 28 May and 3 September 1842 had not produced all the fruits hoped for in clarifying relations with Bishop Pompallier. Colin sent a letter to Propaganda on 27 October in which he dealt with several matters. Among others, he declares very clearly his intention of abandoning the mission in New Zealand. In his response Fransoni reproaches him:

In truth, I do not understand how you can be dissatisfied over your dealings with Propaganda at its general quarters in Rome, when everything has been done to welcome you with great affection, to support your wishes in all ways possible, with the promise of fully pleasing you in those proceedings which cannot, for the moment, be undertaken. But my annoyance was greater than my surprise when I read through the pages you propose to send to Bishop Pompallier. This is to declare a complete break, to cease relations with him and to abandon the mission . . . In case your first affectionate warnings would not succeed, which I can hardly believe, it would not seem suitable to me to have rapid recourse to such an extreme remedy, which would be extremely harmful to religion. It is proper first of all to try other solutions which the Sacred Congregation could attempt in the aforementioned situation . . . I exhort you in consequence with all possible care

---

23.   Mayet 4, 133–4.
24.   Mayet 4, 558–9. 'Parole du père en Novembre 1846.'

to continue to correspond with Bishop Pompallier with the same
spirit of docility, gentleness and peace . . . [25]

The project to divide the original vicariate: 'Overview of Oceania' (May 1842)

Colin sent a plan to Propaganda for the division of the first vicariate and went
in person to Rome in May 1842. He had undertaken the whole work of the
ecclesiastical division of the southern Pacific right from the beginning in 1836.
But the fundamental document on the subject was sent to the Roman authorities at
Propaganda in 1842. Father Jeantin (1824–95), in his biography of Father Colin,
notes in passing: 'this work, which presupposes long and minute studies, was
finished in 1842. He submitted it to Cardinal Fransoni, prefect of Propaganda, in
the following letter, in which shows the flame of strong apostolic zeal.'[26]

It is evident from reading this important document that the father of the
Oceanians had put an incalculable number of hours working on it, because he
shows an exceptional knowledge of the field of the apostolate confided to the
Marist Fathers. We can suppose with a high degree of certainty the collaboration
of Father Victor Poupinel (1814–84), procurator of the Missions in compiling
this work.

In this document, Father Colin gives us the basic reason for all his research
and the subsequent suggestions he thought it his duty to communicate to the
Holy See, in view of the ecclesiastical organization of the islands of the Pacific
Ocean:

> To extend the kingdom of Jesus Christ to the far ends of the earth,
> make the light of the Gospel shine before the eyes of the pagan
> peoples, that is the most ardent desire of Your Eminence; but the
> very special interest you have for the missions of Oceania, and
> the affection you deign to bestow on the religious communities
> which have care of them, makes it a special duty for us to present
> a little account, in which we have tried to collect everything our
> humble knowledge has been able to discover about the present
> condition and immense needs of the peoples confided to our
> frail endeavours . . .

25.   Letter Fransoni-Colin, 10 December 1842. APM 2213/9911.
26.   Jean Jeantin, *Le Très Révérend Père Colin*, volume 3, *Les Missions de l'Océanie*
       (Lyon: Vitte, 1896), 36.

Bishop Pompallier, in New Zealand, is more than absorbed by the urgent needs of those around him to the point that another colleague in the episcopate would be of the greatest usefulness to him, to advance the cause of the truth against the intrigues of error. Until now he has been unable to visit the two priests he had left six hundred leagues away from New Zealand, on the islands of Wallis and Futuna, where Father Chanel has been assassinated. This misfortune, if such it is, must be partially attributed to the impossibility in which Bishop Pompallier found himself of visiting these islands as he had promised the inhabitants that he would. They could have thought he had broken his word, and so the resistance of the chiefs encouraged that of their inferiors.

The account we have reproduced finishes with a note and a wish:

Note: In order to prepare these peoples to receive the gospel, it would be necessary to place at the service of the missionaries, two or three ships manned by Christian captains devoted to this special service. They would go to the different islands, establishing friendly periodic relations, to prepare them to receive missionaries and catechists. They would be charged besides, with bringing help from Europe, correspondence, more evangelical workers. Perhaps also it might be possible to establish by these means a regular service, every year or six months, between Europe and Oceania. In that way what a great facility, enabling the missionaries to receive the gifts of the faithful, and to bring to Europe remarkable things from all these new lands! These means would be in the hands of Our Lord Vicars Apostolic; but they would have to agree in order to get action on them; they have hardly any other way of rapidly advancing the work of God, and paralysing all the efforts of heresy.[27]

In this vast general plan to take the islands of Oceania by assault, so to speak, Father Colin proposed the following general divisions. Notice the astonishing geographical knowledge for that time:[28]

---

27. Letter Colin-Fransoni, 26 May 1842. APM 2213/9915.
28. *Ibid.*

1. The Vicariate Apostolic of New Zealand and islands near at hand
2. The Vicariate of Tonga, Samoa, Viti (or Fidgi) etc
3. The Vicariate of New Caledonia, the New Hebrides, the Solomon Islands
4. The Vicariate of Micronesia and Melanesia.

As well as giving territorial areas very precisely, since he added degrees of latitude and longitude, Father Founder gave details about climate, vegetation, population, etc.

Consulting the *'table of the development of ecclesiastical territories of Oceania'* drawn up by Marist Claude Rozier, one sees that at the retirement of Father Colin in 1854, his plan for each of the ecclesiastical divisions had been carried out, or was in course of being carried out in the case of the Vicariate of Micronesia and Melanesia.[29]

His approaches had a double result:

> - On the territorial plane, a new vicariate was created, one in the centre, which removed Wallis, Futuna, Fiji, Tonga, and New Caledonia from Bishop Pompallier. Furthermore, Pompallier is authorised to choose a coadjutor, which he will do in the person of Bishop Viard (1809–72), who will be appointed on 7 February 1845.
> - At the beginning of 1843, Father Epalle (1808–45) arrived in Europe to report to Father Colin on the state of the New Zealand mission. Bishop Pompallier disavowed him, ordered him not to return, and refused to receive any more Marist missionaries. Hence forward Father Colin will not send anyone to Bishop Pompallier. As to Father Epalle, he was appointed vicar apostolic of the vicariates of Melanesia and Micronesia.

Memorandum of Father Colin, 15 May 1847[30]

In spring 1846, Bishop Pompallier went to Europe to plead his cause in Rome. He arrived there in September. Father Colin went there himself for the fourth time, in November. Both will remain there six months.

Matters were treated slowly. On 1 May 1847, Bishop Pompallier hands in

---

29.   Jean Coste, *Lectures on Society of Mary History (Marist Fathers) 1786–1854* (Rome, 1965), 247–8.
30.   Pierre Allard, *Le Père Colin et les Missions* (thesis, Institut de Missiologie de l'Université Saint-Paul, Ottawa, 1966).

his resignation. But shortly afterwards he begs the Cardinals at Propaganda not to accept it.

Following the resignation presented by Bishop Pompallier, Father Colin writes to Fransoni on 1 May 1847. The secretary of Propaganda appends the following note: *Istanze del sig. Colin Superiore dei Maristi perche sia accettata la rinunzia del Vescovo di Maronea, nuovo progetto di systemazione delle Missioni Occidentali dell'Oceania* (Reasons of Father Colin, Superior of the Marist Fathers, why the resignation of the Bishop of Maronea be accepted, and a new plan for organizing the missions of western Oceania). Colin's plan consists of:[31]

1. creation of an archbishopric at Auckland
2. bishop at Port Nicholson for New Zealand instead of the three divisions proposed by Bishop Pompallier
3. bishop at Wallis, with jurisdiction over the three archipelagos: the Friendly Islands (Tonga), the Navigators and Fiji (Viti)
4. in New Caledonia, a bishop with jurisdiction on this island and over the Hebrides Islands
5. leave Melanesia as it is
6. postpone appointment of coadjutors to another time.

Shortly after this letter Father Colin fell ill and could not present the memorandum to the cardinals of Propaganda until 15 May. In this memorandum he mentions the urgent need for New Zealand to have an English speaking bishop and clergy for English speaking people, because the good of their souls requires that. Then he comes to the ecclesiastical divisions of the country properly so-called: 'In time three or four (dioceses) will be needed. Prudence for the moment seems to advise only two, one French, the other English'.[32] The reasons for this proposal: lack of money, churches, presbyteries, schools, and the still limited population.[33]

In his memorandum Colin replies, among other things, to the problem posed by Pompallier concerning lack of united action among the missionaries. He writes:

---

31.   APM 2341/12591.
32.   Report from 1847, APM 2215/9969.
33.   Claude Rozier, 'Les Missions d'Océanie', in Simon Delacroix (editor), *Histoire Universelle des Missions Catholiques* (Paris: Grund, 1956–1959), volume 3, 375.

To appreciate properly these matters three kinds of unity must be distinguished as being necessary or desirable for the success of any enterprise which requires the collaboration of several people: unity of direction in the one presiding, unity of action and support on the part of the collaborators, unity of feeling on the part of all. For the success of an undertaking such as a mission among unbelievers the first two elements of unity are necessary. The third is highly desirable, can contribute effectively to the success of the undertaking, by the peace and good will it establishes interiorly between the various collaborators, but . . . unless the missionaries cease to have eyes to see and ears to hear there is no hope that this unity of feeling between the Vicar Apostolic and his collaborators will ever exist.[34]

At the end of his memorandum, Father Colin resumes the conclusions of his letter of 1 May 1847 concerning the Oceania project.

The journeys of Father Colin to Rome, 19 June to 27 August and then 29 November 1846 to 25 June 1847 constitute a privileged source for discovering how Father Colin manoeuvred in the world of the Roman curia and the people with whom he related. Father Mayet notes:

[8] All the same, the journey of Very Rev Superior General to Rome in 1846 in the month of July was happy and really providential, for he could make his thoughts known on various points and it was important to do that before the arrival of Bishop Pompallier, which only took place a month later. Then, it was on this journey that Reverend Father made the acquaintance of Rev Father Theiner, priest of the Oratory whose advice he took and whom he had informed about the affairs of our missions . . . Not to mention his insight and prudence, two circumstances above all, made Father Theiner more suitable than anyone else in bringing this matter to a happy and peaceful conclusion. He was connected to Bishop Pompallier by a very sincere friendship since his consecration in Rome in 1836, and he shared the ideas of Bishop Luquet[35] on the organization of the missions . . .

---

34.   APM Rome.
35.   Bishop Jean-Félix-Onesime Luquet (1810–58), Missions étrangères, Paris. He arrived at Rome in 1842 to have the synod of Pondichery, India, approved which centred on the formation of indigenous clergy.

[13] Then in order to unburden his conscience and have nothing to reproach himself with, the Very Reverend General addressed a letter to the Holy Father in which he opened his heart about this sad affair; to this letter he joined copies of some of the New Zealand missionaries. As this was a very confidential letter, Father Colin found means to carry out this pressing duty, that of enlightening the Holy Father without damaging the prelate's reputation. After all these activities, Father felt at peace and even very happy; because he saw that the Society was going to be disembarrassed of a thankless and excessively difficult mission; that is what he told me to say to Propaganda.[36]

Central vicariate

Father Founder discusses the problems of Central Oceania. As reported, the Vicariate of the central area had been created at the request of the superior general of the Marists. This is what Father Jeantin has to say about it:[37] 'When at Rome at this time Father Colin asked Propaganda for the creation of the Vicariate of central Oceania; the proposal was eagerly accepted.'

Vicariate of New Caledonia

Father Colin now proposed the division of the Central Vicariate Apostolic into two parts. The new ecclesiastical division would be New Caledonia, with of course, the neighbouring islands of the New Hebrides:[38] 'In central Oceania: it is very necessary for the good of New Caledonia to appoint Bishop Douarre (1810–53) vicar apostolic of this considerable island and join to his vicariate the neighbouring islands of the New Hebrides.'

Father Colin had already given good reasons for the creation of these two vicariates of the Centre and New Caledonia in his 'General survey of the islands of western Oceania, to serve for determining the boundaries between new missions one could establish':[39]

> A great number of islanders often said to Bishop Pompallier and to his missionaries: we know your people are better; but why did you not come here first? Then we would have been for you.' This talk would be the same among all the peoples of Oceania so we

---

36.   Mayet, 7, 155ff.
37.   Jeantin, *Colin*, volume 3, 48.
38.   Report from 1847, APM 2215/9969.
39.   Report Colin, 26 May 1842, APM 2213/9916.

would see it as extremely urgent to set up these two vicariates apostolic, firstly because the islands which would belong to them are threatened with heresy, which is already occupying a certain number of them; secondly because of the numerous population, the richness and central position of these archipelagos which are going to become in a short time for the rest of Oceania, a hearth of light or darkness, according to whether they are occupied by the ministers of the one or the other (religion).[40]

It is unnecessary to recall at length the situation prevailing at the beginning in Oceania, when Protestants were on an island, Catholics could not be there, and vice versa. It becomes easier then to understand the urgency of the situation Father Colin is talking about.

It is clear that Father Founder is not a dead hand in his approach. On the contrary, he displays great good sense. So the Holy See will create a new vicariate of the centre a short time later.[41]

After the death of Bishop Douarre in 1853, Father Colin went to Rome, and there those in charge at Propaganda asked him for a report on the religious organisation of New Caledonia. Father Jeantin affirms that what they specially wanted was his opinion on the opportuness of finding a replacement for Bishop Douarre, that is, to appoint another vicar apostolic. Father Colin sent this report:[42]

> My own personal opinion is that it is doubtful whether the appointment of a vicar apostolic is a matter of urgency, or even opportune . . . It is to be feared that Father Rougeyron may soon be out of service, and then the Sacred Congregation will be able to provide without inconvenience and with a clearer view of the situation, for the needs of the nascent church of New Caledonia.

As to general organisation, he proposes not to multiply stations, but to keep for the moment the four present ones. There will be four missionaries together in each, and they will spread out around the mission. The superiors of the

40.   *Ibid.*
41.   Simon Delacroix (editor), *Histoire Universelle de Missions Catholiques*, volume 3, 375; *Jus Pontificium De Propaganda Fide* (Rome: Ex Typographia polyglotta, MDCCCXCIX), volume 6, prima pars, 39.
42.   Jean-Claude Colin, letter to Propaganda, 5 July 1854, APM 2215/9978.

four posts will form the prefect's council. The latter will visit the stations at least once a year. No post will be accepted without the consent of the Superior General, because he provides the men, and he needs to have them to open new missions.

The numerous recommendations of Father Colin will serve to prepare a 'General Rule for the Missions of Oceania'.[43] Father Pierre Rougeyron, who arrived in New Caledonia with Bishop Douarre was appointed prefect apostolic until the appointment of Bishop Vidal (1846–1922).

Vicariates of Micronesia and Melanesia

It is again Father Colin who will undertake the evangelization of Micronesia and Melanesia. The Sacred Congregation of Propaganda created these two new ecclesiastical districts proposed by Father in his 1842 report. Father Coste gives a brief description of these vicariates:[44] 'Then, on 19 July 1844, two further vicariates were created: 1) Micronesia, which comprised the islands north of the equator (. . .); 2) Melanesia, comprising New Guinea, New Britain, New Ireland and the Solomons.'

Bishop Epalle, who was their first bishop, will be martyred as he is disembarking on this huge mission.[45] Father Founder, announcing his death to the Society, will say:

> Like me, my dear confreres, you were counting on the zeal and experience of a holy bishop who had already spent a number of years in Oceania; we were thinking that through him the reign of Jesus and Mary would extend rapidly . . . Let us again adore the holy designs of God. To Him alone does it belong to sow, to water and to bear fruit. He has wanted to crown the heroic devotion and erstwhile labours of Bishop Epalle without submitting him to longer trials. We have yet another martyr! He will watch over our confreres who were with him in his apostolate; he will pray for them, and his blood will be a fruitful baptism for these hostile lands. Yes, let us be full of confidence and thanksgiving: one more martyr is one more title to heaven's devotion and graces.[46]

43. Jeantin, *Colin*, volume 3, 341.
44. Coste, *Lectures*, 238. The English translation gives July 18th, here corrected.
45. Armand Olichon, *Les Missions, Histoire de l'expansion du Christianisme dans le Monde* (Paris: Bloud & Gay, 1936), 352.
46. Colin, Circular letter, Lyon, 3 September 1846. APM 2092/7372.

The Founder does not let himself be daunted by difficulties, and he too is aware that the blood of martyrs is still the seed of Christians. So it is still with as great an enterprising zeal that he continues to expand Christianity in Oceania. For example, regarding New Caledonia, he declares: 'When I see that only Brother Blaise[47] has been killed, although they were all just as defenceless among those wolves, that makes me think that God wants them to return'.[48]

The same thing happened in the Solomons: 'It seems to me that in the designs of Providence, we must not abandon the islands which have already been watered by the blood of several martyrs'.[49]

On 7 June 1847, Propaganda rejected the resignation of Bishop Pompallier and decided to create two dioceses in New Zealand. Hearing of this decision, Father Colin thought he should go to the Pope himself and reveal to him the reasons which made him fear a return of Bishop Pompallier to his mission:

> I have decided: I will go to the Pope, if necessary, and I will tell him: very Holy Father, we accept hunger, nakedness, dangers, death, everything except to endanger our salvation, and for that the superior general must be superior general. In Rome there are two parties, that of the bishops and that of the regulars. I have spoken to three of those who are of the first party, one of whom is a bishop: We will give up everything rather than renounce that.[50]

From then on Propaganda hesitated and tried to temporize. But on 29 May 1848, two bishoprics were created in New Zealand, Auckland with Bishop Pompallier and the title of administrator apostolic, for which he must himself find missionaries; the other Port Nicholson (Wellington), consigned to Bishop Viard, with the same title of apostolic administrator and to be held by the Marists. But even after this, difficulties will arise. As for Bishop Pompallier, he will find it very hard to recruit clergy, and New Zealand will strongly resent the result of the difficulties which arose between the first vicar apostolic and Father Colin.

After four days of reflection, Colin finally wrote this letter to Bishop Douarre, dated from Lyon 17 August 1847. This will allow one, I feel sure, to know Father Colin's spirit, and how after having been patient for a long time, he knew how to be firm:

---

47.   Blaise Marmoiton sm, coadjutor brother, massacred on Balade 20 July 1847.
48.   Mayet 7, 629.
49.   Letter Colin-Fransoni, 21 March 1852, APM 2215/9976.
50.   Mayet 4, 669–670.

1. Our decision is taken in respect to New Zealand, the Society is abandoning that mission. It would be useless, My Lord, for you to insist in this matter with the Sacred Congregation. The letters laid before Propaganda in 1843 by Bishop Epalle, and those which I had the honour to lay before his Holiness last June will both suffice to justify us on the subject of our conduct towards Bishop Pompallier. Besides which, a new work is in preparation which will make our proofs more and more convincing.

2. We constantly think that it is indispensably necessary for the little Society of Mary in the foreign missions not to be deprived of a faculty enjoyed by the Lazarists, the Picpus Congregation, the Company of Jesus and others. All these Societies have on the spot representatives of the Superior General with the title of provincials, visitors, Procurators etc, charged with care for observation of the rule.

3. I am not unaware that in Rome certain people would wish that all bodies in the foreign missions might be formed in the same uniform mould, without there being any other link of union and dependence than those which must unite missionaries to the Bishop. It is not for me to pronounce as to whether this uniformity would be desirable and advantageous, but I believe I am not mistaken in asserting that it will never be realisable.

I am and wish ever to be with the most sincere attachment and the most entire devotion and the most profound respect...[51]

Conclusion

After presenting these few texts and their repercussions on the organisation of the ecclesiastical territories of the archipelagos of western Oceania and in the Society of Mary, it seems that the conclusion can only be as follows: Colin played a determining and preponderant role with the Sacred Congregation of Propaganda for the greater good of the evangelization of the Pacific area. His apostolic zeal, his invincible courage, his limitless faith in God helped him not to give way before innumerable obstacles, in order to overcome them for the greater glory of God and the honour of his Blessed Mother.

Jean Coste offers us a paragraph we would like to quote. He declares that after 1842:

---

51.   Letter Colin-Douarre. APM 1466/20880.

> From 1842 onwards when the original vicariate was divided, the
> general tactics and plans for the division and redistribution of
> territories were no longer the concern of any one bishop. It fell
> to Propaganda and Father Colin to take a comprehensive view
> of the problem of the evangelisation of Western Oceania. Here
> Father Colin played a decisive part. It was essentially his plan
> of 1842 that was put into action in the course of the next twelve
> years.[52]

After presenting that general plan to Rome, Father Founder did not stay with
his arms folded, but continued to occupy himself actively for the well-being of
missionaries and missions. On his last journey to Rome, in summer 1854, having
already resigned, Father Colin wrote a letter of thanks to Cardinal Barnabò,
secretary of Propaganda. The letter concludes with these words:

> Here end my feeble efforts to care for the Oceania missions. I did
> love the missions: no one has wanted their success and prosperity
> more than I; no sacrifice on our part had been neglected. It is
> not the cannibalism of the savages which arrested enthusiasm
> or vocations for the missions; misfortune had another cause.
> God has allowed it, keeping for himself no doubt to grant the
> missions in the future more abundant blessings: this I will not
> cease to ask of him in my feeble prayers.[53]

In the following citation taken again from Mayet, Father Colin offers a
remarkable synthesis of his thoughts on the mission. He invites us to see it
with confidence as constituting part of 'the work of Mary': 'Gentlemen, never
egoism, but charity. Let us not say, "it is not my mission, it is the Marists", it is
yours, it belongs to Mary your mother, it is yours.'[54]

There remains one question to which we are obliged to respond. Colin
implicated himself personally: the spiritual and material care of the missionaries,
his taking up a firm position according to which these missionaries were first
of all and above all members of a religious congregation, is all that still part
of the Marist missionary perspective of the twenty-first century? For Colin,
the Society of Mary was an army ranged in battle order under the banner of
Mary, conscious of the risk it was taking but engaged to transmit and defend the

---

52.   Coste, *Lectures*, 249.
53.   Letter Colin-Barnabò, 18 August 1854. APM microfilm.
54.   Mayet 5, 580.

basics of the religious life and the spirit of the congregation. Today we live in a different context with a history behind us and before us, with a future to fight, as the apostolic exhortation *Vita consecrata* on religious life (1996) reminds us: 'You have not only a glorious history to remember and to recount, but also a great history still to be accomplished! Look to the future, where the Spirit is sending you in order to do even greater things.'[55]

Translated by Denis Green SM, Ireland

---

55.   *Vita Consecrata*, number 110.

Colin and the European Powers in the Pacific

John Broadbent

When one comes to tackle the question of Father Colin and the European powers in the Pacific, one is confronted by the fact that his register of letters indicates that the only power he held direct contact with was his native France and that in only certain circumstances.

But first I think we have to ask 'can we discern his attitude to royal or government power or what we in modern times call secular power?' For a Frenchman of his times and background, the altar and king by authority were intricately joined. His family had suffered grievously at the time of the French Revolution (1789) for their traditional views and he was nurtured in that environment which must have stayed with him all his life. Even under the settlements of Napoleon's Organic Articles[1] the attitudes of his boyhood still persisted when he and a number of his fellow seminarians at Saint Irenaeus' Seminary in Lyon heard through the Rector that the Archbishop of Lyon, Fesch, who was Napoleon's uncle had ordered prayers for him to be inserted in the Mass when his star seemed to be waning by losing battles. Colin and his friends risked punishment and possibly expulsion by not carrying out or attending while the prayers were said.[2] Only the Bourbon King represented the one sovereign.

Colin was to live in some of the most tumultuous times in the history of France. We have mentioned the Revolution which formed the first decade of his life on earth. Then there was the forced joining together by Napoleon of the two 'Churches' that had emerged from the Revolution which meant for Colin accepting some bishops and priests who had gone over to the Revolution. The restoration of the Bourbon kings after Napoleon must have seemed to Colin a return to normality except now their absoluteness was gradually eroded by the revolutionary ideas and constitutional parliament.

The revolution of 1830 unseated the Bourbons and put on the throne a compromise cousin who in his time had fought for the revolutionaries, the bourgeois king Louis Philippe (1830–48), whose reign spanned most of Colin's generalate. Louis Philippe was not the strong leader demanded by the various forces swirling around in the vortex of French politics. Then came the more

---

1. Napoleon I (1769–1821), ruling France and parts of Europe from 1799 to 1814.
2. Donal A Kerr, *Jean-Claude Colin, Marist: A Founder in an Era of Revolution and Restoration: The Early Years 1790– 1836* (Dublin: Columba Press, 2000), 116–120.

53

extreme socialism of the 1848 Revolution and the Second Republic carefully led and manipulated by Louis Napoleon Bonaparte, the great Emperor's nephew.[3] Before Colin finished his generalate, the President of the Republic had ratified by plebiscite the Second Empire now as the Emperor Napoleon III.

Fundamentally Colin never seems to have lost his old Throne and Altar mentality, but all these changes of authority on top seemed to have been accepted and not disturbed his equanimity too much. He seems to have accepted the political model that the Legitimate Authority in power is the right one whom one must obey even if those opposing it have a just cause. In this he who always took his lead from Rome and saw Pope Gregory XVI (1831–46) in the 1830 Revolution instructing the Belgian and Polish bishops to tell their catholic revolutionaries to obey Protestant Holland and Orthodox Russia despite their fighting for their and catholic causes. This comes out in one of Mayet's recorded conversations with Colin with a young priest who favoured King Henry V of France. After the exile of King Charles X (1824–30) in the 1830 Revolution, he left his kingdom to his grandson who called himself 'Henry V' but who was replaced by King Louis Philippe. 'Henry V' had still a small following in France. The young priest argued with Colin that Henry V not Louis Philippe should be king of France and Colin defended the legitimate ruler. 'It is to the de facto power that we must submit. The good of the people demands it. Otherwise public peace would be disturbed.'[4]

'The good of the people' was paramount in Colin's thought when in the 1848 revolution the extreme socialist troops entered the Mother House in Lyon. Many of them showed much disdain of the Church and were sympathetic to the striking silk workers many of whom were employed by the Church. Colin ordered these starving workers to be fed and treated with respect. In fact he became their friend and was respected by them in return.

That respect for legitimate authority and a human concern for all the people were the stamp of Colin's attitude. He certainly seemed to feel no need to play up to the constantly changing authority in his beloved France although in his rural apostolate he was noted for getting on well with the civil authorities.

Deeper however than this attitude grounded in experience was his deep-set principle and inspiration from the earliest years - *Quasi ignotus et occultus* (As if hidden and unknown). Mayet remarks: 'He often returned in conversation to the love of his favourite expression – *Quasi ignotus et occultus.*'[5] He never

---

3.   Napoleon III (1808–73), emperor from 1852 to 1870.
4.   Jean Coste (editor), *A Founder Speaks. Spiritual Talks of Jean-Claude Colin* (Rome, 1975) (= FS), Doc 31.
5.   Mayet quoted FS, Doc 57.

sought certainly in secular circles but even in ecclesiastical to be thought of as sagacious, experienced or favoured. Father Poupinel (1815–84) reports his activities in Rome in 1842 where he was by now well respected and even revered. Poupinel, his companion on this journey, says:

> Faithful to his principle of remaining hidden, he never referred to himself as the superior general of the Society, when he was visiting. At the beginning of each visit, he introduced himself as "a Marist Father" when that was necessary . . . One of his reasons for leaving the Hôtel de France was that he would be too much in the public eye. We moved into two small rooms . . . which in his view had the great advantage of keeping us hidden.[6]

After seeing the necessary cardinals and officials he felt he must go to see the Pope. 'I shall have to go but were it otherwise, I would have no difficulty in finding an excuse for getting out of it'[7] reports Poupinel of him.

On his return from Rome, malaria set in and he was intermittently sick which gave him an excuse for escaping the pomp of his own Bishop Douarre's (1810–53) consecration and especially the banquet that followed.

When we see these characteristics of Colin, we can see why he saw no reason for basking in the sun of the rich and powerful. Yet for almost ten years of his generalate he did. The answer could only be some greater good and this we will see.

Apart from that decade, Colin's correspondence indicates only one occasion when he made an approach to the powerful when in 1822, as an enthusiastic supporter of the Marist concept he went on behalf of his confreres to lay out his and their proposals to the Papal Nuncio in Paris. He hoped also to get recognition from the King, Louis XVIII (1814–24), for a society which he reasoned was to give priests, sisters and brothers to educate the young. For various political reasons the Archbishop of Paris advised against seeking the royal assent.[8]

About the time Colin became general, the French Government and their Pacific Fleet became protective of French citizens and missionaries. Koskinen, whose analysis of the situation is probably the best, points out how after the Napoleonic defeat, it took a while understandably for France to recover and

6. Jean Coste (editor), *A Founder Acts: Reminiscences of Jean-Claude Colin* (Rome, 1983) (= FA), Doc 218.
7. *Ibid*, 86.
8. Stanley Hosie, *Anonymous Apostle: The Life of Jean-Claude Colin, Marist* (New York: William Morrow, 1967), 70.

especially match the prowess of the British Navy. During the latter part of the Napoleonic Wars especially after the Battle of Trafalgar there was an effective blockade of ships leaving Europe. This gave the British Protestant missionaries a few decades start in their missionary efforts. When the Catholic Picpus missionaries entered the Eastern Pacific ten years before the Marists in the Western Pacific they were effectively ejected from the 'missionary' kingdoms the Protestants had by now evolved in Hawaii and Tahiti. Koskinen concludes:

> Evidence of the far sightedness of the French is the fact that they appreciated the part played by the missionaries in creating an atmosphere favourable to Britain. Their main attention was attracted to the fact that the sympathy and confidence of the natives towards Britain were particularly visible in the islands where British missionaries had been longest at work.[9]

In actual fact, after the Treaty of Waitangi in 1840 in New Zealand, Britain was virtually only interested in colonies with economic potential until Fiji was ceded to it by the chiefs in 1874 under the influence of Disraeli's more jingoistic politics. That is why in the end Britain did not fight over Tahiti when it was ceded to the French in 1843 even though most of the native inhabitants belonged to the London Missionary Society and Pritchard, their leader, was chief adviser to Queen Pomare IV (1813–77). Taking advantage of Pritchard's absence in England, Commander Du Petit Thouars used the excuse of returning the exiled French Picpus who had retreated to Valparaiso in Chile back to Tahiti as an excuse not only for intervention and threats to the Royal Palace but also annexing Tahiti as a French protectorate. At the time Du Petit Thouars had orders from France to annex the Marquesas as a profitable route between the Americas and Australia. Matsuda goes on to say:

> Tahiti was theoretically annexed to the French state in 1843 by Admiral Abel Du Petit Thouars as a strategic support to naval actions in the Marquesas Islands the previous year. There the admiral had gained rights to establish a whaling station, military outpost and catholic mission.[10]

---

9.   Aarne Koskinen, *Missionary Influence as a Political Factor in the Pacific Islands* (Helsinki: Soumalaisen Tredeakatenean Toimitakaia Annales Academiae Scientiarium Fennice, 1953), 163.

10. Matt K Matsuda, *The Empire of Love: Histories of France and the Pacific* (Oxford: Oxford University Press, 2005), 94–95.

Unsupported by his government, Du Petit Thouars took over Tahiti and in the process restored the Picpus to their mission. La Place, another French Admiral, restored the Picpus to Hawaii. France now in the Marquesas and Tahiti had a bridge-head in its thrust into the Pacific consolidated by New Caledonia on the other side of the ocean in 1853.

Whenever French Catholic missionaries were interfered with or threatened, French naval commanders first issued warnings and tried persuasion, but when necessary they also made demands to emphasize their requests.[11] This very aggressive policy of France was softened by the Tarnac Convention between France and Britain in 1847 and as Koskinen remarks: 'This brief document marked the factual termination of the period of nine years.'[12] The 1848 Revolution strengthened the Convention. However the policy in a slightly less aggressive form was always in the background for several decades later. It benefited the 'Marist' Pacific with not only French corvettes, protection and transport but also decisive interventions in Tonga in the 1850s and lesser but important ones in Fiji and Samoa and Rotuma.

Where Colin fits into this French Policy arising in the 1830s was that he saw in it in his own pragmatic way a means for helping the enormous budget for missionaries' fares, transporting goods and at times naval protection. Hence the large proliferation of letters from Colin to the powerful and as the French were the only powerful Government with which he was dealing we need to see how this entente cordiale eventuated.

The repercussions of this policy began to be heard in Lyon. A letter written by the French Marine Department in 1839 to the Acting Archbishop of Lyon informs him that the missionaries Fathers Petitjean, Viard and Comte (all Marists) for New Zealand will have their fares settled by the Department.[13] One presumes Colin was behind the request. The next letter assuring Colin from Marshal Soult, Napoleon's old general, now Minister of Marine that support will be given by the King's government to these worthy ecclesiastics who with such dedication devote themselves 'to the new apostolate'. He then goes on to tell Colin of the French colony setting out for Akaroa in the South Island of New Zealand need for spiritual help on the voyage out and on arrival he offers any help the missionaries may need and the navy can give.[14] Delightedly Colin wrote to Pompallier even before Marshal Soult's letter but on the strength of the

---

11. Koskinen, *Missionary Influence*, 173.
12. Koskinen, *Missionary Influence*, 181.
13. 6th September 1839; Microfilmes from Archives of Marist Fathers, Rome, situated at Marist Archives 78 Hobson St, Wellington, New Zealand.
14. 16 December 1839; Wellington Archives.

first letter to Lyon telling him this good news and how he could avail himself of French warships and other ships.[15] Just at the moment Colin wrote of course Pompallier was preparing himself for Waitangi and the handing over of New Zealand to British rule at which he would participate. He would receive Colin's letter after Waitangi and would presumably not be as impressed as Colin was, even though in a year's time after receiving Colin's letter he would be benefiting by French naval escort to recover Saint Peter Chanel's body from Futuna.

Numerous letters then criss-cross to the Marine Department on very affable and generous terms. At one stage the union of throne and altar mentality formed in Colin's youth and probably in the background of his whole life is expressed in his letter to Marshal Soult: 'France the oldest daughter of the Church, will always be the glory and the shield of the Faith. Also it is well known that the French character is based on strength and charity.'[16] Colin writes to the chaplain of Marie-Amélie (1782–1866), the devout Queen consort of King Louis Philippe (1773–1850) to help her guide the king in these very same sentiments.[17]

There is even extant a letter from Father Poupinel on behalf of Father Colin to secure free passages for catholic missionaries on the New Zealand Company's vessels sailing to colonise Wellington, New Zealand, answering an advertising of free passages for catholic missionaries on board.[18]

However Colin and those he trained also foresaw the danger of acting as agents of the French Government and its inherent ambiguity. Writing to the aforesaid Queen's chaplain, Colin remarks: 'You understand better than I, Father, how protection from our government which is too open could jeopardise the progress of the Faith because of the English Methodists who are inundating Oceania'. His disciples haven't to tread that narrow line separating protection from being agents of the Government when the two brave first bishops of Melanesia, Fathers Epalle and Collomb prevented their ship's crews especially as one was a French naval escort from taking provoked revenge on the Melanesians in the name of the Gospel and peace.[19]

---

15.   Dated 9 November 1839, in Gaston Lessard (editor), *'Colin sup'. Documents Concernant le Généralat du Père Colin,* volume I, *De l'élection au Voyage à Rome (1836–1842)* (Rome, 2007) (= *Colin sup*), Doc. 97.

16.   Dated 30 November 1839 (*Colin sup*, Doc 106).

17.   Dated 4 December 1839 (*Colin sup*, Doc 109).

18.   Poupinel to Heptonstall, March 1840 (*Colin sup*, Doc 143).

19.   Ralph M Wiltgen, *The Founding of the Roman Catholic Church in Oceania 1825 to 1850* (Canberra, London and Norwalk: Australian National University Press, 1979), 338–341, and 471–2.

This French protection gave rise to a rather wonderful movement which Colin sponsored from the outset, the Oceania Company. It was still in the same vein as Colin's endeavour to aid his missionaries' voyages to the furthest parts of the world from Europe. It apparently arose from a discussion early in 1843 between Bishop Douarre and an enterprising Le Havre shipping magnate called Victor Marziou. Perceiving its rich possibilities Colin sent Epalle to Le Havre to keep it alive. The scheme caught on. Marziou inaugurated the corporation in Paris in 1845. A fleet of Company ships would take manufactured goods from France to the islands, leave them at central depots to be distributed by inter-island schooners, returning with copra, shell, mats, carvings and native artefacts as well as providing free transport for missionaries. Colin's bold lead in promoting the Company and becoming a large shareholder encouraged many others, the famous and even many princes such as King Louis Philippe's son. In Rome many cardinals, archbishops and bishops elsewhere became shareholders. It was a roaring success particularly in procuring the saintly and competent captain Auguste Marceau (1806–51) who wished to make the marine ship at best a floating monastery with the sailors living a monastic life. But the Revolution of 1848 forced financial panic and shareholders withdrew their capital, and Marceau came home with a large debt. The Company was forced to go into liquidation in 1854.[20] Colin's numerous letters and interviews to the rich and powerful were for the purpose of easing missionary expenses and giving his missionaries some protection. Certainly not in the light of his character and spirituality basking in the sun of adulation and admiration. But is that all? Was this Colin's only influence on the European powers in the Pacific? I think we can trace much more influence though it be indirect.

First of all, just by moving his men to certain parts of the Pacific and as we have seen his sponsorship from France, these Frenchmen and missionaries attracted both French shipping and even more French colonial interest in the parts his Society pitched its apostolate, often creating French enclaves in that great ocean. Often too in parts that France would hardly have penetrated, French influence was exercised. A cynical academic friend of mine once said: 'If the French gun-boats hadn't forced your missionaries back, there would be far fewer Catholics in the Pacific to-day.' It was the Marist and Picpus Societies in the Pacific who spread those areas of French influence and in some cases annexation.

Colin too after studying the letters his missionaries sent back, got a very good grasp of their situations and the cultures they worked in and was able to

---

20.   Patrick O'Reilly, 'La Société de l'Océanie (1844–1854)', in *Revue d'histoire des Missions* 7/2 (1930): 227–262.

fill in the Roman authorities as they drew their lines on the map of the Pacific creating Vicariates and missions.

Most particularly it was the men Colin recommended to Rome as bishops who had quite a degree of influence on the European colonial expansion in the Pacific. He was very particular about the men he recommended.[21] Douarre comes to mind in this connection with his attraction to New Caledonia which he tried to found as a mission three times dying in the third attempt. But his lobbying the French Government to make it a colony seemed futile. So he tried the ambitious notion of a Papal colony and even had a certain hearing in Rome. He eventually succeeded when it became a French colony in 1853.[22]

His two bishops of Melanesia, Epalle (1808–45) and Collomb (1816–48), with their premature death as well as those of several of the priests and brothers made Melanesia outside of New Caledonia a fairly impenetrable area for European missionaries and colonisation until the late 1870s and early 1880s. The martyrdom and death of the bishops had a negative effect on all European powers for those years after the deaths who did not dare colonise, while it became a poaching ground for blackbirders and in time Anglicans bringing young boys to Mission Bay in Auckland and later Norfolk Island. Colin's training of these brave and courageous missionaries and selecting their leaders attempting to pioneer the area making European powers and missionaries wary of penetrating it.

Pierre Bataillon (1810–77) who within two or three years of his being made Vicar Apostolic of Central Oceania extended his missionaries to Samoa and Fiji and then when Rome awarded him Tonga, after Pompallier had placed missionaries there, was creating a minority religion to block any idea the Wesleyans and London Missionary Society may have had of missionary kingdoms and hence more British control. Eventually as mentioned above Fiji did become British, but Samoa became German and Tonga became the only independent state in the Pacific Islands fiercely resisting British control.

In actual fact after Britain and France had satisfied their colonial needs by 1855, there was a lull of twenty years when the Marists consolidated and no colonies to speak of were made. Then, after 1870 with two new players in the empires of the earth had been created, Germany and Italy, world trade and empires entered the scramble of colonies until the beginning of the twentieth century.

The connection between this European expansion and missionary movements is, I know, arguable; but there is every indication that Colin's missionary bishops

21.   Mayet in FS, Doc 228.
22.   Wiltgen, *Founding*, 104–6.

set in motion the ground for the movement of the various European powers' interest and take-over of certain areas of the Pacific.

While Colin was not the prime mover in Pompallier's nomination from Rome, the bishops missionaries, almost solely in the early days were Marists. Politically his coming to New Zealand coincided with the eccentric Baron de Thierry, a French man declaring himself King of New Zealand and the expectation of the Nanto Bordelaise Company's attempted settlement of Akaroa and possible taking over the South Island, for France. These and other reasons speeded up Britain's famous Treaty of Waitangi in 1840.

It was Pompallier who dropped Marists at Wallis and Futuna, grateful to find islands not occupied by protestant missionaries which eventuated in the martyr, Saint Peter Chanel (+1841) and Bishop Bataillon, first Vicar Apostolic of Central Oceania. The continued coming and going of French Marist missionaries to these two islands led to their present colonial status with France.

It is not an exaggeration to see Colin's appointees, the religious he formed as being part of this power-play of the Europeans in the Pacific. Remaining at home and not seeking the favour of the Great, Colin's indirect influence on the European powers in the Pacific as it has been shaped in the past two centuries and nurtured with the emerging Pacific nations has been a valuable and enduring one. Colin's only contact with a European power was his own native France, but it was a pragmatic contact not a supporting of France's expansion.

The man who in the spirit of the gospel and Mary of Nazareth formed these missionaries to deepen their faith and their spirituality in order to bear the heat and burden of the days and courageously persevere in one place that wittingly or unwittingly drew European enclaves around them was Colin. These enclaves in their turn drew the European powers to them in the scramble for colonies in the last part of the nineteenth century.

In that sense Jean-Claude Colin may well be seen as the father of missionary effort in Western Oceania and helper of European powers' expansion therein.

Further Archival Documents and Bibliography

Microfilmes from Archives of Marist Fathers, Rome, situated at Marist Archives 78 Hobson St, Wellington, New Zealand.

Allard, P, *Le Père Colin et les Missions* (thesis, Ottawa, 1966).

Aldrich, R, *The French Presence in the South Pacific* (Basingstoke: Macmillan, 1990).

Coste, J, *Lectures on Society of Mary History (Marist Fathers) 1786–1854* (Rome, 1965).

Coste, J (editor), *A Founder Acts: Reminiscences of Jean-Claude Colin* (Rome, 1983) (= FA).

Coste, J (editor), *A Founder Speaks: Spiritual Talks of Jean-Claude Colin* (Rome, 1975) (= FS).

Delbos, G, *The Catholic Church in New Caledonia* (Suva: CEPAC, 2000).

Delbos, G, *L'église Catholique au Vanuatu* (Suva: CEPAC, 2001).

Garrett, J, *To Live Among the Stars: Christian Origins in Oceania* (Geneva and Suva: World Council of Churches and Institute of Pacific Studies, University of the South Pacific, 1982).

Girard, Ch (editor), *Lettres Reçues d'Océanie par l'administration Générale des Pères Maristes Pendant le Généralat de Jean-Claude Colin*, 4 volumes (Rome: APM, 1999) (= LRO).

Hosie, J, *Challenge: The Marists in Colonial Australia* (Sydney: Allen & Unwin, 1987).

Hosie, S, *Anonymous Apostle: The Life of Jean-Claude Colin, Marist* (New York: William Morrow and Co, 1967).

Kerr, D, *Jean-Claude Colin, Marist. A Founder in an Era of Revolution and Restoration: The Early Years 1790–1836* (Dublin: Columba Press, 2000).

Koskinen, A, *Missionary Influence as a Political Factor in the Pacific Islands* (Helsinki: Soumalaisen Tredeakatenean Toimitakaia Annales Academiae Scientiarium Fennice, 1953).

Latourette, KS, *A History of the Expansion of Christianity in seven volumes. The Great Century: The Americas, Australasia and Africa 1800–1914* (Exeter: Paternoster Press, 1971).

Lovett, R, *The History of the London Missionary Society 1795–1895*, 2 volumes (London: Henry Froude, 1899).

McKay, F, *The Marist Laity: Finding the Way Envisaged By Father Colin* (Maristica, 4) (Rome, 1991).

Mangeret, A, *La Croix dans les Isles du Pacifique: Vie de Mgr Bataillon* (Lyon: Annales de Marie, 1932).

Matsuda, MK, *The Empire of Love: Histories of France and the Pacific* (Oxford: Oxford University Press, 2005).

Moister, W, *A History of Wesleyan Missions in all Parts of the World* (London: Elliot Stock, 1871, third, revised edition).

Moorehead, A, *The Fatal Impact: The Invasion of the South Pacific 1767–1840* (London: Hamah Hamilton, 1966).

Neill, S, *A History of Christian Missions* (Harmondsworth Middlesex: Penguin Books Ltd, reprint 1991).

Oliver, D, *The Pacific Islands* (New York: The Natural History Library, Anchor Books, Doubleday and Co, revised edition 1961).

George Pritchard, *The Aggressions of the French at Tahiti*, edited by Paul De Deckker (Auckland and Oxford: Oxford University Press, 1983).

Rozier, C (editor), *Ecrits de Saint Pierre Chanel* (Rome, 1960).

Rozier, C, *La Nouvelle-Calédonie Ancienne* (Paris: Fayard, 1990).

Wiltgen, RW, *The Founding of the Roman Catholic Church in Oceania 1825 to 1850* (Canberra, London and Norwalk: Australian National University Press, 1979).

Colin and Pompallier and the Founding of the Catholic Church in New Zealand

Jessie Munro

This topic has the unspoken subtitle: 'The Rift'. There have been plenty of rifts or at least cracks in church and mission histories and not only between superiors and local bishops.[1] The breakdown in the relationship between Colin in France and Pompallier in New Zealand was a major one.

The intensely compressed nature of New Zealand history, 'running fast and frenetic',[2] is demonstrated remarkably in the first five years there of Catholic mission.[2] All sorts of stresses could prise open a rift: the inexperience of the Society of Mary, its superior general and its mission leader; distance and communication problems from the huge extent and variety of the original mission; the late start of nineteenth-century Catholic mission and consequently big catch-up pressures; the dismay and counterattack of incumbent Protestants; the hardened adventuring mercantilism of the seafarers in the Pacific; the sophistication and strategic acumen of Maori tribal chiefs; the demand for the printed word in the contemporary Maori value system; the sheer costs of a speculative frontier society; the monotony of food—Father Petit's (1797–1858) quip was: 'When you've eaten pork and potatoes eighteen times, you know it's Sunday'; British sovereignty and French nationalism; the costs of trying to be all things to all people at all times, the costs of access, representation, credibility and prestige among chiefs, and sought-after supremacy over Protestants; schooners, barrels of tar, rowboats, printing presses, scarcity of timber, loans and loans on loans, bank failures, berths on ships, and always the mail - missing, overlapping, oh-so-slow or heartbreakingly never written.[3] The demands of the

---

1. For instance, in New Zealand the Anglican Low Church missionaries were alarmed at Bishop Selwyn's Catholic-rivalling High Church practice; in Australia the Irish reacted to Archbishop Polding's overly-loyal promotion of his English Benedictine monastic tradition. In Oceania Bishop Bataillon sent flares up into the sky. In France, Father Jean-Claude Colin had times of stress and confrontation with the Bishop of Belley over diocesan vis-à-vis pontifical status; with Marcellin Champagnat over teacher vis-à-vis coadjutor brothers; with Jeanne-Marie Chavoin over women's agency, and with his successor Julien Favre and other council members over the Constitutions of the Society of Mary.
2. James Belich, *Making Peoples: A History of the New Zealanders from Polynesian Settlement to the End of the Nineteenth Century* (Auckland, 1996), 450.
3. Jan Snijders studies the last aspect in *A Piety Able to Cope: Jean-Claude Colin*

mission, undertaken with such spiritual conviction and human courage, were enormous and any of these factors could act as a wedge.

When the Roman congregation in charge of missions, Propaganda Fide, came to assess the rift, it had a test case on its hands. Under consideration was the demarcation of authority between a vicar apostolic or bishop and the superior-general of his religious mission staff. Jesuit and Franciscan procedures were cited, and the other new French congregation for the Pacific was consulted, the Congregation of the Sacred Hearts of Jesus and Mary ('Picpus' for short after their street address in Paris). They too were having their queries. Catholic foreign mission had been dormant during the generation of revolutionary and Napoleonic upheaval, and policy now needed updating. Varying opinions were given and research made into seventeenth-century precedent. Ultimately the decision was made in Rome to separate, and in 1850 the Marist pioneers of the north crossed the border into their new diocese of Wellington, leaving Pompallier in Auckland with a staff of secular priests.

The theoretical dimension is what in a sense preoccupied Pompallier and drove his decision-making. In essence he was the Pope's representative and answerable to him, and he wrote often and tellingly on the subject. It was a spiritual argument as well as legalistic, only he tended to use the spiritual to justify the legalistic. Colin was equally as loyal to the papacy and equally intelligent, articulate and convincing in his counter arguments on relative canonical responsibilities. Yet the catalyst for Colin was the human dimension: nothing seems to have been as crucial to him as his almost visceral conviction that his men were not in good hands while with Pompallier. Both issues were spiritual and there was overlap. Basically Pompallier addressed conversion and the efficacy of the hierarchy of the Church in obtaining this goal.[4] Colin, who took intensely seriously the responsibility of the Superior as 'the soul of the Society',[5] addressed as well the body, mind and soul of each mission worker

---

and the Marist Missions in Oceania (provisional publication, 2007). He points out the disconcerting, inexplicable lack of letters from home to the first missionaries, especially craved-for news of the Society and family in France.

4.   'Depuis que je suis en mission je ne fais que demander, et je suis bien loin de cesser malgré le gros poids de reconnaissance que je sens pour l'Association de la Propagation de la Foi et tant d'âmes charitables qui m'ont aide en ma personne ou en celles de mes collaborateurs . . . La continuité! La continuité! Jusques à la fin de mes jours je serai un demandeur parce qu'il n'y a pas de pauvres spirituels aussi nécéssiteux que le troupeau et le pasteur de cette mission.' Pompallier to Colin, 14 August 1839, in Charles Girard (editor), *Lettres reçues d'Océanie*, provisional edition (Rome: APM, 1999), volume 1, Doc. 29 (= LRO).

5.   Jean Coste, *The Superior General in the Thought of Father Colin* (Rome, 1992),

in his care, to support them in the primary congregational goal of personal salvation that was the basis of true outreach to others.

This subject is daunting. I have read thousands of pages and marked hundreds of photocopies with post-it stickers saying 'Essential', that are still there looking at me forlornly. Do I concentrate on 'Colin and Pompallier' and analyse the process of the separation of the Marists from Pompallier, which takes us until 1848? Father Kevin Roach's thesis shows how big that topic is.[6] Or choose the 1840–1842 first crisis as representative? Do I capitalise on the recently available edition by Father Girard of the early Marist letters from Oceania and let the voices of those intelligent, perceptive and loyal men be heard more? Brother Edward Clisby's translation of the brothers' letters is a precious companion to this. And so is Father Gaston Lessard's '*Colin sup*', which brings the edited Colin documents beyond the *Origines maristes* to our Pacific period, and includes valuable input from a host of interesting characters: whaling captains and shipping agents—men like Peter Dillon and Daniel Cooper; French Ministers of state and naval captains; mission administrators from Propaganda Fide in Rome, the Foreign Missions in Paris, the Picpus fathers in Eastern Oceania and Benedictines in England—Fransoni, Rouchouze, Heptonstall; laymen like Meynis of the Propagation of the Faith in Lyon; and the Marists in Lyon or Belley—Colin himself, a pithy Maîtrepierre, a young Poupinel learning English . . . These documents show the multiplying, divergent or entwined tentacles of contact Colin and Pompallier and the men had to come to grips with and make decisions from. Especially Colin. Or do I acknowledge the Pacific nature of this topic and leave more room for the role of the people classified into 'regions of those without faith', *chez les infidèles, in partibus infidelium*?

After much hesitation, I have found myself intuitively reversing the title order of Colin, Pompallier and New Zealand, to follow instead an ABC: A for Aotearoa—and 'ariki' (paramount chief), which leads to B for bishop, because that is where I see a big issue, then C for Colin and the crises of communication. Aotearoa first because, given the huge obstacles of the times, it was remarkable how Colin, his Marists and Pompallier founded the Catholic Church in New Zealand so sensitively and courageously, and this achievement is of primary consideration.

42, quoting from Jean Jeantin, *Jean-Claude Colin*, volume 6 (Lyon: Vitte, 1898), 67.

6. Kevin Roach, *Venerable John Claude Colin and the Mission in New Zealand 1838–1848* (doctoral thesis, Gregorian University Rome, 1963); See also Bernard Bourtot, *En l'an 1848: la Société de Marie (Pères Maristes)* (Paris, 2007).

As for B and C, Bishop Pompallier and Colin, superior general, the faith and devotion of the two men are not at issue. There were just grounds for Colin's unease over Pompallier's approach to interpersonal relations, a growing unease leading ultimately to his almost desperate determination to extricate his men by braving out that test case in Rome to establish a template of where a superior-general's authority stops and where a vicar apostolic's takes over.[7] Yet Pompallier rightfully has his honoured place among those who have drafted New Zealand's national ethos and spiritual tradition. His name will always be linked to the statement in our Treaty of Waitangi (1840) guaranteeing freedom of religion for incomers and indigenous alike,[8] and to a gradualist and tolerant approach in Christian witness. His responsibilities were huge from the outset[9] and his initial impact in New Zealand was remarkable. His 1841 'Instructions for the works of the mission' stands as a historical mission document of careful reasoning and insight, which helped form Marist mission perspective. Both men belong in our history.

I have chosen a time span from 1838 to 1842 only, as the differences were already apparent by then and an ongoing pattern discernable. From 1842 to 1848, Colin was wrestling with what he deemed an unsolvable dilemma for the Marists; most of Pompallier's later record in Auckland in the 1850s and 1860s with other clergy, both secular and religious, would serve to corroborate his intuition.

In short order, the Society of Mary had been recognised pontifically and allotted Western Oceania as a mission field for urgent action. The men took their vows, and assisting at the ceremony was newly consecrated Vicar-Apostolic Jean-Baptiste François Pompallier, whose decision at that point not to proceed to take vows as a Marist was canonically reasonable but humanly disquieting. It was a cryptic decision much puzzled over since, by which Pompallier could sometimes claim to be and not be Marist and the Marists for their part to

---

7. Congregational Catholic Mission was reforming in the nineteenth century; the Missions Etrangères was staffed by diocesan priests.
8. As a result of discussions initiated by Pompallier prior to the signing of the Treaty, a statement, now commonly referred to as the 'Fourth Article', was added and read to the meeting before any of the chiefs had signed the Treaty. In translation it reads: 'The Governor says the several faiths (beliefs) of England, of the Wesleyans, of Rome, and also the Maori custom shall alike be protected by him.'
9. Snijders, *Piety*, draws attention to the span of Pompallier's responsibilities and planning.

include or exclude him.[10] What is most important here is that Colin came to feel Pompallier was essentially annexing his men, subordinating their Marist vocation and regarding them as his 'subjects' alone. As bishop he was answerable only to the Holy See. For Colin, they were three-dimensional co-workers of Pompallier as mission leader, with their allegiance to the Holy See through Pompallier <u>and</u> through himself as Father Superior of their congregation. The newness and vulnerability of the congregation made the issue extra-sensitive. In France in May 1840, Father Denis Maîtrepierre tersely summarised in a list of conclusions a long, long letter just arrived from Pompallier, the first letter really to 'set the cat among the pigeons'. Maîtrepierre's sixth point was: 'the vicar apostolic greatly fears the religious state is an obstacle to the dependency he would desire in his priests. Just as previously he was minded to separate out the Marists and have them independent from the episcopate, so now would he like them to be blindly dependent.'[11]

Colin's concern came also from two decisions taken before the first men left in 1836 for Oceania. Pompallier was the head of the mission but was also designated to be Colin's representative in the field as Superior of the Marist men. Their souls, as it were, lay in his hands- *in manus episcopi*, a phrase he would reiterate down the decades with other men.[12] Colin's later vulnerability would be due partly to anguished responsibility at having, perhaps as an act of faith, entrusted his men to Pompallier in that role. He, on the other hand, would serve as pro-vicar, an agent retaining administrative, practical responsibility for

---

10. Colin to Bernard O'Reilly, 22 August 1840, in Gaston Lessard (editor), «*Colin sup*»: *Documents pour l'étude du Généralat de Jean-Claude Colin (1836–1854)* (Rome 2007), volume 1, Doc 189 (= *Colin sup*). Colin says that at the time the Society received papal approval, Propaganda Fide conferred on it the vast mission of Oceania, and ordained one of its members bishop of Maronea and sent him into these distant territories with the title and powers of vicar apostolic. Colin may have been simplifying his explanation to O'Reilly, but he had not yet in 1840 destroyed the papers about the origins. Later, he insists that Pompallier did not belong to the infant Society. See *Origines Maristes* (= OM), Doc 753. Note too that Pompallier recounts telling Fransoni about his 'acte de protestation que j'ai fait pour rester membre de la Société de Marie', 8 December 1836, LRO, Doc 7.

11. Maîtrepierre's conclusions (undated) from Pompallier's letter to JC Colin, Lyon, 14 May 1840, Archive Marist Fathers, Rome (= APM) OOc 418. Both Pompallier's letter and Maîtrepierre's résumé and conclusions are in LRO, Docs 54–56. This quote is from page 425.

12. As shown in the New Zealand correspondence of the Franciscan Friars Minor and the Clercs de Saint Viateur in the 1860s.

men, funds and provisioning from France. This was a function Colin adjusted to rather slowly. The arrangement may have seemed sensible at the outset when such a small band was involved, but was unusual then and presumably an interim measure intended to be readjusted as the mission grew.

The tectonic graunches of this process of readjustment opened 'the rift' and for this to have happened so soon after the establishment of the congregation and its undertaking of foreign mission was traumatic. This rightly has an epic dimension in Marist history and has already been treated in several works including two important theses by Father Kevin Roach and Philip Turner.[13] The thousands of pages I referred to earlier are not even exhaustive coverage. Colin and Pompallier have sometimes seemed like Pacific mountain tops forming islands in a vast sea with the bulk of the mountain range—Pacific peoples, mission fathers, brothers and sisters—largely unseen. Colin would not like being coupled with Pompallier in any summit analogy; his concept of Mary's supportive, discreet, familial leadership in the early church did not call for singling out. He preferred for himself and the Marists to be the foundation unseen below. But as founder figure, as 'Colin sup. gen.', as Venerable Jean-Claude Colin, he inevitably has had a lot of exposure in Marist history.

Alois Greiler at the Second Colloquium on Marist History and Spirituality in 1989 began his paper with an image taken from the well-known French writer Antoine de Saint-Exupéry: 'If you want to persuade people to travel by ship over the great ocean, then don't try to do it by giving them the plans for a ship, a set of tools, and orders to build the ship. If you want to persuade them, then call them together and tell them about the great ocean and arouse in them a longing to sail upon it. Once you have aroused that longing within them, then without any prompting from you they will set about building their ship.'[14]

Father Greiler's point was the all-importance to humankind of personal engagement, commitment, belief and on-going responsibility—a crucial theme in Saint Exupéry's philosophy. For Saint Exupéry this meant being linked in a team: pilot, navigator, mechanic, groundsman, or working alone while knowing you are part of a greater whole—like the Little Prince tending his tiny planet with such simple lonely dignity. Both images speak for the Marist men bringing their faith to New Zealand and staying to earth it in with good foundations. This land is much greater and better because of their longing to do this and the

---

13.   Roach, *Colin and New Zealand*; Philip Turner, *The Politics of Neutrality: The Catholic Mission and the Maori 1838–1870* (thesis University of Auckland, 1986).

14.   Alois Greiler, *Be Men of God in an Age of Unbelief! Mystagogy in Marist Formation and Apostolate*, in *Forum Novum*, 1/3 (1989): 358–378.

ongoing simplicity and responsibility with which they worked, largely keeping their united, simple heart, the *cor unum, cor simplex*, so crucial to Jean-Claude Colin's founding concept.

The forty-one men who passed into or through Pompallier's mission were young, and the first ones had had no congregational formation as Marists. The Constitutions of the Society of Mary were as yet unsettled. Pompallier too was untried; his recent experience had been as a chaplain in Lyon to a small association of laypeople with Marist aspirations. He was a thoughtful teacher and theorist but he had never been in the testing ground of a parish. He was known to like an atmosphere of appreciation, of affirmation. He was the only early Marist affiliate to come from a family of independent means and in Lyon he was in a comfortable, familiar bourgeois environment near the centre of Marian devotion and at the liturgical heart of the city. The fact was that these men didn't have many plans or tools in the initial phases. Fresh from the congregation's very beginnings, they had to rely on their longing.

It is fitting in the Pacific to have a boat story. From Tahiti the *Raiatea* took seven men to Wallis, then five to Futuna, and three to cross the bar into Hokianga Harbour in Aotearoa on 10 January 1838. They were Pompallier, Father Catherin Servant, his former priest companion from their Hermitage days, and Brother Michel Colombon. As Bishop Pompallier, on deck and garbed in purple, sailed on the *Raiatea* up the narrow harbour past the Wesleyans of Mangunu, did he comprehend how aptly suited for him was the name and provenance of the vessel he hired in Tahiti? Ra'iatea, sometimes known as Hava'i, is the sacred island south of Bora Bora in the Leewards, and it was from Ra'iatea that the great navigator high chief and high priest Tupaia, of the exclusive red-clad arioi caste, sailed from Tahiti with Cook on the *Endeavour*. It was Tupaia who communicated with Maori, and it was his mana that impressed them as much as the novelty of the foreigners. It was the hope of seeing Tupaia again that brought canoe-loads of people from near and far to Cook's ship on his second voyage. 'He had become the object of veneration across New Zealand,' writes Anne Salmond, 'a near-mythical figure who had brought these strange vessels from the homeland with their loads of marvellous possessions.'[15]

When Cook arrived in the Bay of Islands and anchored off Motuarohia Island, Tupaia negotiated peace with the Ngä Puhi chief Tupua who was both ariki priest and warrior. His son Patuone, of later Treaty fame, and his daughter Tari remembered the Tahitian. Tari later married Te Wharerahi, the ariki elder brother of Rewa and Moka, who were the patron chiefs of Pompallier's arriving

---

15.   Anne Salmond, *The Trial of the Cannibal Dog: Captain Cook in the South Seas* (London, 2003), 189. See also 35. 135.185.188.

and settling in Kororareka. Peata, the first woman in New Zealand to lead a dedicated life of religion, also belongs in this region and in this intricate story of the entitlement and empowerment of the French newcomers. The issue of Maori agency would become more complex still with the new interplay of rival Christian faiths and rival European nationalities coming from the sudden entry of Catholics and Frenchmen on the scene.[16] It is a crucial part of Pompallier's experience.

The French missionaries came a generation after the first period of trade contact and missionary endeavour, and a decade after Hongi Hika's death brought an end to his devastating warfare and mission hegemony; in fact, they arrived right at the cusp of change when old and new forces in Maori society could be said to be ambivalent, in equipoise. Both old and new needed to be reckoned with, and they found themselves trying to operate in and understand 'complex, equivocal zones of action'.[17]

Papahurihia was one of the significant chiefs welcoming Pompallier that first summer on the Hokianga and holding discourse with him at the sacred rocks at the top of the hill overlooking the Whirinaki.[18] He was the prophet also known as Te Atua Wera, whose traditionally-inspired but new indigenous religious movement was one of the precursors of spiritual change.

Pompallier could benefit from ariki status to make rapid advances for the Catholic mission and Maori did indeed use 'Ariki' to address the Catholic priests.[19] Mary's stars needed to rise fast to orient Maori towards Catholicism

---

16. James Belich writes: 'Maori did not passively receive Europe but actively engaged with it. They chose, adjusted and repackaged the new, in many respects into a less culturally damaging form. They did so with courage and perceptiveness, exploiting a technologically formidable Europe that thought it was exploiting them, separating Europe and its things like a fool and his money. But Maori did not perform this feat as an act of collective wisdom, with an eye on the future and the common good. Instead their goal was the immediate subtribal good, or apparent good. Each group sought to bilk its rivals by exploiting the new resources more effectively, the age-old dynamic.' Ironically, 'rivalry helped spread Europe faster, developing a life of its own'. *Making Peoples*, 154–5.
17. *Ibid*, 431.
18. Whirinaki, Papakawau, Puräkau, Totara Point are only some of the Hokianga names at the birth of Catholicism in New Zealand.
19. For example, this from Garin in 1842: '[Peata] is one of the most keenly devout women you could ever see. She wields a lot of influence with the chiefs, even with the two greatest in this part of the island, Rewa and Moka—she is of a virtue and standing far out of the ordinary in their eyes. A few days ago I was setting off to visit a tribe; she was arriving and from as far off as she could make

because after so many arid years, the Church Missionary Society and Wesleyan missionaries were finally beginning to gain converts en masse. In this they were greatly boosted by the shift of 'currency' from warfare to literacy, from muskets to print. The new covenant of the Bible was gaining legitimacy. As Angela Ballara says: 'By 1834 in the Bay of Islands it was not unusual to see Maori reading their scripture instead of polishing their weapons.'[20]

Catholic worship had 'ariki' elements such as statues, bells, medals and miracles, and especially the sacred nature of the episcopate: the purple, the ring, the mitre, the crozier, the pectoral cross, the benevolent distributing of largesse, the claim of unbroken *whakapapa* back to Christ's commissioning of Peter, demonstrated very effectively by an intricate image of the one true Catholic 'family tree' with Protestant branches and leaves falling by the wayside. Add to that, Pompallier's handsome stature and demeanour, his intelligence, his fluency of expression and quick grasp of language, his beautiful celebration of liturgy, his intuitive sense of diplomacy and politics, his finesse, and his comprehension of customs, which we glimpse through his sensitive 'Instructions' to his missionaries—all this unexpectedly catapulted him past huge handicaps to a position of competitive viability with the Protestants.

And so Pompallier became 'Pikopo', from the Latin *episcopus* or bishop, and Catholic identification seemed to be invested in his person and status. To be 'pikopo' was to be Catholic, whereas the Maori word for Protestant was a generic 'mihinare' from 'missionary'. A 'politic of prestige' was established.[21] In 1841 Father Comte (1812-1899) explained this situation to Colin, listing Pompallier's 'position as bishop which gave him standing in the eyes of all, his role as superior which made him distributor of items sent from France,

---

herself heard, she called out to me: 'Ariki, priest', and she carried on calling out as she came up to the boat. She was wanting to get on board to touch my hand in greeting, but I climbed out onto the bank. She hurried up eagerly, took my hand and kissed it with respect, which she does every time she hasn't come by for a few days.' Garin to Colin, Bay of Islands, 9 August 1842, APM Z 208, 4, paragraph 11; LRO, Doc. 177.

20. Angela Ballara, *Taua: 'Musket War', 'Land Wars' or Tikanga?: Warfare in Māori Society in the Early Nineteenth Century* (Auckland, 2003), 431.

21. Turner, *Politics of Neutrality*, 33.34. See also in Turner, 40: citing M Roquemaurel in Dumont d'Urville, *Voyage au Pôle Sud . . . Histoire du Voyage* (Paris, 1841–46), volume 9, 312: 'The New Zealanders love our bishop, because to them he is good, humane, generous; they perhaps believe in the goodness of God who sent them this holy apostle, but they don't see anything else in religion other than the bishop and the gifts they receive from him; their natural instinct does not go beyond that.'

his objectivity which earned him the respect of the whites, his gestures of generosity to everyone, his love for the New Zealanders'.[22] A whaling captain just back in Le Havre gave his impression from August 1839: 'Monseigneur was then starting the first chapel etc. etc. and I can add what Monseigneur will not tell you; he is not only beloved but adored by the natives, liked and held in esteem by the English and Americans.'[23] The word *adoré* was underlined in the original.

Jean-Claude Colin must have winced reading this. The dilemma for the founder of the Marists is contained in his own words: 'As Mary is the first superior and the model for Marists, the Society ardently desires its members to do their utmost to imitate the beautiful modesty which hides from the eyes of the world the most exemplary of lives. That is why it invites them to do good in secret, to come to like being forgotten by men, and why it orders them to renounce all dignity beyond one's own innate dignity, except in heathen countries.'[24] A dilemma, because in this closing phrase he acknowledged the pull the very visible dignity of a bishop had in the mission field. Just over a year later, possibly anticipating a need to persuade Pompallier over the creation of a new vicariate in Oceania, he would write: 'You know more than anyone else how effective the presence of a bishop is with native people and even heretics; what is more, the episcopate has very special graces that lead to conversion of nations. And in addition I am convinced that here is an excellent means of having more missionaries and aid for the mission.'[25]

The more the mission projected heroic success in narratives with interesting, anthropological descriptions, the more the magazines of the Propagation of the Faith would arouse mission fervour and donations from its readers, and the more the young Society of Mary would build its future increase and stability.[26] Father Louis Rozet (1813–84) graphically described being sponsor, soon after

22. Comte to Colin, 25 April 1841; in the edited version of the *Annales des Missions d'Océanie – correspondance des premiers missionnaires* (=AMO) (Lyon, 1895), volume 1, 538-9.
23. Emile Franque to Colin, 9 May 1840, in *Colin sup*, Doc 165.
24. Colin to Bernard O'Reilly, 22 August 1840, in *Colin sup*, Doc 189.
25. Colin to Pompallier, 6 June 1841. (One copy of this letter goes with Captain Du Bouzey of the corvette *l'Allier* and another via Daniel Cooper. Colin is also forwarding letters from Fransoni, separately, so to give greater chance of their getting through. He informs Pompallier that he has brought up with Fransoni the advantage of creating a new vicariate.) Quote from *Colin sup*, Doc 271.
26. Colin to Louis Perret, 20 November 1840, telling him letters have been published in the *Annales* 'pour ranimer l'ardeur et exciter les vocations'; *Colin sup*, Doc 216.

his arrival, at the 1841 baptism of 'the famous Moka' — *le célèbre Moka.* '[He] wanted a fine-sounding name and one belonging to a great prince. We offered him the name of the pope in their language, *Kerekorio.* They didn't consider it beautiful enough. Finally, after much discussion, they settled on calling him *epikopo*, the name given to Monseigneur, which means bishop. The latter had to go to some length to make them understand that this word denoted hierarchy and dignity of status, and was not a saint's name. At last he got them to accept his baptismal name, Jean-Baptiste, Hoane Papita.'[27]

Dignity in humility, however, was Colin's base-line definition of dignity for the Society of Mary. Before Pompallier's departure in 1836, Colin had written to him: 'Remember the poverty and simplicity of the apostles; they too were bishops and yet they often worked with their hands to provide the basic necessities of life. Simplicity, poverty and zeal must always be the companions of the missionaries of Mary . . . The spirit of the Society is poverty, humility and simplicity. I hope, Mgr, that you will accept this letter with goodwill and that you consider it as proof of my ardent desire to contribute to the success of your apostolate.'[28]

He didn't care for the repeated reference in new missionaries' letters to Pompallier as 'His Lordship', 'Sa Grandeur', or to 'the honour of accompanying His Lordship', 'big words,' he said, 'which ill suit a bishop of New Zealand, a missionary bishop who must *lodge sub paupere tecto*, under a humble roof.'[29] In the copy for publication in the *Annales* of the Propagation of the Faith, he had these phrases deleted as 'being immodest, and not fitting to the spirit of simplicity and evangelism, the spirit of the child of the Holy Virgin'.[30] Colin's theological concept of Mary did not so much isolate Mary in the exalted, privileged position of *Regina Mundi* ('Queen of the world') as focus on her quiet yet active role among the regrouped apostles of Pentecost, the birth of mission, and within the home of Nazareth, the template for human support, union and nurture.

Early in 1840 he quoted to Father Cholleton a passage from Pompallier's letter to Louis Querbes (1793–1859), the founder of the Clercs de Saint Viateur. Was he quietly sounding out his reaction? (Cholleton was now joining the Society of

---

27. Rozet to the Sisters of Saint-Martin-en Coailleux, Opotiki, 10 October 1841, APM Z 208, LRO, Doc 104.
28. Colin to Pompallier, 18 October 1836, in *Colin sup*, Doc 5.
29. Mayet, *Mémoires,* 1, 186–9 (*Colin sup*, Doc 64). Note that Colin would later express concern that there were too many bishops within the society.
30. For instance, Petit to Colin, 3 March 1840, APM Z 208, LRO, Doc 46. Petit is writing on behalf of Pompallier 'qui m'a chargé de vous mettre un peu au courant de nos besoins . . .', 340; also Servant to Colin, 5 March 1840, LRO, Doc 47.

Mary and it was he who, as Vicar General of the diocese of Lyon, had proposed
Pompallier's name as candidate to lead a Western Pacific mission.) Pompallier
told Querbes that chiefs came from vast distances to consult him on matters of
conscience, which he found very moving: What warmth of friendly regard they
have for us! The most distinguished chiefs are the ones coming forward and
proffering themselves to accompany me far off into their forests. One carries the
altar, another the chest of altar vessels; others take charge of food and supplies
for the party of people often numbering twenty-strong. Sometimes I can't help
laughing at the thought of myself alone in these fastnesses with this band of
former cannibals, all of them poorly clad, tattooed and always armed with their
wooden spears or else European weapons. You might think I was leading a band
of brigands; yet I was never the slightest bit afraid in their company, they are
the flock of Jesus Christ following their divine shepherd in the person of his
minister. There was nothing they wouldn't do for me, whether it was our food
which they prepared themselves with minute care, out of respect serving me
mine separately alongside them. They say the prayers with me before and after
the meals and we eat with lightness of heart before setting off again en route. If
there's a stream to cross, the highest-ranking chief argues his pre-eminent claim
to the honour of carrying me on his shoulders, and normally he is obeyed.[31]

Pompallier describes how at night they roll themselves in their blankets and
settle down on the ground. He tries to sleep but says that more often than not,
questions keep coming at him right through the night. This happens time after
time. For the first eighteen months, there was only one other priest in New
Zealand, Father Servant, and he was mainly in the Hokianga and handicapped
by a degree of deafness. Pompallier, despite being in his prime, fit and
intellectually attuned towards understanding his context, must have been over-
stimulated and tired at the same time, and he was ill equipped psychologically
to evaluate his own state of being. Colin was aware of this last aspect, part of
the stamp of Pompallier's character (*sa trempe d'esprit*) that Colin said he knew
from times past.[32] Back in 1837 he had quietly observed: 'the saints who were
best at leading others kept an extremely close watch over themselves'. 'Ask
yourself repeatedly for self-knowledge . . . I have been constantly doing this for
ten years.'[33] Instead, Pompallier would cling nostalgically to this brief time of
chiefly mission for the rest of his life.[34]

31.   Colin to Cholleton, 13 May 1840, in *Colin sup*, Doc 173.
32.   Colin to Fransoni, 18 March 1842, in *Colin sup*, Doc 330.
33.   Mayet notes: 'se défiaient singulièrement d'eux-mêmes', 20–22 November 1837,
       in *Colin sup*, Doc 16.
34.   Turner, *Politics of Neutrality*, 39, notes that the decline of the use of 'ariki'

Both Hokianga and the Bay of Islands were becoming cosmopolitan gathering places. Thomas and Mary Poynton, ex-Australia and Pompallier's first Pakeha hosts, represent the practical, entrepreneurial generation heading across the Tasman. There were already many Maori-Pakeha families in the Hokianga, including that of the ship's pilot who brought the *Raiatea* across the bar. The French Catholic missionaries were not in luck financially with the timing of their arrival. There was the massive inrush of land speculators, especially in 1838 and 1839. Among the land purchases was the New Zealand Land Association settlement, which was a prototype in the Hokianga to the Wellington Wakefield scheme and was causing concern to the missionaries about the incipient harm to Maori from less than scrupulous immigrants. Further inland the family of disaster-prone French émigré Charles de Thierry (1793?–1864) was eking out an existence since 1837 on a tiny bush portion, all that was finally conceded to him of the royal domain that he, the self-styled 'Sovereign Chief of New Zealand', thought he had bought long before. But a French king was a French king even if in fantasy, and a trio of French missionaries could be seen as menacing French papist spies; de Thierry and Pompallier found anti-French feeling mounting among the British.

Support from visiting French naval vessels in the Bay would not have removed this prejudice but did improve Pompallier's standing with Maori.[35] It

---

seems to have coincided with the disclosure of the poverty of the mission from about 1841, and there is no recorded instance of its use after 1843. And 137: 'Naming was highly significant in Maori society: in according the Catholics a title that Protestant missionaries were never offered, the Maori were expressing a deliberate message of hope and confidence in the wealth and power, the mana-tapu, that Pompallier seemed to represent.' Viard noted, to Fransoni on 1 March 1849, Archive Propaganda Fide, Rome (= ACPF) SC IV and in his journal on 9 June and 9 August 1846, APM 669/6 that he has found that the Rewa and Moka had left the faith, the former going over to the Protestants; 'brambles and thorns have taken the place of flowers'. By 1857, Protestant missionaries observed very little 'Popery' in the north. In 1851, Church Missionary Society missionary Burrows reported that Rewa's people at Te Rawhiti had turned to Protestantism. (R Burrows, Annual Report to the CMS, January 1851, copies in POM 33–7, Auckland Catholic Diocesan Archives; cited in Turner, *Politics of Neutrality*, 185–6).

35. Rev H Williams to the Lay Secretary, Paihia, 11 January 1839: 'Our general views of the appointment of the NZ Association you will have learnt are this in your letter of March/38, & since that date our fears have been much increased by the active measures of the French RC [Roman Catholic] Bishop & priests, supported as they are by the appearance of two French Men of War. The first

was straight after his visit with Captain Dupetit-Thouars to Rewa on 7 November 1838, and Rewa's impressed appraisal of the frigate, that the purchase of the first land in Rewa's territory of Kororareka went ahead, land at Maiki bought on 10 November. In July 1839, the mission's headquarters in Kororareka were confirmed when Pompallier bought the shoreline property that bears his name today. The June 1839 arrival of six Marists in a newly bought schooner in shared ownership with the Picpus Fathers also validated a location with good anchorage and ship facilities.

Kororareka was the Western Pacific's main port of call, decidedly secular and ensconced safely across the stretch of water from the Church Missionary Society stations at Paihia and Kerikeri. There were Americans—including black escaped slaves on Nantucket ships, English, Scots, Irish, Portuguese, Italians, Russians and French (as well as 'mixes and matches' such as Americans captaining French whaling ships, and French captains on American whalers). James Belich has written: 'The importance of French and American whalers as agents of contact has been underestimated.'[36] These mingled and traded with Maori, both local and distant.[37]

---

frigate, *L'Heroine*, M Cecille, sailed about three months since to the Chatham Island to revenge the seizure of a French Whaler & the murder of the crew. It was proposed by us that one of us should go on board the frigate & act as interpreter, should it meet with the approbation of the Captain; though we had no reason to think that our proposition would be acceded to owing to the conduct of the RC Bishop. We have felt we should have neglected our duty had we not mentioned our desire under the supposition that the Commander would not wish to punish the innocent with the guilty. Our offer was not accepted, & the frigate sailed in company with three or four whalers to act with him. We have not yet heard the result of this affair. The *Venus*, French frigate of largest class, 550 men, Commandant Du Petit Thouars, 1500 tons, arrived from Tahiti, where she has levied a fine of 2000 dollars on account of the Queen not allowing the RC Bishop & priests who are now here to remain on the island. We have reason therefore to fear that the French may have designs not yet known upon this island, & would therefore urge, most strongly, that the British Government should take immediate steps for the protection of this people.' CNM, volume 11 (1838/40): 301 (Alexander Turnbull Library Ref: 2003-105-119).

36.   James Belich, *Making Peoples*, 138.
37.   Inland Ngäti Tuwharetoa, for instance, held land at Tapeka, the headland at Kororareka near where Pompallier acquired additional property. Tapeka is the name of their wharf at Waihi on Lake Taupo, which has long been a centre of Catholicism as Father Reignier and other Marists, Suzanne Aubert, Mill Hill priests, and Bishop Max Takuira Mariu have attested.

Kororareka was a commercial success story for Maori who engaged actively in shipping and trade with New South Wales especially. Along with a traditional respect for *ariki* priesthood would have been their modern awareness of the temporal clout wielded by a bishop in Christian societies with faith traditions based on apostolic succession—even if the power was more symbolic than real. Many would have known of Anglican Bishop William Broughton who visited New Zealand from Sydney in 1839, perhaps partly to counteract Pompallier's sole occupancy at that point, and of John Bede Polding (1794–1878), Catholic Bishop in Sydney from 1835, who befriended Pompallier en route to New Zealand. Most probably some word of the incoming French bishop reached Maori via Maori shipping before he appeared on the horizon.

Rewa (or Mänu—the name 'Rewa' derived from English 'Rivers') was very instrumental in the founding of the Catholic Church in New Zealand. He had been one of the major 'patron-managers' of the Church Missionary Society in the 1820s and 1830s in Kerikeri, Waimate and then in Kororareka. He had been Hongi's war lieutenant; his elder brother Te Wharerahi was called upon in the ritual peacemaking role. The third brother Moka was a prominent warrior in the campaigns. Their names feature often in primary sources and recent historical analysis has provided insight into their role in both traditional society and in the zone of adaptation and change.[38] They were of the Patukeha sub-hapü of Ngai Tawake in Ngä Puhi, and the chiefly kinship links of the three brothers were extensive and would open doors for the Catholic mission in the Bay of Islands, Hokianga, Whangaroa, Auckland, Bay of Plenty, Waikato, Taupo.

From 1830 Rewa and Moka held power through *utu* over the crucial commercial Kororareka-Te Räwhiti area. In the late 1830s he was still advising the Church Missionary Society (CMS) mission in its outreach 'to the southwards', but then when Pompallier, naval vessels and whalers increased the French presence in the Bay, Rewa chose to become Pompallier's patron for his mission headquarters in Kororareka.

For the next few years Rewa's name was associated largely with Catholicism, including during the all-important negotiations of the Treaty of Waitangi when Pompallier's presence was impressive. CMS printer Colenso (1811–99) overheard Maori remarking: 'Ko ia ana te tino rangatira! Ko Pikopo anake te hoa mo te kawana—He's the great chief! Only Pikopo is the fit companion for the governor.' It is generally accepted that 'the Roman Catholic bishop in canonicals, his massy gold chain and crucifix glistening on his dark-purple-

---

38.   Dorothy Cloher, *Hongi Hika: Warrior Chief* (Auckland, 2003); Judith Binney, *The Legacy of Guilt* (Auckland, 1968); Ballara, *Warfare*.

coloured habit' as Colenso described him,[39] contributed to the argumentation
of Rewa, Moka, Hakiro, Tareha, Wai, Te Kemara and Kawiti on the 'sceptical,
cautious' side. Rewa was the reluctant last signatory at Waitangi.

Pompallier was also aware that Rewa and other chiefs had long been realising
that missionaries could help in peace-making roles. 'New Zealand customs
oblige us to fight,' he said once to Church Missionary Society James Hamlin,
'[but] if you go with us we can make peace in your name.'[40] This is borne out in
the 1841 letter from Father Louis Rozet (1813–1884) at Opotiki in the Bay of
Plenty The chief Tangaroa had told him of his voyage to the Bay of Islands to
ask for a priest and his two-month determined wait there. 'Now that I have one,
he said, now that I have turned to the true faith, I want peace. I want to love all
men. Then in conclusion, he exclaimed: my wealth, my taonga, is the bishop
[*Ma richesse, c'est l'évêque*]'.[41]

After the signing, Rewa went as far as Auckland with Pompallier and
there participated in *hui* resulting in significant non-signatories. Pompallier
meanwhile went on to the Bay of Plenty where Moka had preceded him to set up
stations among his wife's kinship.[42] Significantly, another word is now added to
'ariki' and 'epikopo' in the record. It is 'kawana'. On 14 May 1840, Pompallier
told Colin of the territories now 'turning' to Catholicism. 'To turn' included
'acknowledging that it was the true church, the church of preference, the ancient
church, the mother-church, the trunk that Jesus Christ himself formed . . . it is to
understand that the successor to Saint Peter is the Holy Father the Pope, known
here under the denomination of Kawana tapu nui o Hehu Kerito, (that is, great
and sacred governor of Jesus Christ, the one supreme king of the church), and
that the bishops are the other successors to the apostles, united to the king and
to the visible governor who rules the church in his holy name until the end of
the world when he will return on earth to judge all peoples according to his
works'.[43]

39.   William Colenso, *The Authentic and Genuine History of the Signing of the Treaty
       of Waitangi* (Wellington, 1890).
40.   James Hamlin, Journals, entry for 17 March 1828, quoted in Ballara, *Warfare*,
       111.
41.   Rozet to the Sisters of Saint-Martin-en Coailleux, Opotiki, 10 October 1841,
       APM Z 208, LRO, Doc 104.
42.   Pompallier stayed in '17 des tribus principales dont les autres sont des dépendances
       par alliance de parenté'. Pompallier to Colin, 14 May 1840, APM OOc 418.1,
       LRO, Doc 53.
43.   *Ibid*, 388.

In the immediately post-Waitangi world when the treaty was still circulating, the words *kawana* and *kawanatanga* were on everyone's lips. The analogy would be effective. The origin of the word 'governor' in Latin *gubernator* or helmsman had been explained to some Maori; once again the image of great *ariki* navigators held meaning for the ship of state or the barque of the mission. Pompallier, also a *kawana tapu* by succession, was at the apex of his mission achievement.

But, ironically, this was the very moment the cracks opened up. Colin now comes to the front of the stage. In late April 1840, while Pompallier was away, the men as Marist colleagues took the opportunity to confer, take stock and write uncensored letters, measured yet poignant, to their father superior back in France: first the elder missionary Servant, writing with the knowledge and input of Baty, Petit and Epalle; then Petit writing separately.[44] Servant—the anonymous priest with Pompallier at Waitangi on 5 February—and Brother Michel had sometimes been cowed by the vehemence of Pompallier's fault-finding wrath, by the exigencies of his authority—or if not cowed, silenced by their own loyalty to the obedience they had promised and which he exacted religiously.

Servant's letter to his 'dear father in Jesus Christ' was to 'be opened only by the very reverend superior general of the Society of Mary'. In it he simply let Colin know of the tenuousness of the reported rush to conversion, the impossible promises to supply priests, their solitude and suffering, the growing poverty, especially with more missionaries on hand to feed and more stations to supply, the mismanagement and arbitrary handling of money, the lack of consultation, and above all his concern for the four other men in the islands of Oceania.

From the outset, Colin had invited them to tell him everything that affected them and asked Pompallier to encourage them to do so.[45] Pompallier once explained one reason for checking what was written, apart from an inherent right, when he advised Colin to be cautious about mission correspondence submitted for the *Annales* of the Propagation of the Faith. The English translation was

---

44. Servant to Colin, 26 April 1840, APM Z 208, LRO, Doc 50.
45. Colin to Bataillon, 31 July 1838, in *Colin sup*, Doc 44: 'Please take the opportunities and write to me from time to time. Have no fear revealing your troubles and your joys. If I can do nothing practical, I will pray and have others pray. In any case everything that concerns you concerns me; I want each one of you to write to me individually of your woes and misfortunes, the dangers and risks to body and soul you run, so the spirit of the Society, union, courage, the spirit of faith and prayer are safeguarded among you all. Always stay well united and submissive to Bishop Pompallier.'

available in Sydney and had been cited in the Sydney newspapers read by Protestants. Passages with more than a whiff of Catholic or Gallic triumphalism would be inadvisable. He also suspected that sometimes their mail was blocked or tampered with by similar anti-Catholic or anti-French agency, which was one reason he favoured entrusting his mail to French whalers—until he discovered that the whaling ships might circle the oceans many times with their letters before making it back to France.

But the checking of mail came largely from a deep-seated need in Pompallier to control and, yes, to manipulate while hiding behind the rights of the episcopate. This is what I mean when I say that Colin probably felt his men were not safe with Pompallier in a regime of dual obedience, maybe psychologically not even at all. The urbane kindliness of Pompallier's personality and the reasoning behind his approach were acknowledged and appreciated by his men, but they could not relax with him as they came to be wary of his over-heightened self-consciousness, and to know the totality of that urge to control—hugely exacerbated by the cross-cultural reinforcement of 'ariki'—to the detriment of the mission and the erosion of their own selves.

These Marists were fervent, traditionalist Catholics recreating faith after the Revolution years through revivalist missions in the towns and villages of central France. They were nevertheless inheritors of 'liberty, equality and fraternity', and this legacy contributed to the inclusiveness and brotherliness of the Marist ethos. Even allowing for self-abnegation, in no way could they accept as their due the demeaning and distancing treatment an 'ariki' Pompallier often dealt them, especially the brothers who were sometimes contemptuously referred to by Maori as kuki, cooks or slaves. In April 1841, Cardinal Fransoni of Propaganda Fide would write to Pompallier: '[Your dignity does not] suffer if at times you seek counsel from those sharing your labours and your ministry, and if you act toward them as an equal and a colleague, rather than a superior, so that all things may be accomplished in the Lord and in charity.'[46] By not acting in that manner, Pompallier's dignity did suffer in essence when unimpressed Petit could say tartly: 'he spat straight up in the air, no wonder he's had to wipe his face.'[47]

According to Philip Turner, 'Pompallier consistently alienated his priests. His belief in the inherent personal sanctity of his office led him to husband

---

46.   Fransoni to Pompallier, 12 April 1841, quoted in Ralph M Wiltgen, *The Founding of the Roman Catholic Church in Oceania: 1825 to 1850* (Canberra, London and Norwalk: Australian National University Press, 1979), 235.

47.   Petit: 'Mélange d'observations sur le Temporal et le Spirituel de la Mission en General' [1842], APM 669/4; quoted in Turner, *Politics of Neutrality*, 142.

his authority jealously, at times pettily, refusing to take advice from is men or to delegate responsibility. Priests who showed resourcefulness in their actions were more likely to be castigated for their presumption than praised for their initiative.' He certainly does not seem to have talked much about the men personally as friends and companions[48] or shown unqualified enthusiasm for major accomplishments on their part[49] such as the delivery of an up-to-the-minute press or Yvert's skill in printing. 'Instead, his hypersensitivity to criticism earned him from Petit the nickname 'Don Quixote of the Episcopate'.[50] Funny, apt and tragic because, right through the 1850s and 1860s, obedience would remain as Pompallier's main criterion for approval and advancement of a 'subject'.

This element of regulation was a factor also in Colin's disquiet about the stamp of Pompallier's character. Colin recalled that when Pompallier had become spiritual director at the Hermitage in the early 1830s, he drew up a whole lot of rules [*il fesait force règles*] and was involved at that point in a move to separate out the fathers from the brothers. He was fixated on the issue of rules, and when he was not chosen as superior of his fellow priests, he arranged a transfer to Lyon and the chaplaincy at La Favorite, where 'he set to once more to compose yet again a plethora of rules for that little group.' This admittedly was a later, biased interpretation from a completely disillusioned Colin.[51]

In 1836 Colin had asked Pompallier to watch over his missionaries, to seek all possible means of 'maintaining union amongst them, peace and a holy gaiety' and to consult willingly with them for their opinions: 'it will keep them interested in your undertakings and contribute to unity. Feel for them a father and mother's visceral caring.' (In fact, reading letter after letter written to Colin over the years from his men, I am struck by the unaffectedness of their style, the intelligent directness of their rapport with him, the trust and affection as well as respect, a respect in which there is no fear.) But Colin's very next sentence in his 1836 letter to Pompallier had been: 'You are their bishop and their superior;

---

48.   There are exceptions. He does say that Viard has skills in language. He sensibly wants Fiji to be the next vicariate as it is one language only.
49.   Another exception: 'telle a été ma joie dans le Seigneur . . . lorsque la petite goélette qui tranportoit nos sujets, a paru . . . 14 juin dernier'. Pompallier to Colin, 14 August 1839, LRO, Doc 29.
50.   Turner, *Politics of Neutrality*, 192.
51.   'Là, se livrant à son zèle, M Pompallier se mit à composer encore pour cette petite réunion une foule de règles.' Mayet, *Mémoires*, in OM, volume 2 (Rome, 1961), 455.

they doubly owe you obedience and respect.'[52] Colin now believed they urgently needed to be released from this duty. His companions in France recognised a quality of discernment in him, a talent for going straight to the heart of the matter; once he had drawn his own conclusions, he would not be able to make a weak compromise.[53]

With the 1840 letters, the floodgates opened and the resulting correspondence over the next decade would build up a picture of men, united among themselves still as Marists and not contemplating leaving the congregation to continue with Pompallier in a diocesan capacity, loyal to him as their mission leader and aware of his talents but making judicious observations on varying issues according to their own insights. They now had a Marist superior in New Zealand. Mission stations in Hokianga, Tangiteroria, Whangaroa, the Bay of Plenty were manned and grapes grew but poverty would always be an issue. A graceful schooner was bought and soon sold at great loss; through the labour of the brothers and Maori helpers, the rammed earth printery rose slowly while Pompallier was away fetching the remains of Pierre Chanel from Futuna; Petit-Jean (1811–76) went off to Sydney for help and brought back a miniature ark-load of animals to sustain them; Epalle likewise left to try and sort out matters in France and in Rome; in 1845 Archbishop Polding unsuccessfully attempted to be a facilitator in Sydney between Epalle for the Marists, and Pompallier. In Rome other vicariates in the Pacific were founded by Propaganda Fide and staffed by Marists; Pompallier argued sensibly for a linguistic and cultural basis for grouping the vicariates. The capital of New Zealand was taken to Auckland and the once-thriving Kororareka slumped; Kororareka was in fact sacked in the March 1845 attack by Hone Heke and Kawiti and the subsequent British retaliation—Kawiti's cloak would be laid on Pompallier's shoulders in the aftermath; Pompallier departed shortly afterwards and would not return until 1850 when he settled in Auckland and hardly ever again set foot anywhere else in New Zealand.

Pompallier and Colin's was the first major nineteenth-century mission dispute. Missionary congregations were swelling in number and Rome had to be careful in establishing policy around the issues of authority. The fine details of the argument and settlement seem somehow irrelevant to the crux of the matter: Colin essentially could not, would not trust Pompallier whose mindset remained fundamentally unaltered. Reconciliation was impossible, and by 1848 the breach between Pompallier and the Marists was complete.

---

52.   Colin to Pompallier, 18 October 1836, in *Colin sup*, Doc 5.
53.   'Le talent d'aller directement au fond des choses', Mayet, *Mémoires*, in OM, volume 2 (Rome, 1961), Doc 752.

The years of struggle took their toll on both men, as sheaves of correspondence testify, all eminently quotable documents essentially circling the same treadmill. The missionaries moved south. Garin and Claude-Marie would now be identified with Nelson; Reignier, Forest, Basile and Florentin with Hawke's Bay; Petit-Jean, Yvert, Viard with Wellington; Séon with the Hutt Valley; Pezant, Lampila, Euloge and Elie-Régis with the Whanganui River. They have earned their place in our memory. So has Pompallier. The wharf piles of Father Petit's wonderful tidal mill at Puräkau may be quietly shrinking away but the Puräkau church, taken on the Hokianga tide to Motuti, now shelters the remains of the first Catholic leader in Aotearoa-New Zealand. There is no sense in blame on either side now; there were too many extenuating circumstances. The taonga was in the founding. As Anne Salmond writes, understandings are never final: 'the spiral is still spinning ... the past never ends.'[54]

---

54.   Salmond, *Between Worlds* (Auckland, 1997), 517.

Colin and Melanesia[1]

Hugh Laracy

Joseph Thomassin (1818–91) was one of the pioneer Marist missionaries to the islands in the south-western corner of the Pacific. From Sydney in January 1854 he addressed a sad letter to his superior Father Colin in Lyon. It was a critically barbed assessment of a major apostolic failure:

> Ten years ago our mission to evangelise the islands of Melanesia got under way. It was a glorious launching, one laden with high hopes; with a large and ardent company led by a guide respected for his experience. And what is the result of it? It has entailed much cost, loss and suffering, without any successes or conversions. May our successors be more fortunate than us.

In seeking to explain the debacle, Thomassin acknowledged the inherent difficulties that faced a few strangers trying to change the habits of belief and behaviour of people with customs so different from their own. 'That would take a great many years'. Even so, he went on, much of the blame for the failure must lie with the missionaries themselves, for demanding too much too soon:

> It is true that the natives are not easy to convert. He who is impatient with them is wasting his time. Our lack of success among them derives, perhaps, less from their primitiveness than from the lack of a true apostolic spirit among the missionaries. They hear, but they do not understand the words of the divine master, 'behold, I send you as lambs among wolves'. And Saint John Cryotome tells us 'remain lambs and you will tame the wolves; but if you shed that skin the wolves will eat you'.

Giving point to his comments, Thomassin referred to several of his former superiors in the unhappy enterprise. The first was Bishop Jean-Baptiste Epalle (1808–45), whom he deemed to have been naive, lofty and impractical: 'he thought himself to be a great administrator because he built and destroyed at

---

1. Published in French: *Le RP Colin, les Maristes et le Vicariat de Mélanésie (1845–1853)*, in *Société d'Etudes Historiques de la Nouvelle-Calédonie*, Bulletin no 154 (2008): 65–86.

will a thousand castles in Spain'.[2] This was a view not inconsistent with Epalle's own contention, made on the basis of three years work among the Maoris of New Zealand, that 'the Oceanian is disposed to Catholicism and nothing else is needed to win him but steadfastness and fearlessness in the face of privations, especially hunger'. It also accords with the ambitious proposal for setting up two new vicariates, one north and one south of the equator that Epalle proposed to Church authorities in Rome in August 1843. Ambitious as it was, though, such a scheme also fitted in large measure with one that the more circumspect Colin himself had already proposed in May 1842.[3]

The other objects of Thomassin's criticisms were Jean-Pierre Frémont (1810–64) (whom he considered ineffectual) and Xavier Montrouzier (1820–97) (whom he considered naive and disorganised), each of whom held authority in the mission at various times and places. Frémont, already pro-vicar to Epalle, had been elected 'Provincial' by his colleagues after the bishop's death in the Solomon Islands in 1845. And Montrouzier, named pro-vicar by Epalle's likewise ill-fated successor Jean-Georges Collomb (1816–48), was left as 'deputy-Provincial' on the island of Murua (or Woodlark) in 1848, when Collomb took Frémont and two other Marists to found a second post on the island of Umboi (or Rooke), nearer to the alluring vastness of New Guinea.[4]

Thomassin's aspersions of 1854 were not the first harsh comments he had made about the management of the mission. In 1849, after the collapse of the Umboi adventure and the return of the survivors (two out of four) to Murua, he had expressed similar misgivings to Colin. Nor was he alone in his strictures. And in June 1849, his confrère Pierre Trapenard (1813–92), with whom he and Brother Gennade Roland (1817–98), had recently made a second foundation on Murua, was also scathing of Frémont and Montrouzier. 'I see', Trapenard wrote 'the mission to Melanesia falling in ruins because of a lack of direction

---

2.   Thomassin to Colin, 6 January 1854, in Charles Girard (editor), *Lettres Reçues d'Océanie par l'administration Générale des Pères Maristes Pendant le Généralate de Jean-Claude Colin*, volume 3 (= LRO 3) (Rome: APM, 1999), 877–886. Translations from French are my own (HL)

3.   Hugh Laracy, *Marists and Melanesians: A History of Catholic Missions in the Solomon Islands* (Canberra, 1976), 15–6; Ralph M Wiltgen, *The Founding of the Roman Catholic Church in Oceania, 1825 to 1850* (Canberra, 1979), 235–8, 287–291. Now also Ralph M Wiltgen (+ 6 December 2007), *The Founding of the Roman Catholic Church in Melanesia and Micronesia, 1850–1875* (Eugene, Oregon: Pickwick Publications, 2008) (published after this article was written).

4.   Wiltgen, *Founding*, 475; LRO 3, 434. Hugh Laracy, 'Xavier Montrouzier: a missionary in Melanesia', in JW Davidson and Deryck Scarr (editors), *Pacific Islands Portraits* (Canberra, 1970), 127–145.

[administration] because I am convinced that with such men at its head it is impossible for it to last'. Nor was that the limit of his gloomy presentiments:

> When calling in at Aneityum [New Hebrides, May 1848] I had the opportunity to appreciate that the mission to New Caledonia was not in great shape, that disorder was rife among the various members, that Father Rougeyron and Father Roudaire could not stand each other, that each wished to be the sole pro-vicar [in Bishop Douarre's absence], that the brothers did not agree with the priests, nor among themselves, [and] that among the priests each did as he wished.

Nor, he went on, did the mission to New Zealand offer much hope under the leadership of Bishop Pompallier.[5]

One salutary feature of such comments is that they illustrate for posterity the personal and temperamental differences, and the diversity of opinions—and even antagonisms—that can exist within an ostensibly homogeneous group of people ('Marist missionaries') engaged in a common, and traditionally hallowed, cause: in this case that of spreading the Gospel of Jesus Christ. Given human individuality, such disparities are not surprising. But the fact that they are on record, and that they thereby offer an inside view of the unfolding narrative of events that will eventually be crystallised as 'history' means that they warrant close examination. To start with, it should be recognised that the missionaries' criticisms and misgivings and disaffection did not imply any rejection of their apostolic vocation. Their abundant correspondence is replete with comments on the need to maintain the regular observances and pious exercises of religious life, in order both to conform to the due ordering of their vowed state and to sustain them amidst very difficult circumstances. Prayer was an act of piety, but it was also highly practical. In a situation where success was to be measured more by continuance in being than by a high baptismal score, the observance of the religious Rule was vital for survival. In February 1847 Cyprien Crey (1823–47) wrote in this vein to Denis Maîtrepierre (1800–72), who had been his novice master:[6]

---

5.   Thomassin to Colin, June 1849; Pierre Trapenard to Colin, 21 June 1849, in LRO 3, 464–8, 471–4. Claude Rozier, 'Un Essaie de Mission Catholique à Anatom (Nouvelles Hébrides), 14 mai 1848—fin [23me] février 1850', in *Journal de la Société des Océanistes*, 22 (Décembre 1966): 1–10.

6.   Cyprien Crey to Maîtrepierre, 16 February 1847, in LRO 3, 319.

> I assure you, Father, that one year of novitiate is not too long to prepare a missionary to manage a mission like ours. The best missionary is the best religious; the best religious is he who made, when he could, the best novitiate. Without that one does not acquire the training without which a missionary, especially when left to himself, is unable to hold to his exercises of piety.

In 1848, from Umboi, Frémont observed of his confrères, 'piety sustains them'.[7]

An allied sentiment to that of not relying unduly on temporal means of support was the prevalent acceptance of being killed. In 1847, addressing the thirteenth contingent of Marists preparing to depart for the Pacific, Colin said:[8]

> You are going to leave your homeland, your relatives, your friends, everything, to save souls, and to suffer martyrdom. Oh yes, if it is not a martyrdom of blood, it will be a martyrdom of hunger, a martyrdom of thirst, a martyrdom of pain, of anguish, of tears.

These sentiments, bolstered by the fact that the death of Pierre Chanel on the Polynesian island of Futuna in 1841 had been followed by the wholesale conversion of the island,[9] were echoed by the Marists assigned to the more difficult islands to the west, who are the focus of the present discussion. In October 1847, commenting on the killing of a Marist in the Solomon Islands, Collomb expressed the hope that his death would inspire rather that discourage more missionaries.[10] Referring to the same incident (in which three of them had been killed), his colleague Montrouzier, who had himself been wounded with a spear and had expected to die for his apostolic cause, wrote that the prospect of martyrdom ought to be an attraction, not a deterrent.[11]

---

7.   Jean-Pierre Frémont to Colin, 11 July 1848, in LRO 3, 434.

8.   Jean Coste (editor), *A Founder Speaks: Spiritual Talks of Jean-Claude Colin*, Rome, 1975, 419.

9.   Hugh Laracy, 'Saint-Making: The Case of Pierre Chanel of Futuna', in *New Zealand Journal of History*, 34/1 (2000): 145–161.

10. Jean-Georges Collomb to Jacques-Marie Crozet, October 1847, in LRO 3, 369.

11. Léopold Verguet to Colin, 5 January—28 February, 1846; Xavier Montrouzier to Jean-Baptiste Jacquet, 17 December, 1847; in LRO 3, 182.397.

As for Montrouzier's tendency to be abrupt and imperious and impatient in his manner, which Thomassin saw as contributing to the failure of their undertaking, he himself confessed that failing to Colin in 1849:[12]

> . . . my character, harsh and caustic, renders me unsuitable to be a superior. God has not given me the gift of winning hearts. I lament this fault, which I have long tried in vain to remedy. Accordingly, it seems to me necessary to charge someone else with the horrible burden of the mission.

That admission survives in the records along with statements that Frémont and Montrouzier distrusted the pioneering capabilities of Savoyards (such as Ducrettet, and the deceased quartet of Crey, Paget, Collomb and Villien), whom they deemed to be indigenously inclined to melancholy. Be that as it may, mismanagement and personal differences are not sufficient to explain the failure of the undertaking that began with the advance into the Solomons in 1845, and that ended with the retreat from Murua in 1853.[13] Incidentally, with a pleasing irony, Montrouzier would later write a gracious life of his critic, Thomassin.[14]

To understand the fate of their enterprise, it must be appreciated that in moving up the chain of islands extending from New Guinea to New Caledonia, the Marists were entering what was, at least for strangers, a notably dangerous and difficult-to-live-in region. Conventionally known as Melanesia, it was one of the three broad divisions of the Pacific islands promulgated by the French navigator J-S-C Dumont d'Urville in 1832.[15] The other two sections were Polynesia and Micronesia.

Melanesia was characterised by diversity, fragmentation and multiplicity; by a lack of large-scale social cohesion and uniformity. It was a region that contained many large islands; and was inhabited by people speaking a multitude

12. Montrouzier to Colin, 14 May 1849, in LRO 3, 458.
13. Montrouzier to Colin, 14 May 1849, Thomassin to Colin, June 1849; in LRO 3, 452, 467–8. Wiltgen, *Founding*, 486. J Paget, *Le P Paget (1816–1847): de Sonnaz à San Christoval* (Chambery, 1915), 12, 19.
14. Xavier Montrouzier, *Notice sur le RP Joseph Thomassin, Missionnaire Apostolique de la Société de Marie et sur les Premières Missions de la Mélanésie qui ont été le Théâtre de son Apostolat* (Saint Louis, [New Caledonia], 1892), 107.
15. 'Jules-Sébastien-César Dumont d'Urville, On the Islands of the Great Ocean', in *Journal of Pacific History*, 38/2 (2003): 163–174. It was Dumont d'Urville who coined the term 'Melanesia'.

of different languages, and who lived in small, mutually hostile political units, and in whose consciousness lay a pervasive belief in the efficacy of sorcery and in the power of numerous spirit beings. Moreover, with the exception of New Caledonia, it was a region of endemic malaria.[16] As pioneer would-be settlers in that area, dependent on infrequent and irregular shipping and living among people who, at most, had known but scant contact with Europeans—and who had no reason to feel intimidated, or even particularly impressed, by them—the Marists were singularly vulnerable, especially in the less frequented northern islands.

The history of what they did and experienced there is, like any history, not an isolated one. It is part of a conceptual and organisational narrative that is centred on Europe but which has a wider embrace. To fathom that some definition of terms is required. The 'Pacific' (a usage long challenged by the term 'South Sea'), wherein the Marists found their theatre of operation, was so named from Magellan's comfortable traverse of that ocean, which he entered via the strait that bears his name on 28 November 1520. From the 1820s the term 'Oceania', which originated in France, came increasingly to be applied to that maritime immensity. Hence, when Catholic ecclesiastical jurisdiction began purposefully to be extended to what was also referred to as the 'the fifth part of the world', first the vicariate apostolic of Eastern Oceania (1833) and then that of Western Oceania (1836) were created. By the 1840s, with its popularisation by Domeny de Rienzi, in a widely-read ethno-geographical description of *Océanie*, first published in 1836, d'Urville's classification had become fixed.[17] Thus, as the division of Bishop Pompallier's domain continued (a process required for improved management as well as being driven by internal conflicts) more precise and up-to-date labels were employed. Admittedly, the two southern components of d'Urville's 'Melanesia', New Caledonia and the New Hebrides, were incorporated in the vicariate of Central Oceania in 1842 (from which they were detached in 1847), but that still left New Guinea and the Solomons to be dealt with.

---

16.   Ian C Campbell, *Worlds Apart: A History of the Pacific Islands* (Christchurch, 2003), 30–1.

17.   Thomas Ryan, '"Le Président des Terres Australes": Charles de Brosses and the French Enlightenment beginnings of Oceanic anthropology', in *Journal of Pacific History*, 37/2 (2002): 184. Oscar HK Spate, 'South Sea' to 'Pacific Ocean': a note on nomenclature', in *Journal of Pacific History*, 12/3-4 (1977): 205–11. In 1830, Rome established the 'Prefecture Apostolique, of the South Sea Islands', which was soon superseded by the vicariates of Oceania. Wiltgen, *Founding*, 23-51.

As early as May 1842 Colin had proposed a five-way division of Western Oceania, involving a vicariate of New Guinea, which would include the Solomons.[18] In August 1843, visiting Rome to report on the difficulties in New Zealand, Epalle endorsed that scheme, but employed the more inclusive term 'Melanesia'. He also suggested 'Micronesia' for northwest Oceania (excluding the Marianas, which fell under Philippines' jurisdiction).[19]

After considerable discussion, these proposals, with Epalle's terminology, were accepted by Propaganda. On 16 July 1844 the Vicariates Apostolic of Melanesia and Micronesia were decreed into being.[20] Already, in April, Colin had, with some reluctance, accepted responsibility for staffing a third vicariate and, much against the nominee's inclination, had recommended Epalle as Vicar Apostolic. In so doing, he conceded approvingly that it was not the work that Epalle feared but 'the prospect of such a dignity'. On his part, and being familiar with the conflicts of authority that had arisen with Pompallier and Bataillon, Epalle insisted on tying himself more firmly to the Society of Mary by taking the vow of stability before being made a bishop. The first Marist (by sixteen years) to take that vow, he was consecrated in Rome on 21 July 1844.[21]

On 18 January 1845 Bishop Jean-Baptiste Epalle sailed from London for Sydney, accompanied by twelve other Marists, six priests and six brothers, and one other priest, Claude Jacquet (1812–47), who had absconded from his diocese of Lyon to join the party. The eleventh missionary departure, it was the largest single group Colin ever sent to Oceania. As for Jacquet, he was professed in the Society of Mary on 19 March 1847, a month before he was killed in the Solomons, aged 35.[22]

When Epalle's company reached Sydney on 21 June 1845 they were met by three other Marists whom Colin had sent ahead to open a supply centre, a Procure, for the expanding operations in Oceania. During the four months they spent in Sydney Epalle made strong efforts, as he had earlier done in Europe, to gather information about the vicariate of Melanesia. It would have

---

18. Wiltgen, *Founding*, 235–8.

19. *Ibid*, 290–1. Colin referred to Melanesia and Micronesia in 1844, *ibid*. 297–8.

20. *Ibid*, 304. For the time being the 'third vicariate' was to subsume both Melanesia and Micronesia, and Epalle was to be given a coadjutor (in the event Collomb) who would assist with Micronesia.

21. *Ibid*, 298. Coste, *A Founder Speaks*, 230; Jean Coste (editor), *A Founder Acts: Reminiscences of Jean-Claude Colin* (Rome, 1983), 198–201.

22. Coste, *A Founder Speaks*, 368; Collomb to Crozet, October 1847, in LRO, 368. For details of missionary departures, see LRO, volume 4 (Rome: APM, 1999), 15–27.

been inconceivably irresponsible of him to have done otherwise. Indeed, he wondered if he was not 'relying too much on human opinions'. [23] He need not have worried. The yield—from exiguous sources, in both places—was slight. The published information available was mainly geographical and, like the verbal advice, did not come from sojourners long familiar with the area—for there were none—but from ship-resident transients. Therefore, the expedition, buoyed by Epalle's optimism and the fact that Protestant missionaries had not yet ventured north of the New Hebrides, called for fortitude and faith as substitutes for knowledge. It was undoubtedly risky, but not on that account to be dismissed as foolhardy. Finally, on 23 October 1845 they left Sydney aboard a chartered schooner, the *Marian Watson*.

Epalle's overall plan was ambitious. Before leaving France he said he was aiming for New Guinea.[24] This was an objective that accorded with Colin's preference to concentrate his limited resources on Melanesia rather than over-reaching into Micronesia, but not on the scale that Epalle envisaged.[25] Excited by the prospect of preceding other European settlers, who would bring 'not only infidelity but heresy and unbelief' into 'this fine part of Oceania', Epalle hoped '*quam primum* [without delay] to station communities of three or four priests and as many brothers' in various places, 'one in the Solomons, one in New Britain, one in New Ireland and at four or five in New Guinea', each of which might soon be the core of a diocese. Colin's response to these prodigal expectations (Thomassin's 'castles in Spain'), which called for a minimum of forty-two missionaries and considerable expenditure, was cautious.[26] A detached commentator might, however, be excused for diluting any inclination to censure the bishop by recalling a line of poetry from Epalle's contemporary, Robert Browning:[27] 'Ah, but a man's reach should exceed his grasp / Or what's a heaven for?' Or one from the New Zealand laureate, Thomas Bracken:[28] 'Poor souls with stunted vision /Oft measure giants by their narrow gauge.'

---

23.   Wiltgen, *Founding*, 287, 291.
24.   Epalle to Propagation de la Foi (Lyon), 23 March 1844, APM (Archivio Padri Maristi, Rome), OMM 000 Melanesia and Micronesia; Epalle to Colin, 15 December 1844, Epalle to Fransoni, 2 January 1845, Epalle to Propagation de la Foi, 2 January 1845, OMM 411 Mgr Epalle. Wiltgen, *Founding*, 287, 291, 307.
25.   *Ibid*, 298–9, 306–9.
26.   Epalle to Colin, 15 December 1844, Epalle to Fransoni, 2 January 1845 (copy), APM, OMM 411 Mgr Epalle. Wiltgen, *Founding*, 292–3. Ralph M Wiltgen, *A Difficult Mission*, in Norman Ruffing (editor), *The Word in the World, 1969* (Techny, 1969), 11.
27.   *Andrea del Sarto* (1855), l.97.
28.   *Not Understood* (1879).

Besides, had not Saint Paul commended 'Christ's fools', and attendant risk-taking; and had not Saint Peter been matter-of-fact about martyrdom?[29]

In any case, the bishop's immediate intentions became less grandiosely explicit once he reached Sydney. 'I see great advantages,' he wrote, 'in commencing at a [small] place of which we can make ourselves complete masters'.[30] Father Jean-Louis Rocher (1809-94) reported to Colin that, on the advice of a trading captain named Blackland, Epalle would first investigate San Cristobal in the southern Solomons; then, he would deposit two priests (Thomassin and Jacquet) at Ponape, in response to a request by a settler from there (James Hall, himself a Protestant) who had visited New Zealand in 1842. Ponape was to be a chaplaincy for the Europeans settled there, while Micronesia generally was seen as a possible refuge for Pompallier if he was forced from New Zealand. En-route though, Epalle would scout for suitable base sites elsewhere in Melanesia.[31] It was a quixotic enterprise, visionary and faith-driven, but in the circumstances it could scarcely have been otherwise. It reflected bold assumptions not unlike those that had driven Captain Cook (to go 'as far as it [is] possible for man to go'); or John Williams of the London Missionary Society ('I cannot content myself within the narrow limits of a single reef'); or which would drive George Augustus Selwyn, the Anglican Bishop of New Zealand, to inaugurate his Melanesian Mission in 1849 ('I hope in ten years to shake hands with the bishop of Borneo').[32]

The dangers for the Marists were remarked on by the French Consul in Sydney. Referring to Epalle, he wrote: 'I was struck by the vagueness of his plans'. As already intimated to Colin, these were to explore his domain and then to set up a base on some small island—possibly Waigeo, off the western tip of New Guinea, but which lay on the shipping route between China and Australia.

---

29. I Corinthians 3:18; I Peter 4:12–19.

30. Epalle to Colin, 12 July and 17 August 1845, APM, OMM 411 Mgr Epalle.

31. Epalle to Colin, 22 October 1845; Jean-Louis Rocher to Colin, 4 December 1845, Etienne Chaurain to Colin, 2 March 1846, in LRO 3, 171, 175, 217. Wiltgen, *Founding*, 263, 303. By 1840 about forty Europeans lived on Ponape, David Hanlon, *Upon a Stone Altar: A history of the Island of Pohnpei to 1890* (Honolulu, 1988), 60.

32. John C Beaglehole (editor), *The Journals of Captain James Cook*, volume 2, *The Voyage of the 'Resolution' and 'Adventure', 1772–1775* (Cambridge, 1969), 322; Richard Lovett, *The History of the London Missionary Society, 1795–1895* (London, 1899), volume 1, 256; Hugh Laracy, 'Selwyn in Pacific Perspective', in Warren Limbrick (editor), *Bishop Selwyn in New Zealand and the Pacific* (Palmerston North, 1983), 121–135.

The consul, Jean Faramond, continued:[33]

> I pointed out to him the dangers to which he was exposing
> himself in landing in the midst of savage people . . . But I knew
> in advance that my warnings were useless, he placed himself
> at the mercy of Providence and regarded it as a culpable lack
> of confidence in divine power to arrange his voyage according
> to the ordinary rules of human prudence. I accompanied him to
> his ship . . . I was following him with Archbishop [Polding's]
> Vicar General [Abbot Gregory] to whom I said 'There is a good
> missionary that we shall never see again. He will be dead with
> his companions before six months.' 'That would be a great
> happiness,' he replied. 'It is the blood of martyrs which makes
> religion prosper. Look at Futuna, a missionary was sacrificed
> there and today the entire island is Catholic'.

In the circumstances, though, there were so few certitudes for the missionaries
to rely on that thinking big was probably the best way to think.

The narrative of their venture has been often told.[34] Epalle and his party of
seven priests and six brothers left Sydney on 23 October 1845 in a chartered
trading vessel, the *Marian Watson*. They travelled via New Caledonia, where
Marists had been stationed since 1843. There they left one of their number,
Brother Bertrand, but were joined by two *canaque* catechumens. Then, on 2
December, they dropped anchor off the southeast coast of San Cristobal. Four
days later, seeing no expanse of flat land, and preferring some place more central,
Epalle decided to go north to Santa Isabel, to Thousand Ships Bay, which had
been charted by d'Urville in November 1838 and which was described in the
second edition of Rienzi. There, after misreading local political rivalries, Epalle
was mortally wounded on 16 December. Consequently, under the direction of
Jean-Pierre Frémont, who was also seriously wounded in the attack, the

---

33. Cited in Hugh Laracy, 'Roman Catholic "Martyrs" in the South Pacific 1841–55',
    in *Journal of Religious History*, 9/2 (December 1976): 194; Wiltgen, *Founding*,
    330–1.
34. Léopold Verguet, *Histoire de la Première Mission Catholique au Vicariat de
    Mélanésie, 1844–1848* (Carcassonne, 1854); Antoine Monfat, *Dix Années en
    Mélanésie: Etude Historique et Religieuse* (Lyon, 1891); Laracy, *Marists and
    Melanesians*; Claude Rozier, 'La Première Mission Catholique aux Iles Salomon',
    in *Journal de la Société des Océanistes*, 17 (1961): 15–23.

survivors retreated to San Cristobal where they settled on the southwest coast at Makira harbour, which they named Port Sainte-Marie.[35]

When the *Marian Watson* left there at the end of March, two missionaries, Chaurain and Brother Prosper also said goodbye to the Solomons. With them was Montrouzier, who was going to New Caledonia to recuperate from a spear wound. Even so the prospects of making a settlement seemed reasonable, but malaria and inter-village hostilities remained a threat. When Jean-Georges Collomb, Epalle's intended coadjutor turned successor, visited for a week in February 1847 he found his confrères in a debilitated state. When he returned in August having gone to New Zealand to receive Episcopal consecration from Bishop Viard (1809–72), and having just experienced murderous attacks on the mission stations at Balade and Pouebo in New Caledonia, in which Brother Blaise Marmoiton had been killed, he found an even worse situation.[36] One priest (Crey) had died of fever and two priests and a brother had been killed. With little to hope for at San Cristobal, Collomb then led his troupe northwards towards the ever beckoning New Guinea, to Murua. Charted by a Captain Grimes of the *Woodlark* in 1836, this island had a favourable reputation among certain traders in Sydney, and he had already decided to try his luck there. From New Caledonia he informed Colin of this, adding:[37] 'I have written to the consul at Sydney, to M Lavaud, Governor of Tahiti, and to Admiral Thomelin at Valparaiso so that if anyone thinks to have us visited by a warship they will know where to find us.'

The islanders at the anchorage of Guasopa on Murua welcomed the Marist 'knights errant' (Frémont's term) on 15 September 1847, but more from the hope of material gain rather than from any interest in religious doctrine.[38] Eight

---

35.   Claude Jacquet to Para [Zacharie Paret], 26 January 1846; Montouzier to his parents, 30 January 1846; Frémont to Colin, 22 February 1846; Chaurain to Colin, 2 March 1846; in LRO 3, 184–196, 203–7, 212–236. Montrouzier to Henri Montrouzier, [January/February 1846], APM, Correspondence Missionaires avec Administration Generale. GL Domeny de Rienzi, *Océanie*, was first published in 1836, and the second edition in 1843.

36.   Georges Delbos, *The Catholic Church in New Caledonia: A Century and a Half of History* (Suva, 2000), 68–73; Lillian G Keys, *Philip Viard: Bishop of Wellington* (Christchurch: Pegasus Press, 1968), 60–1.

37.   Collomb to Colin, 6–8 May 1847; Collomb to Jean-Marie Crozet, October 1847; Montrouzier to Gabriel Montrouzier, 13 October 1847; in LRO 3, 348-9, 368–378, 391–2. Montrouzier to his parents, 15 July 1847, APM Montrouzier correspondence, personal file. Collomb thought of going to Buka. Collomb to Colin, 21 August 1847, APM, OMM 411.

38.   Frémont to Colin, 11 July 1848, in LRO 3, 434; Montrouzier to Gabriel

months later, prompted by the lack of progress, and by impatience grounded in the assumption that the truth of their message should be obvious to people of goodwill, Collomb and three confrères departed to establish a second station on Umboi, within sight of New Guinea. Alas, the people there were no better disposed and malaria was again troublesome.[39] When Montrouzier came up from Murua in May 1849, he found that Collomb and Grégoire Villien had succumbed to fever. So he took the two survivors, a priest and a brother, back to Murua where affairs had continued to deteriorate.[40] Moreover, the situation was exacerbated by personal tensions and by Montrouzier's inflexible insistence on the observance of the Rule. In June, therefore, Brother Aristide returned to Sydney while Fathers Trapenard and Thomassin shifted from Guasopa to a new post at Uaman (or Waman). They stayed there for fourteen months until driven back by a famine that was ravaging the island, and which was probably due to people being unable to attend their gardens on account of sickness introduced by the series of visits by Europeans.[41]

Meanwhile, as the Marists endured discomfort, dissension and disappointment on Murua, their fate was being decided on the other side of the world. The Society of Mary had not been founded as a foreign missions society. And the strife with Pompallier and, later, the losses in Melanesia (the glory of martyrdom notwithstanding), forced Colin to review Marist commitments. He sent no more missionaries to Oceania after 1849. The turning point in his thinking can be dated to August 1847, when he told a Marist audience that 'we must try to consolidate the Society in Europe' and that he would welcome other congregations into its mission fields: 'Jesuits, Vincentians or whoever they be'.[42] Subsequently, on at least five occasions between July 1848 and September 1850 Colin wrote to the Congregation of Propaganda asking that the Marists be discharged from the vicariate of Melanesia.[43] He was not seeking to withdraw his men in a hurry and conceded that they should stay where they were until replacements had been

---

     Montrouzier, 18 August 1850, Montrouzier to his parents, 3 September 1850, APM, Montrouzier, Correspondence, personal file; Monfat, *Dix*, 288.

39.   Grégoire Villien to abbé Villien, 10 July 1848, APM, OSM 208. Also, in an edited version, in *Annales de la Propagation de la Foi*, 22 (1850): 101–6.

40.   Montrouzier to Colin, 14 March 1849; Thomassin to Colin, June 1849; in LRO 3, 450–5, 464–8. Note: Colin himself had contracted malaria, in Rome in 1842. *A Founder Acts*, 100–1.

41.   Montrouzier to Colin, 14 May 1849, 16 June 1852, Thomassin to Colin, 6 January 1854; in LRO 3, 453–5, 804–5, 880; Laracy, *Montrouzier*, 136; Wiltgen, *Founding*, 486.

42.   Coste, *A Founder Speaks*, 403–5. Wiltgen, *Founding*, 541–2.

43.   Wiltgen, *Founding*, 522, 541–2, 546.

found and settled in. As late as August 1850 he even secured the appointment of a prefect apostolic, to provide formal ecclesiastical leadership for them. Frémont was elected to this post in June 1851.[44]

About the same time, Colin learned that Cardinal Fransoni (1775–1856) had at last found a replacement for the Marists in Melanesia, members of the newly-founded Milan Institute for Foreign Missions.[45] Ironically, when word of this development eventually reached the island in May 1852, to be followed on 8 August by the Italians themselves, the fortunes of the mission appeared to have taken a turn for the better. This was a result of a two weeks visit to Sydney in August 1851 of five young men accompanied by Montrouzier. So impressed were they with what they saw that they returned wishing 'to build Sydney at Murua'. This desire generated an incipient conversion movement. In August 1852 there were sixteen catechumens. So the Marists stayed on with the Italians, and even introduced them to Umboi.[46] But a year on the promise had receded. Apart from a handful of individuals, the Muruans had again turned against the missionaries, who were also being severely troubled by fever. In November 1853 therefore, the last three Marists in the vicariate of Melanesia — Thomassin, Frémont and Brother Gennade, all of them Epalle 'originals' — left Murua for Sydney.[47] The Italians, with two dead out of seven, lasted two more years. In March 1855 Brother Giuseppe Corti died on Umboi, and in August Father Giovanni Mazzucconi was killed at Murua.[48]

44.	Rocher to Colin, 26 February, 30 May 1851; Frémont *et al*, 'Act d'élection', 18 June 1851; in LRO 3, 714, 736, 742. Rocher to Colin, 8 August 1851, APM, OP 458 Rocher Epistolae.

45.	Wiltgen, '*Founding*', 546, states that Fransoni did not inform Colin of this until 21 August 1851, but Colin's correspondence indicates otherwise. Colin to missionaries of Woodlark, 23 June 1851, APM, Epistolae Variae, Generalium Societatis Mariae; Colin to Rocher, 25 October 1851, OP 458.2; Colin to Frémont, 19 January 1852, 410 Sancta Sedes. Colin to Giuseppe Marinoni, 30 July, 27 September 1851, archives of Pontificio Istituto Missioni Estere (PIME), Rome, volume 28.

46.	Jean-Louis Rocher to Colin, 23 August 1851, 30 August 1852, APM, OP 458 Rocher Episolae; Pierre Trapenard to Colin, 23 January 1853, in LRO 3, 844; Colin to Marinoni, 13 January 1853, PIME, volume 28. For more fully documented accounts of these events, refer Laracy, 'Montrouzier', and Laracy, *Marists and Melanesians*.

47.	Frémont to Colin, 9 January 1854, in LRO 3, 887

48.	Rocher to Julien Favre, 1 June 1855; Rocher to Victor Poupinel, 8 September, 20 December 1855, 20 June 1856, APM, OP 458 Rocher Epistolae. The general superior of the Milan missionaries hoped in vain that the death of Giovanni

The Marist assault on Melanesia had achieved none of its goals. Of the nineteen missionaries who entered the vicariate under Colin's aegis four were killed, three died of illness, two were seriously wounded, four left the Society; and the Faith had not been planted there by 1855.[49] As a final assessment though, to see the mission as amounting to little more that an unremitting source of bad news for Colin, is being unduly myopic. For, despite its costs and shortcomings, the Melanesia venture can, at least in hindsight, be vindicated on several counts. It can even be seen as a glory of Colin's generalate. To his credit, it must be acknowledged that Colin dealt generously with the undertaking, and that in managing it he leavened piety with pragmatism. For instance, in an effort to provide better shipping services for his missionaries and to ease their hardships, he backed an islands trading venture, the *Société de l'Océanie*. Although short-lived, it was very useful on several occasions. Besides, while he despatched three parties of missionaries to the vicariate of Melanesia between 1845 and 1847, he also prudently engineered a retreat as their operation foundered.[50] For their part, his envoys set a high standard of self-sacrifice. It was one that, among much else, consistently led them to refuse to sanction any reprisals against their attackers (and which, it may be suggested, might be worthy of imitation in the various parts of modern-day Melanesia that are wracked with bitter internal divisions).

Historical dredging also salvages numerous other, and appreciably more substantial, relics from this melancholy episode. One is the vast archival deposit of letters which, while being predominantly concerned with the missionaries, also contains much that is of enduring worth about the culture and history of the people they encountered. Of related interest are the first two books published by long-term residents of the Melanesian region (excluding Fiji). One is a history

---

Mazzucconi, like that of Chanel on Futuna, might prompt 'the sudden conversion of the island'. Marinoni, 24 September 1856, in *Annales de la Propagation de la Foi* 29 (1857), 42. Nicholas Maestrini, *Mazzucconi of Woodlark: priest and martyr* (Hong Kong/Detroit, [1984]).

49.   Those who left the Society were Verguet, who became a priest of the diocese of Carcassonne; the brothers Charles Vincent and Optat Bergillon who left Sydney and returned to France in 1846 and 1850 respectively; and Prosper Rouesné, a brother who worked in New Caledonia, before leaving from there in the late 1850s. Information from Brother Edward Clisby fms.

50.   Patrick O'Reilly, 'La Société de l'Océanie (1844–1854)', in *Revue d'Histoire des Missions*, 7 (1930): 227-62. Wiltgen, *Founding*, 300–1, 306–7, 436–8, 486–7. Stanley W Hosie, *Anonymous Apostle: The life of Jean Claude Colin, Marist* (New York, 1967), 181–4. Hugh Laracy, 'Marists as Mariners: The Solomon Islands Story', in *International Journal of Maritime History*, 3/1 (1991): 61–5.

of the Solomons episode by Verguet (1854), and the other is a botanical work on Murua by Montrouzier (1857). Verguet also produced water-colour paintings of named people and places in Santa Isabel and San Cristobal, and also in Sydney and in the Bay of Islands.[51]

Fittingly, the story of the vicariate of Melanesia also has a place in the history of later ecclesiastical developments. Significant here, if only emblematically, is Puarer of Murua. Already acquainted with the Marists, he subsequently attached himself to the Italian priests. When they, in turn, left Murua he accompanied them to Sydney (where they lodged with the Marists) and then in 1857 went with them to Hong Kong, where they established the Catholic Church. Probably in Sydney in mid-1857, Puarer became the first identifiable baptised indigenous Christian of New Guinea or the Solomons.[52]

More evident however, is an institutional legacy. In 1875 Cardinal Franchi of Propaganda wrote to Julien Favre (1812–85), Colin's successor as Superior General, advising him that Propaganda had never intended to withdraw the vicariates of Melanesia and Micronesia from Marist administration.[53] Favre did not take the hint, but in 1881, responding to a French colonisation scheme for New Guinea, Cardinal Simeoni, assigned those regions to the Missionaries of the Sacred Heart. Then, after New Guinea began to be sub-divided in the 1880s, more missionaries were sought for the Solomons. Further pressure from Propaganda and the pleadings of Cardinal Moran of Sydney and of Bishop Vidal of Fiji, at length led the Marists to again accept that responsibility. At first Bishop Couppé of Rabaul wished to retain the northern half of the group, which had fallen to Germany under the Anglo-German imperial agreement of 1886. But Vidal, although fearful 'of seeing the Protestants go first to plough their furrow in the soil soaked with the blood of Marist martyrs' — among whom he

51. Verguet, *Histoire*; Xavier Montrouzier, *Essai sur la Faune de l'ile de Woodlark ou Moiou* (Lyon, 1857). Hugh Laracy, 'Léopold Verguet and the Aborigines of Sydney, 1845', in *Aboriginal History*, 4/1–2 (1980): 179–83.

52. Rocher to Poupinel, 20 June 1856, Rocher to Bataillon, 4 July 1856, Rocher to Favre, 7 August 1856, APM, OP 458 Rocher Epistolae. Raimondi to Marinoni, June 1856, *Annales de la Propagation de la Foi*, 29 (1857): 42–56. Maestrini, *Mazzuconi*; Thomas F Ryan, *The Story of a Hundred Years: the Pontifical Institute of Foreign Missions (PIME) in Hong Kong, 1858–1958* (Hong Kong, 1959), 10–1. Timoléone Raimondi, who baptised Puarer, became the first bishop of Hong Kong in 1874. Bishop Pompallier tried to bring the Italians to New Zealand. Pompallier to Marinoni, 7 September 1857, archives PIME, volume 28.

53. Favre to Franchi, 12 October 1875, APM, Epistolae Varie, Generalium Societatis Mariae.

included three who had vanished while attempting to evangelise the Polynesian outlier of Tikopia—demurred. He did not want Santa Isabel, which lay within the German sphere, 'to be snatched from the Marists', although he later relented on that point.[54] Finally, after much discussion and paperwork, in 1897 and 1898, respectively, prefectures were decreed for the South and the North Solomons. Then, in 1898 and 1899, again respectively, and again following political demarcation lines, the South was entrusted to Marists from British-ruled Fiji and the North to Marists from German-ruled Samoa.[55] With these arrangements, the ecclesiastical configuration of the former vicariate of Melanesia came to resemble that envisaged by Epalle nearly sixty years before.

But that does not exhaust Colin's bequest. There are still other ways in which the Melanesia adventure has helped shape the growth and activities of the Society of Mary. At least four of the missionaries originally assigned to that field by Colin were later re-deployed to help establish the mission firmly in New Caledonia.[56] And others of their confrères contributed significantly to the spread of the Society elsewhere. In 1852 Etienne Chaurain (1819-87), who had been near Epalle when he was attacked, and who had acquired a good knowledge of English while staying at the Procure in Sydney was appointed on that account to the newly opened Marist house in London, where it was thought that 'he will be useful, and even necessary'. Similarly, Jean-Louis Rocher, who was based at the Sydney procure from 1845 to 1864, was appointed there in 1864. That house, Saint Anne's, Spitalfields, intended as a residence for missionaries en route to the Pacific, was to be the germ of the later provinces of England and Ireland.[57]

---

54.   Persico to Nicolet, 26 August 1891, Nicolet to Persico, 30 November 1891, 29 December 1891,Vidal to Simeoni, 15 December 1891, APM 410 Sancta Sedes; Nicolet to Martin, 19 December 1891, Martin to Ledochowski, 25 May 1895, OSM 208; Martin to Ledochowski, 17 February 1897. Vidal to Moran, 21 January 1894, Catholic Archdiocese of Sydney, Archives, Moran correspondence. Ralph M Wiltgen, 'A Difficult Mission'; Hugh Laracy, 'The First Mission to Tikopia', in *Journal of Pacific History*, 4 (1969): 105–110.

55.   Hugh Laracy, 'Church and State in German Samoa: the Solf-Broyer Dispute', in *New Zealand Journal of History*, 12/2 (1978): 159–161. With the adjustment of borders by the Anglo-German agreement of 1899, part of the North Solomons was placed within the British Protectorate.

56.   Colin to Rocher, 7 October 1853, APM, OP 458.2. The four were Fathers Frémont, Montrouzier and Thomassin, and Brother Prosper. There may have been others: Claire O'Brien, *A Greater than Solomon Here: A Story of the Catholic Church in Solomon Islands, 1567–1967* (Honiara, 1995), 92,135,199.

57.   Established as a single province in 1889, England and Ireland became separate provinces in 1952.

Again looking to the Pacific, in 1859 Father Favre noted that in the interest of their missions the Marists needed to be established in Ireland.[58]

In like manner, the Sydney procure itself, which Colin was prompted to establish because of the imminent departure of Epalle and his party in 1844, also has played a major role in Marist history. Not only has it continued to serve the needs of Marists throughout the province of Oceania that emerged from Colin's investment in the Pacific, but that provinces' headquarters were linked to the procure in Sydney from 1898 to 1971. Moreover, the Procure of 1844 also proved to be the genesis of the future Australian province (1938) of the Society of Mary.[59]

Paradoxically, then, it would seem that Colin's Melanesia gamble has succeeded after all. Also paradoxical, especially in the light of his disciple Epalle's concern to occupy the vicariate of Melanesia in advance of the agents of mammon and of heterodoxy, is the fact that when the Church was eventually being established in New Guinea and the Solomons half a century later, that process occurred in conjunction with, and in part because of, those very same forces. Forces, incidentally, whose operations were also shaping the future for the peoples of those islands in so many other ways. But those are other stories.[60]

---

58. Poupinel to Rocher, 13 June 1850, APM, OP 456.2. Hugh Laracy, 'Les pères maristes and New Zealand: The Irish connection', in *Journal de la Société des Océanistes*, 105 (1997): 187–198.

59. John Hosie, *Challenge: The Marists in Colonial Australia* (Sydney: Allen & Unwin, 1987), 29–30, *passim*.

60. 'When Catholic missionaries, again Marists, returned to the Solomon Islands in 1898, it was as part of a well established and steadily growing movement of European contact. Their security was less problematical than half a century before and points of contact with the islanders had multiplied'. Laracy, *Marists and Melanesians*, 35.

The Contribution of the Marist Teaching Brothers and the Marist Coadjutor Brothers to the Foundation of the Catholic Church in Western Oceania

Edward Clisby FMS

In outlining the contribution made by these two groups of brothers within the Society of Mary during the generalate of Father Colin, 1836 to 1854, I will also attempt to show how the relationship between the two developed during this period, and to describe how the brothers generally and the priests of the Society related to each other in the context of the missions.

I approach this topic at a period when the name *Society of Mary* was still understood by many of the first generation of priests, brothers, and sisters as applying to all the branches envisaged in the original Marist project of 1816.[1] The name might have been appropriated officially by the branch of priests when it was approved by Rome as a congregation of pontifical right in April 1836, but it is clear that Colin and the other pioneers had not abandoned hope at this stage of eventually realizing the original vision. Certainly, Champagnat (1789-1840) had not. One has only to read his spiritual testament, dictated on his deathbed in May 1840.[2] For nearly the whole of the period we are dealing with, his brothers acknowledged Colin as their superior general, and did not regard themselves in any way as separate from the Society. Indeed, it was only in 1852, when his generalate was almost at its end, that Colin renounced his right to overall supervision of the teaching brothers.[3] All the Little Brothers of Mary sent out to the Oceania missions during his time as general left France long before that. Thus we should not be surprised to find the missionary brothers in their correspondence referring to their place in the Society or signing themselves *SM*. It is in the older, inclusive sense they have inherited from their founder. If this has given later historians a headache, that is our problem, not theirs.

---

1. For example Jean Coste, *Lectures on Society of Mary History (Marist Fathers) 1786–1854* (Rome, 1965), the first three chapters, and Antoine Forissier, *For a Marian Church: Marist Founders and Foundresses* (Middlegreen: St Paul's, 1992).
2. Brother John Baptist, *Life of Joseph Benedict Marcellin Champagnat* (Bicentenary edition, Rome, 1989), 235–8, Jean Coste and Gaston Lessard (editors), *Origines Maristes (1786–1836)*, volume 1 (Rome, 1960), Doc 417.
3. Coste, *Lectures*, 194.

Yet there is no doubt that there was a problem, and that it persisted until the latter part of last century when research into the origins of the Society of Mary and its early history made clarification necessary, in this area as well as others. The work of Fathers Jean Coste (+1994) and Gaston Lessard in *Origines Maristes* ('Marist Origins'), published in four volumes between 1960 and 1967, and that of Brothers Paul Sester and Raymond Borne on the *Lettres de Marcellin Champagnat*, two volumes in 1985 and 1987, had as one of their many valuable spin-offs the sorting out among the brothers sent out to the Society's missions in Oceania between 1836 and 1861, of those who came from the ranks of Champagnat's Little Brothers of Mary (PFM), and those who were properly coadjutors or lay brothers with the priests of the Society. Thus, of the total of forty-four whom Colin was responsible for assigning to the missions during his generalate, twenty-six are now recognised as belonging to the PFM and eighteen to the Marist Fathers.[4] Even at the Hermitage, motherhouse of the PFM, no unquestionably clear distinction was made between the two groups, even after the formal separation of brothers and fathers in 1852. Brother François (Gabriel Rivat, 1808–81), the new general of the brothers, at the general chapter that year, indicated that the PFM serving in the missions would continue to do so under the guardianship of the fathers, while remaining members of the brothers' congregation.[5] But in the letter he wrote to Father Victor Poupinel (1815–84) a few years later in 1857 asking the newly appointed visitor general of the missions to look after their interests too, he listed among the recipients of his circulars several of the coadjutors, on the grounds that they had done at least part of their novitiate at the Hermitage, or had been in some way associated with it.[6]

At the time Champagnat made his vows with 19 other priests in the newly constituted Society of Mary in September 1836, the professed PFM numbered some 105 spread among thirty-two establishments, including one at Belley.[7] While the vast majority of them were teaching, there was also a significant number engaged in other works, such as administration and formation, as well as in the various trades and occupations necessary for the running of such a large establishment as the Hermitage and supporting and supplying the schools. The three brothers at the Capucinière in Belley were at the service of the fathers

---

4.   For an overview of this question from the PFM/FMS viewpoint, see the appendix to the writer's article, 'Marist Educators in the Pacific 1836–1870', in *Marist Notebooks*, 13 (July 1998): 78–80.
5.   *Ibid*, 79.
6.   *Ibid*.
7.   Frère Avit, *Annales de L'Institut*, volume 1 (Rome, 1993), 188.

in much the same way. The figure given by Brother Avit Bilon (1819–92) in his *Annales de l'Institut* covers only those brothers who had passed through the Hermitage. It does not include another five recruited either at Belley or in Lyon for the service of the priests and their works.[8] Yet these too were considered part of the branch of the brothers, and when Champagnat received his official appointment as superior of the brothers in the Society the following September, they were, at least in theory, under his control.

Although the 'Rule' Colin composed at Cerdon envisaged *fratres adjutores* (coadjutor brothers), dedicated to manual work, and although the man recognized as the Society's first coadjutor brother, Jean-Baptiste Cartier (1799–1880), the later Brother Eugène, had joined the Colins at Cerdon as early as 1819,[9] it was not felt necessary to consider any form of organization for these brothers until the 1830s. By this stage, the increase in the number of priests and their communities, and the arrival of other men interested in serving the Society in the capacity of coadjutor brothers, had given Colin cause to pay serious attention to this issue. It was not, of course, a question of starting something new. Champagnat already had a flourishing organization and a tested formation program, and his men were available for the service of the fathers. It was his aim that his brothers should be able to take on any work or office required of them in the Society.[10] Colin was not, therefore, looking to set up another organization or a different training program. What he proposed, in a letter to Champagnat in February 1832, was to form a separate group within the Marist brothers, who would be primarily at the priests' service and would be known by a separate name as 'Joseph' brothers.[11]

The correspondence between the two founders over the next few years between 1832 and 1835 reveals a certain evolution in Colin's thinking about the place of the coadjutor brother in the Society. This was, in part at least, forced on him by the reluctance of the brothers generally to countenance the idea of having separate sorts of brothers in the same body. We will see how he attempts to compromise at the same time as his ideas become more definite. In April 1832 he volunteers to have the Joseph brothers formed at Belley, with the help

---

8. Bernard Bourtot, *Les Frères Coadjuteurs de la Société de Marie sous les généralats Colin et Favre 1836–1885* (Document SM, 57) (Saint Priest, 2001), 7.

9. *Ibid.*

10. John Baptist, *Life*, 422.

11. Letter of 3 February 1832, Doc 102 in *Origines Maristes (1786–1836) Extraits concernant les Frères Maristes,* Rome 1985, 217, (= OME). Avit gives summaries of this and following correspondence on pages 88–93 of the *Annales.*

of an experienced brother from the Hermitage.[12] Two years later, in September 1834, apparently no closer to his goal, he intends to send two of his brothers to the Hermitage to do their novitiate and receive the habit.[13] One of the two is Cartier, who enters in November, receives the habit in January 1835 and makes annual profession in April, before returning to Belley.[14] In January 1835, Colin raises the question of a distinctive costume: brothers engaged in manual work should not wear the white *rabat*—the mark of a teacher—and carry a rosary on their belt instead of wearing a profession cross. He also wants a brother destined for manual work to spend more time during the novitiate engaged in such work. He floats the idea of having two of his men receive the habit at Belley while belonging to the Hermitage.[15] One of these is certainly François-Xavier Girod (1802–76), Brother Marie, but Champagnat obviously does not agree, since in April the same year, Colin informs him that he is sending Girod to the Hermitage to take the habit.[16] It is interesting to note that he already has a religious name. Writing to him in October, in reply to doubts he is having about the nature of his vocation as a brother, Colin tells him that a brother can be both a Marist brother, when he is teaching, and a Joseph brother, when he is engaged in manual work, and that the employment is the only distinction.[17] But from what we have read, this is clearly not the case. It would appear that Colin had plans for Marie and hoped to keep him. In fact, the brother opted for the classroom and spent the rest of his life as a PFM.

Between 1835 and 1839 then, we see a general pattern emerging. Beside the PFM routinely assigned to the fathers to meet the needs of their establishments, of which Puylata in Lyon (1836/37) is the most significant, there is a smaller group of brothers, recruited by the priests specifically as coadjutors, who do their novitiate at the Hermitage, receive the habit there, and are professed as PFM, but return to work with the fathers. A notable exception is Jean-Xavier Lacroix (1808–88), who is received as Brother Xavier at Puylata in 1836. He is professed in the Society in December 1841, and is thus the first brother Colin receives as a coadjutor and forms outside the Hermitage.[18] In the summer of 1839 it appears that there are ten brothers engaged in the service of the fathers, either at Belley or Puylata, six of them PFM from the Hermitage, two PFM,

---

12.   Letter of 8 April 1832, OME, 220.
13.   Letter of 4 September 1834, *ibid*, 271.
14.   Bourtot, *Frères Coadjuteurs*, 177.
15.   Letters of 7 and 17 January 1835, OME, 277, 279–80.
16.   Letter of 23 April 1835, *ibid*, 283. For Girod, see note on preceding letter, 280.
17.   Letter of 3 October 1835, *ibid*, 285.
18.   Bourtot, *Frères Coadjuteurs*, 7.

including Eugène, from Belley, and two others, Xavier being one, recruited and formed independently of the Hermitage.[19]

Nevertheless, further correspondence between Colin and Champagnat during this period reveals that there were some fundamental differences in their conceptions of the role of the brother in the Society. These came to light when Colin began receiving requests for brothers to take over the role of sacristan in certain centers of Marian pilgrimage, notably Fourvière in Lyon, where two were asked for in August 1837, and Verdelais in the Bordeaux diocese, just entrusted to the Society, where Father Jean-Baptiste Chanut (1807–75) wanted one the following year.[20] Colin obviously expected a positive response when he passed on these requests to Champagnat, but this was not a work the latter considered in conformity with the aims of his institute. He must have made this clear, since a letter from the superior general at the end of October 1837 upbraids him for being 'too fixed on certain points' in his ideas, and gives him the ominous warning: 'I am meditating a major reform in the government and direction of the brothers.'[21] Champagnat's brothers did not, all the same, provide sacristans for Fourvière. Colin was more pressing in the matter of Verdelais. He wrote several letters and, in this case, Champagnat appears to have thought it best to adopt delaying tactics, hoping his superior would eventually grow tired of asking. But in February 1839, an exasperated Colin addressed him with what the annalist, Brother Avit, describes as a 'severe and singular admonition', commanding him under obedience to provide the brother for Chanut, and accusing him of never having been able 'to properly understand the order and the aim of the Society.'[22] His statement that one of the main purposes of both the brothers' and the sisters' congregations was to serve the needs of the fathers so that the latter could the more freely give themselves to the salvation of souls, indicates clearly the gap between the two. Avit comments that Colin had become so obsessed with the idea of 'servant Brothers and preachers' that he had fallen into the fault he had earlier accused Champagnat of, that of having too fixed ideas.[23] Verdelais did not get its brother either, not because Champagnat would not respond, but because Chanut fell from favor and the request was not repeated.

---

19. *Ibid.*
20. Letters of 7 August 1837 and 22 February 1839, *Correspondance Passive du Père Champagnat* (Rome, 1993, Cepam (Centro de Estudios del Patrimonio Marista) (= CPC), 113, 159, summarised in Avit, *Annales*, 91–2. Chanut had worked with Champagnat at the Hermitage.
21. Letter of 27 October 1838, CPC, 125.
22. Avit, *Annales*, 92.
23. *Ibid*, 93.

Considering these differences, and the fact of Champagnat's deteriorating health, Colin decided that the simplest solution would be to detach his coadjutors from the Marist brothers and attach them definitively to the branch of the priests. He put this proposal to the vote at a special session at the end of the priests' retreat at Belley in September 1839. A majority voted in favour of the formal separation of the two groups. From that moment, the PFM ceased to regard Belley and Puylata as among their establishments.[24] Some, at least, of their brothers in the service of the fathers were given a choice as to which group they wanted to belong to. Two returned to the Hermitage, while the four others stayed with the fathers. The initial group of coadjutors of the Society therefore numbered eight. Champagnat had been among those who voted against the motion, and he was disappointed with the result. As he was only too well aware of the probable difficulties in store if the situation remained unchanged, this may seem surprising. What it appears to suggest is that he was willing to make the compromises necessary to maintain the union. Yet when the vote went the other way, he accepted without reservation. It was he who in February 1840 counselled the reluctant Brother Timothée Valla (1803–71) to continue in the service of the fathers as a means of binding the two branches together.[25] Colin also hoped to maintain contact between the two groups by having the coadjutors continue to do their novitiate at the Hermitage. But Champagnat and his brothers did not find this acceptable.[26] From early 1840 it was clear that the fathers themselves would have to take responsibility for the formation of the coadjutors and their admission to vows.

From the correspondence it would appear that it was the brothers themselves, or at least the senior ones whom Champagnat regularly consulted on such matters, who had the decisive impact on the direction eventually taken. History seems to prove that in this they had a firmer grasp of what was in the best interests of both groups than either of the founders. It says something for Colin that he was able to recognize this. We must admit that some of the early brothers, such as Avit, are rather critical of Colin in this connection. It seems to me that they were inspired by the super-sensitive loyalty to their founder which animated Brother Jean-Baptiste Furet (1807-72) when he was hauled over the coals later in 1856 for his excessively critical portrayal of Fathers Rebod and Courveille in his *Life* of Champagnat.[27] Nevertheless, relations between the two groups, although

---

24.   Bourtot, *Frères Coadjuteurs*, 9.
25.   Letter of 1 February 1840, Paul Sester (editor), *Letters of Marcellin JB Champagnat 1789–1840*, volume 1 (Rome, 1991), 544.
26.   Letter of 29 February 1840, in CPC, 185.
27.   See Favre's letter to Francois, 17 September 1856 in OM 2, 763–4. Some

necessarily more limited, do not seem to have suffered after the division. The case of Brother Jacques Peloux (1818–63) offers an interesting example. Jacques entered the Hermitage in July 1843, but made his vows with the coadjutors in September 1844. Either he had entered with the intention of becoming a PFM and then transferred to the coadjutors, a very simple procedure at the time, or he had been sent by Colin to do part of his training at the Hermitage before being professed as a coadjutor. There is no documentation to help us arrive at a conclusion.[28] Either way, however, it shows a great readiness on both sides to serve the other's interests. Jacques left for the missions in October 1844, so perhaps being destined for that work had something to do with his rather ambiguous situation. While his later correspondence shows close links with the Hermitage, it is clear that he belongs in the ranks of the coadjutors rather than to the PFM. In the case of another of the missionary brothers, Paschase Saint-Martin (1819–53), however, it is equally clear that when Colin sent him to the Hermitage from Lyon in January 1845, he intended him to be enrolled among the PFM, and that is indeed where he ended his days.[29] An example from the other end of our period shows that this close relationship continued. Gabriel Lagardelle (1826–95) was received as a coadjutor in 1849 and professed in 1854. He left for Oceania the following year. François includes him in his list of 1859 as recipient of his circulars, but we have no idea of what constituted his connection with the Hermitage or the Little Brothers of Mary.[30]

At the time of the separation, there were also seven PFM working with the priests in the missions of Oceania. Contrary to a later common assumption, these men were not affected by the new arrangement. They had left France not as coadjutors but as catechists, in keeping with the aims of their congregation.[31] This is the case with all those PFM who followed them. Whatever their actual function in the missions, it was in the capacity of catechists that they differed from the coadjutors who started coming after 1841. The PFM contributed to

---

modifications were made to the first volume of the *Life* to accommodate the criticisms of the Fathers.

28. See the note on Jacques at the beginning of Dossier 539–10, *Frères Coadjuteurs,* APM.

29. See his biography in Mayet, *Mémoires,* volume 1, 483–5.

30. François to Poupinel, 17 January 1859, translated by Edward Clisby in *Letters from Oceania 1859,* part 7 (Auckland, 2005), 351 (= LO and part).

31. See, for example, the introduction to the Prospectus issued in December 1840 in *Circulaires des Superieurs Généraux,* volume 1, 341. This fact, which is to the forefront in the correspondence of Colin, Champagnat, Pompallier, of the brothers themselves, and later of François, Louis-Marie, and Poupinel, appears to have been forgotten by their successors.

the Oceania mission as members of the wider Society of Mary up to 1852, and afterwards as partners in a joint work with the Marist Fathers and Brothers under the umbrella of the Society. Despite the fact that, for a variety of reasons, they stopped sending men out to work directly with the fathers after 1860, this partnership continued through the presence and work of the remaining missionary brothers and ended, in some cases, only with their deaths. That is why the Oceania missions can be seen as part of a common or shared history, and why the Society of Mary can justifiably include these men in its necrology. The mission is, in fact, the only work in which the original vision of the Society can be said to have been realised, at least in part.

Any assessment of the contribution made by the brothers, catechists and coadjutors, to the foundation of the Church in Western Oceania has to take into consideration both direct and indirect involvement in the work of evangelisation. During our period, direct involvement in this work, in the form of catechesis and teaching, was largely the preserve of the PFM. Rome appears to have been of the opinion, in 1842 at least, that since the brothers of the mission served as catechists they were 'hardly less efficient than [the priests] in propagating the faith.'[32] Rome was labouring under something of a misapprehension at the time, because both the temporal needs of the mission and the policies of the vicar apostolic, Pompallier, and of some of his priests, meant that the time the brothers generally were able to give to catechizing was severely restricted. Where they did have the opportunity, however, as with Marie-Nizier Delorme (1817–74) on Futuna, and Élie-Régis Marin (1809–72) in various parts of the North Island of New Zealand, Cardinal Angelo Mai's observation seems a just one. The same could be said of Lucien Manhaudier (1815–72) in the short-lived Rotuman mission and later of Charise Gras (1819–84) in Samoa.[33] Yet despite Rome's expectations, and the personal hopes of the brothers themselves, they did not make any significant contribution as a group to the direct work of evangelisation. Was Colin's decision to have seven of his brothers destined for Oceania professed as 'catechist brothers' in Lyon in 1847 and 1848 an

32.   Quoted in Ralph W Wiltgen, *The Founding of the Roman Catholic Church in Oceania, 1825–1850* (Canberra: Australia National University Press, 1979), 240.

33.   The evidence can be found in their correspondence and in the testimony of the priests they worked with. See, for example, the writer's article, *Marist Educators in the Pacific 1836–1870*, 62–3. Only one of them, however, has found a biographer. See Joseph Ronzon, *Jean-Marie Delorme, Frère Marie-Nizier* (Lyon, 1995).

attempt to redress the balance?[34] All we know for certain is that none of the seven is remembered as a catechist. They made their contribution in other areas, Sauveur Conil (1816–78) as a printer on Wallis, Aimé Mallet (1811–97) later as procurator for the mission of New Caledonia, and Joseph Reboul (1822–1910) as a builder and blacksmith for the same mission.[35]

As time went on, elementary schooling went hand in hand with catechising. Various PFM are associated with both Maori and English schools attached to the New Zealand procure in the Bay of Islands, and at the Auckland school in the 1840s.[36] By the 1850s most missions had at least the beginnings of schools. And there were more ambitious projects. In New Zealand, Monsignor Philippe Viard (1809–72) realized Pompallier's vision of a college on Auckland's North Shore by the end of 1849. He informed the governor, Captain Grey, in January 1850 that he intended to employ some of the brothers in teaching technical subjects to the Maori students. They may indeed have started doing so, but at the end of April they joined Viard and the other Marists in moving to the new diocese of Wellington.[37] In Central Oceania in 1847 and 1848, the vicar apostolic, Pierre Bataillon (1810–77), established two colleges, one at Lano on Wallis to train catechists, and eventually seminarians, and the other at Kolopelu on Futuna, appropriately named the Hermitage, for the training of catechists and brothers.[38] Both colleges employed brothers, Lano mainly as domestics, Kolopelu as teachers and instructors. By the end of 1850 there were thirty students at the Hermitage from Wallis, Futuna, and New Caledonia. Neither institution survived the transfer of key personnel over the next few years. Though none of the students became brothers, many provided valuable services to the mission in Samoa, Tonga, and New Caledonia, as well as on Wallis and Futuna, as catechists and general helpers. The contribution made later by the brothers at the Sydney procure and at Bataillon's seminary at Clydesdale falls outside the scope of this study.[39]

34. Coste, *Lectures*, 190.
35. See their brief biographies in *Alive in Memory. Recalling our Marist Predecessors in Oceania 1836–1984*, Oceania Province, or in the later revised edition, *In Memoriam* (Suva, 2001).
36. Clisby, *Marist Educators*, 65.
37. *Ibid*, 70–1.
38. *Ibid*, 71.
39. For a study of the Hermitage on Futuna, as well as the brothers' roles at Villa Maria and Clydesdale, *ibid*, 171–3. The latter are well covered by John Hosie, *Challenge The Marists in Colonial Australia* (Sydney: Allen & Unwin, 1987), particularly chapters 9 and 17.

Another work closely associated with evangelization was the printing and distribution of gospel texts, prayers, catechisms, and related works. In New Zealand, a printing press was installed at the Procure and began operation in October 1842. It was run by a lay missionary, Jean Yvert (*1796), assisted by two brothers, Emery Roudet (1819–82) and Luc Macé (*1813). The latter was the first professed coadjutor sent to the Pacific and the only one in New Zealand until the 1860s. In the five years it operated in the north, the press produced a number of works of great value to the mission, including several catechisms, the text of Saint Matthew's Gospel, prayers for the Mass, the Way of the Cross, the Rosary, other prayers and hymns, and a list of the Popes.[40] On Wallis, where a press was set up at Lano in 1847, Paschase was employed with helping to run it and training young islanders in printing. But it came into its own the following year when Sauveur, a professional printer, arrived to take it over. He produced catechisms, a dictionary, a Latin grammar and plain chant, among other things.[41] It would be difficult to overestimate the value of the Catholic press in the work of spreading the faith and countering the propaganda of the Protestant missions, and therefore the contribution of the brothers—and lay missionaries—in this area during these years.

It was in their work as coadjutors with the priests more properly that the brothers generally made their most valuable contributions to the foundation and building up of the Catholic Church in the Pacific. In his initial instructions to Champagnat about the choice of men for the missions, Colin stated: 'They must be good religious, grounded in virtue, reasonably well instructed in their faith as well as able to turn their hands to a variety of lesser occupations.'[42] From the beginning, it was the 'lesser occupations' that were to take up the greater part of their time and energy. The first mission stations, isolated, under-resourced, and under-manned, found the brothers indispensable for their material maintenance. Clearing ground, erecting buildings, laying out gardens, planting and harvesting crops, raising livestock, getting in supplies, providing food, clothing and footwear, growing vines and making wine – these were just some of the things brothers were expected to do at the beginning. It must be admitted that some of the first PFM missionaries were more adaptable in this than others. The correspondence of Claude-Marie Bertrand (1814–90), whose mother was a first cousin of Champagnat, reveals the problems facing a frustrated catechist in New

---

40.   Michael O'Meeghan, 'The French Connection', in *New Zealand Historic Places*, no 44 (November 1993), 7.
41.   See his entry in *Alive in Memory,* 37.
42.   Letter of 11 April 1836, OME, 317–8.

Zealand.[43] Apart from Joseph-Xavier Luzy (1807–73), a jack-of-all trades, most of the first brothers had to do their apprenticeships in the mission. The group sent out at the end of 1840, the largest during Colin's generalship, however, did include specialists: a tailor, a bootmaker, a blacksmith, as well as two laymen, an architect and a printer. Most of the coadjutors, who started coming from 1841, were tradesmen. But unless appointed to a large establishment such as the Procure in the Bay of Islands or in Sydney after 1845, or the New Caledonian reductions from 1854, they too had to perform a variety of functions. No wonder that writing from Rotuma early in 1851, Lucien, a PFM, stating that the brothers being often occupied 'with trades they know nothing about', recommended that they should be provided with a collection of manuals or an encyclopaedia of arts and trades.[44] Builders, of course, were notable exceptions.

The employment of the brothers in these occupations had a very important side-effect for the mission. The peoples of the Pacific were not in the beginning interested in the spiritual benefits promised by the missionaries, but they were impressed by the material ones offered by the presence of a European tradesman among them. Jean-Baptiste Épalle (1808–45), the later vicar apostolic of the Solomons, recognized in 1840 that a brother could contribute more to the work of the mission in New Zealand by attracting people through their trades and services than by direct catechising.[45] Joseph-Xavier made himself useful on Wallis by acting as barber, doctor, dentist as well as carpenter and smith. He showed the people his tools and how to use them, planted cotton and taught them what to do with it, made and mended clothes, and generally won the favour of both king and people, thus preparing the way for their conversion. Father Jerome Grange went so far as to claim that 'a brother in the islands, especially in the beginning, is *more useful than a priest*, and if Wallis is converted, it is rather to Brother Joseph than to Father Bataillon that we owe it.'[46] In Tonga, where Wesleyan missionaries were firmly entrenched and there was strong

---

43. Father Servant's description of him in 1841 as 'pious and willing but neither robust nor adroit' sums him up well. Unable to do the catechising he preferred and later to study for the priesthood, he led a rather frustrated life, but found some consolation in teaching catechism in his old age in Nelson. Servant's observation can be found in his letter to Colin of 20 December 1841 in Charles Girard (editor), *Lettres Reçues d'Océanie par l'administration Générale des Pères Maristes Pendant le Généralat de Jean-Claude Colin* (= LRO), volume 1, 1836–1841 (Rome, APM, 1999), 819.

44. Letter to Poupinel, 1 January 1851, APM, copy supplied by Father Schianchi February 2003.

45. Epalle to Colin, 31 August 1840, LRO, volume 1, Doc 66.

46. Letter to Colin, 3 July 1843, LRO, volume 2, 760, where italics in original.

resistance to Catholicism, an important factor in getting the Marists tolerated, if not accepted, was the reputation achieved by Attale Grimaud (1809–47) as doctor and surgeon in his four years there.[47] Attending the sick and the dying was a ministry valued by the brothers since it gave them the opportunity of administering baptism, often surreptitiously. In Attale's case, since he was a sick man himself, it probably contributed to his early death. In the case of Marie-Nizier it undoubtedly saved him from sharing Chanel's martyrdom.

Once conversions had been made and a Christian community established, the missionaries saw their task to 'civilise' the people, that is teach them how to cultivate European plants, raise livestock, build healthier and more comfortable houses, read and write, and so on, a process in which the brothers also had an important part to play. Although Joseph-Xavier was training boys on Wallis in carpentry and building as early as 1843, it was toward the end of the decade in most missions that the fruits of their work could be seen. In New Zealand, when Viard visited the Otaki mission late in 1850, he found a school, an almost completed flour mill, and productive fields and orchards. During the year or so Élie-Regis and Euloge Chabany (1812–64) were stationed there, two more flour mills and a timber mill were built. Élie also planted vines, but as in the other places he had planted them, he did not stay long enough to enjoy their fruit.[48] If Colin had been able to make a tour of the Society's missions at the end of his generalate, he would have found at Auckland an imposing church and a college, both in stone, in the Bay of Islands the wooden printery and storehouse just as visitors see it now as the Pompallier Mission, and at Apia in Samoa and at Matautu on Wallis, the beginnings of two cathedrals in stone, as well as the various smaller churches scattered around the islands. The Apia cathedral in particular is associated with Jacques Peloux, a carpenter and mason, and certainly among the most notable of the brother builders.

As Jean Coste has pointed out, Colin was so committed to the missions that he sent out the best of his men, from among the brothers as well as the priests.[49] He was prepared to take unprecedented steps in furthering this aim. For example, he allowed Luc Macé to make perpetual profession in the Society although he had not completed his term of formation and, most un-canonically, made it conditional on being sent to the missions.[50] In fact, once Luc found himself

47.   Antoine Monfat, *Les Tonga ou Archipel des Amis, et le RP Chevron* (Lyon, 1893), 224, 227f.
48.   Letter to Colin, 1 February 1852, quotation translated by Edward Clisby, *Marist Brothers and Maori 1838–1988* (Auckland: Marist Brothers, 2001), 47.
49.   Coste, *Lectures*, 249.
50.   Bourtot, *Frères Coadjuteurs*, 11.

in Wellington in 1854 working for a European settler Church, he obtained dispensation from his vows and left the Society. When Pompallier was pressing the need for more priests at the end of the 1830s, Colin encouraged one of the brothers, Pierre-Marie Pérénon (1804–73), who had been a seminarian before joining the PFM, to resume studies for the priesthood.[51] Thus while working at the Procure in the Bay of Islands, the brother continued his studies. But in 1846 ill health forced him to return to France, where he rejoined his confrères and went back to teaching. Success in Oceania was gained at great cost. Among the brothers, eight died before 1855, five PFM and three coadjutors, while ten left the Society, five of each. Among the dead, two died at the hands of local peoples, Hyacinthe Chatelet (1817–47), a PFM, in the Solomons in April 1847, and Blaise Marmoiton (1812–47), a coadjutor, in New Caledonia in July the same year. If the 'blood of martyrs' is indeed 'the seed of Christians', then the brothers, no less than the priests, are among the foundation stones of the Church in Oceania.

Writing in his *Annales* some years later, Avit gives some of the reasons why the superiors of the PFM decided to stop sending brothers to work with the fathers in the missions:[52]

> . . . the situation of our Brothers in Oceania was precarious and very difficult. They had gone as catechists, and this appealed to their zeal. Once arrived in the missions, the Fathers had considered them and treated them as servants . . . These Brothers found themselves isolated from one another, in the company of Fathers who sometimes treated them badly, even left them alone often enough, and forced to spend weeks, entire months, without being able to assist at holy Mass or frequent the sacraments . . .

Although these criticisms are made from the point of view of the PFM, some of them apply equally in the case of the coadjutors. In assessing how brothers and priests related to one another in the missions, we have to ask how valid are the criticisms voiced by Avit.

First of all, we have seen that conditions in the missions at the beginning, apart from the policies of individuals, favoured if not demanded the employment of the brothers as coadjutors rather than as catechists. We should not forget that priests in stations by themselves often had to perform the same tasks since they

---

51.   See Pierre-Marie's letter to Francois, 25 February 1841, translation in LO (2), Letter 22.
52.   Avit, *Annales*, volume 2, 372.

rarely had the means to afford hired help. Secondly, isolation from confreres and irregular access to the sacraments were problems shared by the priests. They were among the complaints Colin regularly made against the vicars apostolic, and the main reasons why he stopped sending men to the missions after 1849.[53] It is somewhat ironic, however, that the brothers were making the same reproaches to the Society a decade later, and using the same reasons to justify their refusal to contribute further personnel to the missions. In the case of the PFM, community life and catechetical ministry had become non-negotiable matters.

Complaints of being considered and treated as servants, though, and of being badly treated by some priests, are common to both groups of brothers, and are amply substantiated from the correspondence. Claude-Marie speaks for a number of the brothers when he informs Colin in January 1843: 'To tell you plainly, my good Father, and in a few words, we are here in New Zealand as servants, and treated even worse than those in France . . . The natives who witness these scenes only too often have a low opinion of us and give us the names – slave, cook, person of no standing.'[54] It is true that the brother had mainly in mind the irascible Maxime Petit (1797–1858) in charge of the Hokianga station, a dedicated missionary but one his fellow-Marists, priests as well as brothers, found it difficult to work with. The unfortunate Claude-Marie spent more time with him than most. It was not just a difference of temperament, however. We are well aware of the rigid hierarchical structure of the Church of the period, reinforced in France by reaction to the revolution and the excesses perpetrated in the name of 'liberty, equality, and fraternity'. A certain exalted clericalism is evident in the attitudes of some of the priests as well as those of their bishops, notably Pompallier and Bataillon. For such, brothers were barely a step above the average layman. This is not to say that the brothers were always models of obedience. Champagnat, whose father had been an official of the revolutionary regime, albeit a moderate, was much less caste-conscious than the majority of priests, and introduced among the brothers ideas and attitudes that did not sit well with many of his fellow-Marists. Some of the younger missionaries towards the end of our period probably had cause to complain about the excessive independence shown by some of the pioneer brothers.[55]

---

53.   Coste, *Lectures*, 249.
54.   Letter of 22 January – 2 February 1843, in LRO, volume 2, 577–8.
55.   In a letter to Colin from Kolopelu in 1850, Laurent Dezest reports that Bataillon was complaining that Joseph-Xavier had usurped his position and that of the superior, Charles Mathieu, in the house. 14 September 1850, in LRO, volume 3, 679.

Yet certainly, from the case of Michel Colombon (1812–80), the first brother
in the New Zealand mission, who left in 1840, to that of Jean Taragnat (1816–
78), one of the first in New Caledonia, who departed in 1852, the attitudes and
conduct of some of the fathers proved a major factor in the loss of brothers to
the mission. As Attale put it in a letter of February 1844, not writing about his
own situation: 'The hardships a brother experiences himself are burden enough.
If he is not supported by the charity of those who ought to show him such, how
will he persevere?'[56]

Relations between priests and brothers also suffered when the needs of
the mission took precedence over the requirements of religious life. In New
Zealand, Pompallier found it politic, in order to impress status-conscious Maori
and class-conscious English, to draw clear distinctions between priests and
brothers, making the latter wear lay clothing and take their meals apart from
the priests. If this helped clarify the ranking of the personnel of the mission, it
did a great disservice to the religious status of the brothers.[57] In this respect, at
least, the bishop did not live up to Champagnat's expectations that he would
show himself a father to the brothers.[58] But it is clear that this did not count for
much in the thinking of either Pompallier or Bataillon, or indeed of some of
their priests, more imbued with missionary zeal than religious spirit. It was not
an attitude shared by the superior general. Addressing some of these problems
in his circular of 21 November 1840, Colin writes to his missionary priests:[59]

> As for those who are your companions and who are by custom
> called Brothers, let this term retain its full meaning for you.
> Love them like brothers, regard them as children and be fathers
> to them. In our houses in Europe we are happy to have them
> at our tables, to foresee their needs, and ease their burdens by
> sharing them. More than once I have seen our fathers working
> in the kitchen, serving at table, washing the dishes to help out
> a brother who is indisposed. The Society is directed by the
> same spirit here and there. I am convinced that there as here the
> brothers are regarded as members of the same body.

---

56. Letter to Colin, 15 February 1844, translation in LO (3), Letter 44.
57. Clisby, *Maori*, 27.
58. See Champagnat's letter of 27 May 1838, Sester, *Lettres*, volume 1, 369.
59. Letter of 21 November 1840, in Gaston Lessard (editor), *Colin sup* (Rome, 2007),
     Doc 218.

Yet the same correspondence that lets us know of the problems allows us as well a glimpse of the good working relationships, friendships, and solid community spirit which were characteristic of the missions generally and which also played a part in winning souls for Christ. Marie-Nizier and Pierre Chanel on Futuna, Élie-Régis and Jean-Baptiste Petitjean (1816–76) at Whangaroa, Attale and Joseph Chevron (1808–84) in Tonga, Sorlin Gentes (1818–1903) and Jean-Baptiste Bréhéret (1815–98) in Fiji are good examples of such partnerships. Pierre-Marie's idealistic portrayal of community life at the Bay of Islands in the early 1840s, Claude-Marie's description of the exhilaration felt by all at a gathering of eleven Marists for retreat at Tauranga in 1846, Jacques' account of a joyful reunion in Apia at Easter 1848 of over 30 missionaries, fifteen Marists, four Lazarists, and twelve Sisters of Saint Vincent de Paul—the latter on the way to China—help us to see another, and certainly fuller, part of the picture.[60] Even in tense situations, it was the ideal of unity emphasized by Colin that prevailed. When the conflict between the coadjutor Jean Taragnat and his superior, Gilbert Roudaire (1813–52), on the Isle of Pines in 1849, threatened to get out of control, it was the brothers, led by his fellow coadjutor, Prosper Rouesné (*1816), and Bertrand Besselles, PFM (1814–90), who took steps to defuse the situation and restore peace.[61] The soundness of this network of relationships is nowhere better demonstrated than during the six or so years from 1849 to 1855 when no missionaries, priests or brothers, were sent out to Oceania. Despite enormous pressures—the high mortality rate from disease and massacres, and the failure of missions in Melanesia, civil war and the attempts of Bataillon to detach his Marists from the Society in Central Oceania, the challenges of reshaping the mission in New Zealand in the wake of the conflict with Pompallier—the Society remained true to its origins, surely telling testimony to the spirit of unity and dedication among all its members in the Pacific.

For most of the brothers, PFM at least, Colin as superior general, would have remained a venerable, remote figure, to be glimpsed only occasionally and from afar on visits to the Hermitage in France or sometimes during the annual retreats. For the missionary brothers, on the other hand, he was someone closer and more familiar. He had taken part in choosing them for the missions and had, where possible, had a personal talk with them before their departure. His circulars to the missionaries were addressed to them as much as to the priests. It is evident that he took his responsibility for them very seriously, as much after as before 1842, when Rome refused to recognize the PFM as one body with the Society. Their correspondence, which is not negligible—at least thirty-fve

---

60.   Letters 41, 61, and 76 in the 'Letters from Oceania' series.
61.   Prosper to Colin, 5 April 1851, in LRO, volume 3, 720.

letters to him alone between 1840 and 1854 – shows a definite filial openness and trust. Marie-Nizier, in a letter of 13 June 1849, conveys the general attitude when he writes: 'I am overjoyed at finding a fresh opportunity for letting you know how pleased I am to be able once more to communicate with the kindest of fathers!'[62] Had Colin done only this for the missionary brothers, he would have deserved the gratitude and respect of the Little Brothers of Mary.

---

62. Marie-Nizier to Colin, 13 June 1849, translation in LO (4), 221. Marie-Nizier wrote a number of letters to Colin, some after his term as superior general had ended. See 'Les Lettres de Frère Marie-Nizier', présentées par Frère Joseph Ronzon (1994).

Jean-Claude Colin and Women Missionaries

Catherine Jones SMSM

The thinking and practice of Father Colin on women missionaries may be traced to the earliest Marist Missions in the Bugey Mountains in France. It was there that **Marist spirituality developed as essentially a missionary spirituality,** traced out on paper in the little presbytery of Cerdon as Father Colin worked on the Constitutions, tramped out in the missions in the Bugey, as it was later in the missions of Oceania. His brother Pierre Colin (1786–1856) summed it up in his words of October 1824: 'Today, the little Society of Mary begins'.[1]

This paper will be built up around four case studies that illustrate something of the relationship between Father Colin and four groups or individual women missionaries.

Jeanne Marie Chavoin (1786 – 1858) and the Marist Sisters

It was also evident in these Bugey missions, that they were the work of the priests—first of all from Cerdon, and later with the team of missioners based in Belley. Where were the Marist Sisters at the time? How were they involved in these missions? Jeanne-Marie Chavoin and Marie Jotillon (1791–1838) had joined the Colin brothers in their ministry in Cerdon in 1817. Over the next seven years others joined them until, on 8 December 1824 Chavoin was elected their superior, taking the name of Mother Saint Joseph, and the first ten sisters took the habit in the little parish church of Cerdon.[2] Earlier that same year she had written to Bishop Devie (1767–1852), asking that the sisters move to a larger centre . . . I think there is here a clear missionary intention, even if not stated. The following year, in late June 1825, they set out on their three day 'missionary journey' to Belley.

There is no indication that the sisters travelled with the mission band on these Bugey missions, or that they took an active part in either the preaching or

---

1. Jean Coste and Gaston Lessard (editors), *Origines maristes*, (Rome, 1960-1967), Doc 114, 1.
2. Marie Challacombe, *By a Gracious Choice: The Story of Jeanne Marie Chavoin Foundress of the Marist Sisters* (Rotorua, 2001); Historical Committees of the Marist Fathers and Sisters, *Correspondence of Mother Saint Joseph, Foundress of the Marist Sisters (1786–1858)* (Rome, 1966) (= CMJ); Historical Committees of the Marist Fathers and Sisters, *Index Mother Saint Joseph, Foundress of the Marist Sisters (1786–1858)* (Rome, 1977) (= IMJ), 118.

the catechesis outside their ministry in Cerdon, and from 1825 at Bon Repos. It was perhaps their way of living 'unknown and as if hidden' supporting the missioners by their prayer, their sacrifices, and no doubt a good meal and the laundry on their return!

The decade 1825–1834 was one of steady growth and expansion for the Marist Sisters. 1834 was also a turning point for Colin and the clerical Marist aspirants. It was the year that Colin submitted his plan for a united Society of Mary under one superior general—a plan that was roundly rejected by Cardinal Castracane (1779–1852), Rome, as the monstrosity of 'a cart with four wheels'.[3]

Despite this set-back, events moved rapidly for the priest's branch of the Society. In December of 1835 the Sacred Congregation for Propaganda decided to create the vicariate of Western Oceania. In February 1836 Father Colin accepted to provide missionaries for this vicariate, confirmed on 29 April with the Brief of approval, *Omnium gentium.* Jean-Baptiste Pompallier (1801–71) was appointed vicar apostolic and ordained bishop on 30 June in Rome. On 16 August, Pompallier presided over the clothing ceremony and profession at Bon Repos . . . It is hard to imagine they did **not** talk about the forthcoming departure for Oceania!

By year's end, after the election of Colin as superior general and the first professions on 24 September, the first band of missionaries, under the leadership of Bishop Pompallier set out for Oceania. But there were no Marist Sisters on board. Pierre Chanel's sister was at Bon Repos, and he wrote optimistically to her: ' . . . When the time comes for some of you to come out to Polynesia . . . '[4]

By the time the mission band reached Valparaiso in July 1837, Pierre Chanel's (1803–41) enthusiasm was more realistic: ' . . . His Lordship [Pompallier] is at present not sufficiently established in his mission to put in a request for sisters to the Congregation of the Blessed Virgin.'[5]

But by 1840, Pompallier was begging Father Colin:[6] 'Send me priests in large numbers and even more brothers, and soon sisters too. I need fifty priests

3.   Donal Kerr, *Jean-Claude Colin, Marist : A Founder in an Era of Revolution and Restoration: The Early Years 1790–1836* (Dublin: Columba Press, 2000), 270.
4.   Pierre Chanel and Dominique Chanel, 21 Nov/23 Dec 1836, in Missionary Sisters of the Society of Mary, *Our Pioneer Sisters from Correspondence 1836–1885*, volume 1, First Departures 1836–1860, Letters numbers 1–126 (Rome: General Administration, 1973) (= OPS), Doc 1.
5.   Pierre Chanel and Dominique Chanel, 23 July 1837, OPS, Doc 2.
6.   Pompallier - Colin, 14 May 1840, in Charles Girard (editor), *Lettres Reçues d'Océanie par l'administration Générale des Pères Maristes Pendant le Généralat de Jean-Claude Colin* (Rome: APM, 1999), volume 1, 391.

for NZ, twenty for Fiji, twenty for neighbouring islands; and money to buy a ship and three good printing presses'.

Father Philippe Viard (1809–72), who co-signed the letter to the Society for the Propagation of the Faith (Lyon), had written along similar lines to Colin (1842):[7] 'Many of the young girls want to consecrate themselves to God . . . They pester us saying: 'Come, write off to your head-chief in Lyon, asking him to send us young women to instruct us'. If, among the women you send out when you judge the time is ripe . . . ' Note that Viard leaves it to Colin **to judge when the time is ripe**.

Father Jean Forest (1804–84), writing from the Bay of Islands, New Zealand (1842) is much more pragmatic:[8] 'Devoted women such as our own splendid sisters would do marvellous good in the main centres . . . These sisters could take care of the youngsters, train them to work instruct them . . . [in the margin] Moreover, the sisters would take care of our linen which we find gets more unwearable every day; it is falling to pieces and there is no one to patch it for us.'

Two years' later, (1844) Forest is of a different opinion conveying the wishes of Bishop Pompallier to Epalle (1808–45):[9] 'Reverend and dear Father, His Lordship, Bishop Pompallier . . . told me to inform you of the following which is very important that you know, namely: . . . 2. Do not send any sisters out here. There is no possibility of their doing good here yet, without great, very great opposition on the part of our rival missionaries or on the part of the English Government which is apt to take offence quickly.'

So here is Colin back in France getting very mixed messages: 'Send us women missionaries . . . do not send us women missionaries'. At the same time, there is growing alarm at the dangers the missionaries have faced: the martyrdom of Chanel on Futuna in 1841, the death of so many others through tropical diseases, difficulties of support and supply, opposition from protestant rivals and foreign governments. These men had taken on a missionary commitment with very little preparation or formation. Finally the judgment from Pope Gregory XVI in 1844 indicated that the time was not yet ripe. Colin, in his understanding of Marist obedience to the Pope, would have placed great import on that decision from Rome.

Let us backtrack for a moment to 1839, when Colin transferred his base as Superior General to Puylata with Father Victor Poupinel (1815–84) appointed as his secretary. That same year the Marist sisters moved into a house in Lyon

7.   Viard - Colin, 8 November 1842, OPS, Doc 7.
8.   Forest - Colin, 2 June 1842, OPS, Doc 6.
9.   Forest - Epalle, 3 February 1844, OPS, Doc 9.

belonging to Pauline Jaricot.[10] Jaricot herself had been living at Lorette on the hill of Fourvière since the mid 1830s. Geography here is crucial. They are all within reasonable walking distance of one another. It is hard to imagine how they did **not** encounter one another from time to time, and exchange conversation on the missions of Oceania. During this time, until 1842, Colin continued to be involved in the running of the sisters' congregation, for example, the admission of postulants, transfers of sisters, opposition to new foundations, personal property of the Sisters.[11]

From 1842, following his visit to Rome and yet another refusal of his plan for the Society, Colin gradually withdrew from involvement in the organisation of the Sisters, and by 1845 they were effectively a diocesan congregation, and no longer the feminine branch of the Society of Mary.[12] There was a growing conflict between Colin and Chavoin, not only over organisation and mission, but also in the writing of the Rule for the Sisters.

The Sisters, however, did not lose their interest in the missions of Oceania. It was stimulated by the occasional visit from French missionaries. One was Reverend Guillaume Douarre (1810–53) who, the day he made profession in the Society, 8 September 1842, also received his nomination as coadjutor to Bataillon, (whom he had ordained on 3 December 1843 on Wallis), and vicar for New Caledonia. Douarre visited the Sisters in Belley in January 1843, several of whom were from his home diocese of Clermont, and celebrated Mass for them on several occasions:[13] 'One day he gave a sermon on faith which thrilled them - they were filled with apostolic zeal and joy, and longed for the day when they would be called upon to cross the seas and help God's work in foreign lands'.

They also promised the support of their prayers and sacrifices . . . but it is evident that they were also interested in going to the missions themselves, not just offering him 'a spiritual bouquet'.[14]

---

10. IMJ, 122.
11. Jean Coste, *Lectures on Society of Mary History* (Rome, 1965), 194.
12. *Ibid*, 195–6.
13. Historical Committees of the Marist Fathers and Sisters. *Recollections: Mother Saint Joseph, Foundress of the Marist Sisters (1786–1858)* (Rome, 1974) (= RMJ), Doc 154.
14. A footnote in the French version of RMJ (Doc 154) comments on the relationship of Bishop Douarre with the Picpus Bishop Etienne Rouchouze, Vicar Apostolic of Eastern Oceania since 1834. In 1842, Rouchouze was in France on a recruitment drive for his vicariate, and was obviously convinced of the value of women religious missionaries in his vicariate. No doubt they talked over this project together. On 15 December 1842, Rouchouze set sail from Saint-Malo

It seems also that Bishop Douarre did not follow up on this initial enthusiasm once he left for Oceania. It is not known if he spoke of the matter with Colin before leaving for Oceania, nor is there any indication of future correspondence on the subject, either with Colin or with the Sisters. During his 18 months in France from April 1847 to October 1848, he did not return to Belley.[15]

Again in 1844, there was much talk of the missions at Bon Repos,[16] perhaps in response to the Letter from the Women of Ouvea, published in the Annals of the Propagation of Faith the previous year.[17] In April 1844 Father Mayet (1809–94) had written to the missionaries in Oceania that several Sisters were anxious to join them in their work. However in a July consultation of Bishop Epalle with Pope Gregory XVI about sending Sisters to Oceania, the Pope replied that the time was not yet ripe for that.[18]

There is a key text of this period[19] which throws light on the attitude of Father Colin on *Women's vocations for Oceania* [see Appendix]. What can we discover from this text with regard to Father Colin's attitude to women missionaries?

We see here some key principles of discernment of the missionary vocation:

- *Four/five years* . . . vocation standing the test of time . . . perseverance in the desire for mission . . . yet must act . . . cannot postpone indefinitely — *let them make haste*. However, Colin uses the desire of women to leave for the missions, as an incentive to encourage his own men! [1]
- *Added with a laugh/joked with her/teasing* . . . how to interpret this seeming lack of seriousness with which Colin responded to these women? Embarrassment, uncertainty, a way of postponing a decision, yet through all these he speaks *in a kindly way* [3]
- *Did not wish to give this person any advice* — a certain indifference, freedom about the results . . . would not encourage, nor discourage. However, he can rejoice in the final outcome: the *Te Deum* [2] [5]

---

with his new missionaries: six priests, eight brothers and ten sisters. The ship and all on board were lost at sea, somewhere near the Falkland Islands, the last sighting probably in March 1843, cf Ralph M Wiltgen, *The Founding of the Roman Catholic Church in Oceania 1825 to 1850* (Canberra: Australian National University Press, 1979), 311–9.

15. RMJ, Doc 154, footnote 11, 236-7 (French version).
16. IMJ, 124.
17. *Annales de la Propagation de la Foi*, 15 (1843), 415-6.
18. IMJ, 124.
19. Jean Coste (editor), *A Founder Speaks: Spiritual Talks of Jean-Claude Colin* (Rome, 1975) (= FS), Doc. 126, October 1846, 'Women's vocations for Oceania', Text: see Appendix.

- *Attitude to Bishop Bataillon*r respects his authority and independence in recruiting staff for his missions [2,4]
- *God has not entrusted me with this task:* Colin does not see it within his competence as superior general: is this abdication? Does it also reflect what was happening in his relationship with the Marist Sisters at this time?[20]

  Colin does not intend such women missionaries to be religious: *They would not take the religious habit, nor make vows.* [4, 8]
- *Let no Marist ever say "Off you go". . . but never let him discourage them either. The first would be imprudent and improper, the second might be opposing the will of God.*[21] *For who knows his plans? I would not be surprised if he intended to make use of such a means.* Openness to the surprise of the will of God revealed only slowly. [5]
- *Realism about prayer*: difference between *several hours in prayer* in Lyon, and the realities of apostolic prayer in the missions.[22] Yet he suggests that *their salvation would be in less danger out there than in France.* [2, 9][23]

These years were also a time of deep questioning for Father Colin on the missions to Oceania. Between 1836 and 1849, he had sent 74 priests, twenty-six Little Brothers of Mary and seventeen coadjutor brothers. Of these, twenty-one had died by 1854, a profound loss for the new Society of Mary.[24]

---

20.   Coste, *Lectures*, 194-6.
21.   Reminiscent of the attitude of Gamaliel in the *Acts of the Apostles* chapter 5: 34f; and which was a key principle in Protestant missiology of the post-Reformation period.
22.   As Perroton would discover, and confide to her friend Mademoiselle Bioletti: ' . . . what prayers! . . . They are colder than January in Lyon . . . I will make them fervent', Perroton - Bioletti, 26 October 1861, OPS, Doc 251.
23.   This document echoes an earlier reply Colin had made to Propaganda Fide about 1842: 'When Propaganda made me the offer of the mission in Kaffraria [South Africa] my response was: "I dare neither to accept nor to refuse: in accepting I should be afraid of intruding in a mission to which God was not calling us; and in refusing, I should fear that I was letting God down and letting these poor souls down . . . I beg your Eminence to be kind enough to allow us time to pray and reflect upon the matter", Jean Coste (editor), *A Founder Acts: Reminiscences of Jean-Claude Colin by Gabriel-Claude Mayet* (Rome, 1983) (= FA), Doc 214, 5, ca 15 February 1842).
24.   Coste, *Lectures*, 249–50.

Pauline Jaricot (1799–1862)

Pauline Jaricot, who never set foot in the missions of Oceania, was nevertheless an extraordinary missionary and is included in an essay on Father Colin and women missionaries.

Pauline Jaricot[25] was born in Soucieu-en-Jarrest on 22 July 1799, but her family later moved to Lyon, to Saint Nizier Parish. This was an amazing missionary parish, where she had the rare privilege, as a lay woman, of being buried in a church. She lived most of her life in Lorette, on Fourvière Hill, just beneath the chapel so loved by Marists. The track up the hill passes through her property. Contemporary of so many other missionary women, Anne-Marie Javouhey, Jeanne Jugan, Claudine Thévenet, Madeleine Sophie Barat, she heard the missionary call early in her life, and founded the Society for the Propagation of the Faith in Lyon in 1819 . . . when she was barely twenty years old! Besides her practical financial support for the foreign missions and publication of missionary letters in the *Annales* of the Society, her mission was also one of prayer, for example, the *Living Rosary*, and of social commitment, for example, the cause of the *canuts* during social unrest in Lyon in 1831 and 1834. She thus linked both 'foreign' missions and the mission 'at home'.

Colin's biographer, Jean Jeantin (1824–95),[26] describes a meeting between Colin and Jaricot in 1823, on his return from Paris where the Nuncio had rejected the idea of the Marist project. Donal Kerr concludes that Pauline Jaricot rekindled Colin's conviction of God's intervention in his life and gave him fresh courage. Stan Hosie comments: Colin's meeting with Jaricot was an experience that he spoke of more than once. She told him to take courage: 'The Society of Mary is going to succeed; it will give much glory to God'.[27]

---

25. Information summarised from the standard biography by George Naïdenoff, *Pauline Jaricot: Heroic Lay Missionary* (Dublin: PMAS, 1988; Paris: Mediaspaul, 1986).

26. As narrated in Kerr, *Colin*, 184-6: 'Alone and in a pensive mood, he was walking along one of the quays of Lyon when suddenly a respectable woman approached him and said to him: Father could you come to my house for a moment? He accepted that invitation. After seating him, she said to him without any preliminaries: Father the thoughts that are running through your head just now greatly displease God. His goodness has given you three great graces in your life . . . God who gave you such great graces can give you even greater ones. Have courage and confidence then. So she told him all he must do to respond at that time to the holy will of God. I did not say yes or no to her but simply "thank you Madam" and I went away.'

27. Stanley W Hosie, *Anonymous Apostle: The Life of Jean Claude Colin, Marist*

Both authors note that 'Colin did not visit her again'. There was not a lasting dependence on her encouragement. It was a providential encounter at a time of great need in his life. However, the relationship with the Society for the Propagation of the Faith continued. It was a key source of finance for the first missionary departure in 1838, as well as ongoing financial support for the missionaries in Oceania. The *Annales* regularly published the letters of the missionaries, and in this way contributed to the recruitment of missionary vocations. The Society of Mary regularly reported to the Propagation of the Faith, and occasionally appointed Marists to work with them in mission awareness and fundraising in France.[28]

Marie Françoise Perroton (1796–1873), Sister Marie du Mont Carmel

Colin's only recorded words about Marie Françoise Perroton are significant, writing to Bishop Bataillon in January 1846:[29] 'I cannot but admire the courage of Mademoiselle Perroton whose zeal has urged her to go out to the Wallis Islands. I did not have the pleasure of meeting her for I was not informed of her departure prior to her embarking. But I am told that she is a woman of quite extraordinary worth and virtues, who will be of immense help to the women out there. I have no hesitation in recommending her to you.'

The virtues Colin highlights show he understands the missionary vocation well: courage, zeal that 'urged her to go out', 'quite extraordinary worth and virtues', 'of immense help to the women.' Others would remark later that these virtues sprang from an intense inner life of 'intimate union with God'.

These are certainly a valid expression of the key elements of a Marist spirituality, coming to us from Colin, and reflected in the constitutions of all branches of the Marist family: humility, forgetfulness of self, love of neighbour and love of God.[30]

Perroton[31] was born in Lyon in 1796 and brought up, like Pauline Jaricot, in the missionary parish of Saint Nizier. She was committed to the work of the Society for the Propagation of the Faith, and finally heard the call of Oceania

(New York: William Morrow and Company, Inc, 1967), 73.

28.   FA, Docs 215, 269, 314.
29.   Colin (Lyon) - Bataillon (Wallis), 10 January 1846, OPS, 12.
30.   SMSM Constitutions (1984) number 47.
31.   Information summarised from several biographies of Perroton by Marie Cecile de Mijolla SMSM, as well as texts edited by Sisters Mary Emerentiana and Marie Ancilla.

in reading the letter from the women of Ouvea, published in the *Annales* in 1843.[32]

Coming up to fifty years of age, she did not hesitate to answer this call, and wrote to Captain Auguste Marceau (1806–51) asking for a berth on the *Arche d'Alliance*, which set out from Le Havre on 15 November 1845, the twelth departure of thirteen Marist fathers and brothers destined for the missions of Oceania. It is from this letter to Marceau, not to a religious superior, but to a ship's captain, that the Missionary Sisters of the Society of Mary (SMSM) find the core of their missionary commitment:[33] 'My firm wish is to serve on the mission fields for the rest of my life.'

The voyage took over a year, with a significant stopover in Tahiti, where Marie Francoise Perroton received news from Father Julien Eymard (1811–68) that she had been enrolled 'in the Society of your Third Order'.[34] Before leaving for Oceania, she had consulted Eymard, and signed her name in the locket at the shrine of Our Lady of Fourvière. Practical arrangements had been made through Poupinel, Mission Procurator. These two Marist Fathers were her closest contact with the Society of Mary in Lyon during the generalate of Father Colin.

After a four-month spell in the Marquesas and Tahiti, the band of missionaries continued westwards; Marie Françoise Perroton arrived in Wallis late October 1846, much to the surprise of Bishop Bataillon. However, a few months later he could admit to Colin:[35]

> I was not really annoyed to see Mademoiselle Perroton arrive at Wallis . . . She will be a real asset to the mission; but this is enough for the moment. Do not send out any other women unless we ask for them. Futuna is the only place where we would like to see some good young women or sisters for the education of girls. However, wait until we write to you again after we have visited Futuna. In the meantime you can form your own ideas about all this. We certainly would not want any fanatical or unreliable people out here. Mademoiselle Perroton seems to have what it takes to succeed.

32. *Annales de la Propagation de la Foi*, 15 (1843), 415–6.
33. Perroton - Marceau, [summer] 1845, OPS, Doc 11.
34. Perroton - Eymard, 2 August 1846, OPS, Doc 13.
35. Bataillon - Colin, 10 December 1846, OPS, Doc14.

Colin was well informed about the expected ministry of these women missionaries, as well as the qualities required. I think it is fair to say that Bataillon had already discovered that Mlle Perroton was neither fanatical nor unreliable. Perroton continues in her correspondence with Eymard:[36]

> I am not counting on receiving any assistance, and frankly I would say that despite all the tedium I feel in living alone, I still would not advise anyone to leave her homeland to join me here, unless it were a question of religious which would alter the case, for in my opinion religious would do an immense amount of good here, especially working with the women and children. Bishop Bataillon has his own ideas about this, however. He thinks that the time has not yet come for this step.

Father Charles Mathieu (1809–56), appointed to Wallis in 1843, also expressed his appreciation to Colin:[37]

> You recommended Mademoiselle Perroton to me: she is indeed an excellent woman. The one drawback is that she is all alone which is too distressing a position altogether for a woman. She helps us with the care of the sick and looks after our linen and clothes. She is very active, prudent and intelligent, but she cannot undertake any important work for the simple reason that she is alone . . . What we would need for the start would be some good young country girls, strong, and with good common sense, able to grow what they need to live on, and in so doing, teach their pupils to work, in their turn.

From 1849 Colin sent no further missionaries to Oceania. The decision to send missionaries again to Oceania—both men, and the women who were later known as the 'Pioneers' of the SMSM—was taken only after the election of the second superior general, Father Julien Favre (1812–1885) in 1854.

The main source on the relationship between Colin and Perroton, are from the letters edited in *Our Pioneers*, Volume 1, and the more complete texts of her letters edited in June 2001.[38]

---

36.   Perroton - Eymard, 6 October 1847, OPS, Doc 16.
37.   Mathieu - Colin, 26 August 1849, OPS, Doc 20.
38.   Mary Emerentiana Cooney SMSM - Marie Ancilla Grosperrin SMSM, *Letters of Marie Françoise Perroton Sister Marie du Mont Carmel from 1845 to 1873*

For the period of Father Colin's generalate there are eight letters written between 1845 (the letter to Captain Marceau) and 1853: two of these are written to either a friend or an 'unnamed lady' and the remaining three to Eymard, one to Poupinel, and one to them jointly. Bearing in mind that Father Poupinel was both procurator for the missions, and secretary to Colin, we may be able to assume that Colin would be aware of their contents. There is no record of any correspondence of Colin to Perroton.[39]

Colin was aware, through correspondence from Captain Marceau, of the loneliness Marie Françoise Perroton suffered, and the obstacle that this was to sending women missionaries. In 1847, Captain Marceau wrote to Colin:[40] 'Perhaps I shall have to bring back Mademoiselle Perroton, who up to the present, has shown heroic courage but who has really too much to endure, being alone as she is. Indeed I cannot help thinking that the time is simply not yet ripe for women to become missionaries, unless it be that they come out with their families.'

Did this reflection from a trusted worker for the missions in Oceania influence the decision to send no more missionaries?

By the time we hear from Marie Françoise Perroton again, in 1859, she speaks of Father Poupinel who had announced his forthcoming arrival in Futuna 'bringing . . . helpers and companions all devoted to Mary',[41] the first of the Pioneers of the Missionary Sisters of the Society of Mary.

But that story goes beyond the generalate of Father Colin.

(TOMMO, 1, numbers 1–60, Rome, 2001).

39. Sister Mary Emerentiana and Father Gaston Lessard reflected on the six-year gap in the correspondence of Perroton from 1853 to 1859. It is hard to believe she did not write to anyone during this period, which would probably indicate a loss of correspondence. There are also significant events of that period: in 1853, the general chapter of the Marist Sisters, during which Chavoin resigned, and the election of Mother Ambrose as the second superior general; in 1854, the resignation of Colin and election of Favre as second superior general of the Fathers; in the same year the resignation of Father Eymard as Director of the Third Order and his departure from the Society of Mary in 1856 to found the Society of the Blessed Sacrament; 1854 was also the year that Bataillon sent Perroton to Futuna, with a longer term project for Sydney but which never materialised; in 1858 the death of Chavoin, and with that the dream of missions in Oceania. There is also the wider context of the major reorganisation of the vicariates in Oceania. Any of these events may have affected this loss of correspondence from these crucial years; the correspondence resumes on 8 March 1859.

40. Marceau - Colin, 23 March 1847, OPS, Doc 15.

41. Perroton - Favre, 8 March 1859, OPS, Doc 121.

Indigenous women missionaries in Oceania

What was happening in Oceania with regard to the emergence of religious missionary life for Oceanian women? Did Colin know of these women missionaries, and what was his attitude to them? In 1845, the very same year that Marie Françoise Perroton set out for Oceania, the Sacred Congregation Propaganda Fide issued the instruction, *Neminem profecto*, which outlined the thought of Pope Gregory XVI on the organisation of missionary activity. It contained a recommendation on the establishment of seminaries for the training of local clergy . . . but does not seem to have made any recommendation on the formation of missionary religious. Yet initiatives in new forms of religious life for mission were emerging in Oceania.

The earliest known religious missionary was Peata Hoki, of New Zealand.[42] This Maori woman of chiefly rank, niece of Nga Puhi chief Rewa, was baptised by Bishop Pompallier in 1840. Widowed at the age of nineteen, she then worked alongside the Marist missionaries playing a key role in the establishment of the Marist mission in the Bay of Islands. She was, in a sense, one of the first interpreters of the Maori culture for the French missionaries. She also acted as a mediator and peace-maker in the difficult time of first culture contacts between the Maori and Europeans. She travelled throughout the country, as catechist and teacher: we know this because her name turns up regularly in baptism and confirmation registers as sponsor of those receiving the sacraments of initiation. There are occasional references to her in the early Marist correspondence to Colin and other Marists in France,[43] so he would have known of her, but we do not know what he thought of her.

Closely associated with the Marist missionaries, Peata was one of the women who travelled to Wellington in 1850 with the newly appointed Bishop Philippe Viard, who had known her since his earliest mission days. She did not, however, make religious profession in the congregation he hoped to establish in Wellington at that time.[44]

---

42. Jessie Munro, *The Story of Suzanne Aubert* (Auckland: Auckland University Press Bridget Williams Books, 1996), 81–86; and Jessie Munro, 'Ko wai a Peata? Ko Hoki ia. Who was the woman 'of uncommon virtue' and 'great influence with the chiefs'?' (Unpublished paper presented at Pompallier Symposium, Kororareka, New Zealand, April 2004.)

43. For example, Garin to pupils of Meximieux, 12 June–17 July 1841 (Girard, Doc 91); Garin to Colin, 9 August 1842 (Girard, Doc 177), as quoted in Munro, 'Ko wai a Peata?'

44. Michael O'Meeghan, *Steadfast in Hope: The Story of the Catholic Archdiocese of Wellington 1850–2000* (Palmerston North: Dunmore Press, 2003), 18; Jean

The story of Peata Hoki is closely linked with Suzanne Aubert, who arrived in New Zealand in 1860. They both took vows in Bishop Pompallier's newly established Congregation of the Holy Family in 1862, and is thus the first known indigenous religious profession in Oceania.[45] However, once again this post-dates Colin's generalate.

In Central Oceania, during the time of Father Colin's generalate, new forms of religious life for mission were evolving.

On Wallis, from 1846–1854, Perroton gathered around her a group of young women who supported her in her work, especially in the catechesis of children and adults, as well as care of the church and the priests' domestic duties.[46] When she left for Futuna in August 1854, two young women, Nominata from Rotuma and Eulalia from Tokelau went with her and lived in community with her there. Already we see the first experience of international community for mission that is characteristic of missionary communities today.

After the departure of Marie Françoise Perroton for Futuna, these lay communities on Wallis continued under the guidance of Suzanne Pukega at Luketuno and Amelia Claudia at Aleka. Both of these were still functioning at the time of the arrival of the Pioneers in 1858, but seem to have dispersed after that.[47]

Also on the horizon were Sara Fuasea, who lived in community with Perroton on Futuna from 1854, and Silenia Tipai, both of whom went to Sydney in 1867 for their religious formation. They eventually made profession in the Third Order Regular of Mary, and served in the missions of Samoa and Tonga.

Coste, *Vocations Féminines pour l'Océanie Mariste sous le Généralat (sic) du P Colin* (Rome, polycopy, 1970).

45.   Munro, *Aubert*, 81. When this congregation was disbanded on the departure of Bishop Pompallier in 1868, Peata Hoki spent some time with the Sisters of Mercy in Auckland, then returned to the Bay of Islands. Soon after that, we lose trace of the story. At the same time, Suzanne Aubert left for the Marist mission in Hawkes Bay, and was eventually professed in Third Order Regular of Mary (TORM) in 1884. In 1892, this New Zealand 'branch' of TORM became the Daughters of Our Lady of Compassion (Munro, *Aubert*).

46.   Marie-Cécile De Mijolla, *Une Lyonnaise Marie Françoise Perroton (1796–1873): Missionnaire en Océanie–A Woman from Lyons Marie Françoise Perroton (1796–1873): Missionary in Oceania* (Rome, 1997), 74.

47.   Frédéric Angleviel, *L'apostolat Féminin à Wallis et Futuna (1837–1886): Des Catholiques Lyonnaises aux Sœurs Autochtones,* in Jean Comby (editor), *Diffusion et Acculturation du Christianisme (XIX–XX siècle) Vingt-cinq ans de Recherches Missiologiques par le CREDIC* (Paris: Editions Karthala, 2005), 355–382, here 359–360.

They deserve a place among the Pioneers of the SMSM. These early attempts at community life for the service of mission were a significant moment in Marist mission history.[48]

Fascinating to note that there is an even earlier initiative[49]: a community formed in Futuna in 1851, that is, before the arrival of Perroton and her companions. There is even a religious house, as described by Father Catherin Servant to his parents. Colin would probably have read about it, since all correspondence from Oceania, including that for family, went through the General Administration. There were chants composed to describe the life and the work of the community; these young women sang of taking a vow of poverty (*voto mativa*), committed to being poor, their eyes open to the misery of others. According to Servant, they lived in community and devoted themselves to reading, recitation of the rosary, religious chant, care of the church and sacristy. They also carried water to the presbytery, and prepared kava for the missionary.[50]

Conclusion

Jean Coste[51] makes the following conclusion about women missionaries at the end of Father Colin's generalate: It was apparent that:

- women were indispensable for the success of the apostolate to the women of Oceania;
- isolated initiatives, like that of Marie Françoise Perroton cannot suffice;
- the Fathers (Colin at least) were not disposed to sending Marist Sisters;
- other religious congregations could be requested for New Zealand (Viard and the Mercy Sisters), but that would be more delicate in the vicariates that were entirely Marist.

---

48.   These early experiences of religious community life for mission paved the way for the eventual religious commitment of Sara Fuasea and Silenia Tipai, who went to Sydney in October 1867 with Sister M de la Merci to prepare to enter the religious life. They both made profession there in 1878 as Third Order of Mary of the Missions of Oceania (TOMMO). In December 1880, Silenia, now Sister Marie Saint-Victor (Malia Vika), took the habit of the TORM, made a vow of obedience to Bishop Lamaze and was missioned to Tonga where she lived and worked until her death in 1902. Sara, Sister Marie du Mont Carmel, also made profession in TOMMO in 1878 and worked in Samoa until 1903, when a mental breakdown required that she be repatriated to Futuna (cf OPS, volume 4, 257–8, 285–6).

49.   Angleviel, *L'apostolat féminin*, 359–360.

50.   Catherin Servant SM (1808–60), quoted in Angleviel, *L'apostolat féminin*, 359.

51.   Coste, *Vocations Féminines pour l'Océanie Mariste*, 2–3.

According to Father Coste, Father Colin himself had hesitated for two main reasons:

- Oceania was not well known; there were dangers; as well as the possibility of calumny by the Protestants;
- reticence to take on the responsibility of women (as we saw in our study of FS, Doc 126).

What is the legacy of Father Colin in his relationship with women missionaries for mission today?

Collaboration for mission

Father Colin was hesitant about this, but there are profound lessons in his way of being in mission that call Marists to collaborate for mission. There is a need to think more 'family',—both lay and vowed—rather than just an isolated branch of the Society of Mary, and to plan consciously for closer collaboration in ministry, convinced of the 'gracious choice' that has called us to our Marist vocation.

Marist collaboration for mission will also have a special focus on youth. Pauline Jaricot was not even twenty years of age when she launched the Association for the Propagation of the Faith. Imagine if she could inspire a similar missionary dynamism in the youth of today!

Exploring Colinian themes for mission together

In the missions of the Bugey, Colin and his first companions tramped out the key Marist insights for mission in their time. How can those themes of Colinian thought be expressed in a new way of collaboration for mission? Themes such as:

> **Being something of Mary's presence in the Church coming to birth: Hidden and unknown** as a fundamental missionary attitude 'so as not to impede God's action'.[52] For the Missionary Sisters of the Society of Mary, this is in the chapter on mission, rather than the chapter on Marist spirituality.
>
> **What might this mean for us today:** Our attentive way to being present to people, standing alongside, rather than in front or commanding attention. It means being on the frontiers of mission, where 'the church is coming to birth'.
>
> **Intimate union with God**, rooted in the Hebrew and Christian

---

52.   SMSM Constitutions number 20.

scriptures, an essential theme in Colinian thought,[53] is taken up in all the life documents of the Society of Mary in its different branches.

What might this mean for us today?
It includes the consistent and disciplined commitment to nurture the inner life of prayer, in particular the daily examen of awareness, developing a sense of awe and gratitude for the gift of life and our vocation, facing courageously our resistance to intimate union with God, and daily responding to the invitation to share in the mission of God.

Intimate union with God is of particular relevance to SMSM in our missionary context. Our 2001 General Chapter examined carefully 'Living in violent situations'[54] that marks so many of the situations in which our sisters live and work daily: the Great Lakes region of Africa; the simmering violence of poverty in Latin America; the rapid deterioration of civic and political life in the Pacific: in Papua New Guinea, the Solomon Islands, Tonga and Fiji; the urban and domestic violence of New Zealand.

How do we continue to live in 'intimate union with God' in these situations?

Instruments of divine mercy, bonds of communion
This is recurrent theme in Marist missionary life, linked to the previous theme:

> *It is in a deep experience of God, personal and communal, and by trying to live daily the Gospel values of communion and reconciliation, that we become witnesses to God's love and instruments of divine mercy, sharing with Him in the transformation of society and its total liberation in Christ.*[55]

Reconciliation is a key component of mission, and it applies to family life, the wider social and political scene, as well as all multi-cultural or multi-faith situations. Sirin Phathanothai, daughter of a famous Thai politician, who was sent as a young girl to be brought up in Maoist China, throws light on a key

---

53.   FS, Docs 45.2; 63.2; 64.1–3; 132.8–12; 162.5; 182.37–42.
54.   Missionary Sisters of the Society of Mary, *Living in Violent Situations*, VIII General Chapter 2001, Rome.
55.   SMSM Constitutions number 26.

Marist theme in mission today:[56] 'If I am a bridge between worlds, I'm all too aware now of the chasm that bridge must cross. Indeed, both to span and to reveal that chasm is the commitment I have made.'

Marists in Oceania

During Colin's generalate, Oceania was on the receiving end of missionaries. Today, all four vowed branches are sending missionaries far beyond their local churches: Marist Fathers in the Philippines; Missionary Sisters of the Society of Mary in Algeria and Latin America; Marist sisters in the Philippines and West Africa; Marist brothers and their new *mission ad gentes* project. But where are the lay Marists? How can they be included in these missionary initiatives? Mission is not just 'where' but 'how'. What are the specific gifts and insights that these Pacifican and Marist missionaries bring to the vocation of the Society of Mary?[57] Marists also have a continuing role within the Pacific churches. There are pressing missionary needs still here in Oceania. Do we have eyes to see them?

Jean-Claude Colin could never have imagined the diversity and range of the Marist mission in Oceania, and in particular the role that women missionaries, inspired by his vision and commitment, have played in that mission. He will continue to guide us as we look for ways to live his vision into the future in greater collaboration with lay Marists, in the search for deeper meaning of key themes in Marist spirituality, and in the expanding role of Pacifican Marists in leadership of the Society for mission.

Appendix: Colin in *A Founder Speaks*, Rome, 1975, Document 126 - a key document: October 1846, *Women's vocations for Oceania*

[1] In October 1846, Reverend Father Superior spoke of a lady who had come to see him and who wished to go to Oceania. 'For four or five years now she has been harrying me to give my consent.' And he added with a laugh, 'Messieurs, let those who wish to go to the aid of these people make haste, for they are going to be outstripped by the weaker sex!'

[2] He had not wished to give this person any advice and had told her that he did not think any prudent priest could encourage her to go. He added, 'But if one fine morning they told me she had gone, I would bless God and say

---

56.   Sirin Phathanothai, *The Dragon's Pearl: Growing up Among Mao's Reclusive Circle* (London: Simon and Schuster, 1994), 518.

57.   See the comments about a 'Marian Church' by Craig Larkin in *Maristes: Un Lien Entre les Pères Maristes de France de Leurs Amis* no 183 (2ième trimestre 2007).

my *Te Deum.*' He spoke to her often and joked with her. He told her, 'Here you spend several hours in prayer, but if you went out there you would have around you day and night a crowd of savages who must be dealt with. Goodbye to the hours of prayer!' And he would laugh, teasing her. This lady told him that Bishop Bataillon wanted her to go. He replied that bishop Bataillon was a bishop but that he personally had nothing to say on the subject.

[3] And so Father Colin spoke to her in a kindly way, neither encouraging nor discouraging her, and he even told her that if she was going to embark he would gladly agree to see her.

[4] He recommended us strongly to follow the same approach. 'How', he said, 'could I take it upon myself to send out women like that? God has not entrusted me with that task. As for Bishop Bataillon, he is a bishop and he can provide for his flock by whatever means he sees fit.'

[5] 'Messieurs, I say that not without reason, I do so purposely. Let no Marist ever say to these women "Off you go." But never let him discourage them either. The first would be imprudent and improper; the second might be opposing the will of God. For who knows his plans? I would not be surprised if he intended to make use of such a means.'

[6] Then he spoke about Mlle Perroton who had gone out on the latest ship, on her own initiative and without consulting the Marists. [Footnote by the editor: In fact she had consulted Fathers Eymard and Poupinel before her departure in November 1845, but these latter advised her against speaking to Father Colin. On 10 January 1846, he wrote to Bishop Bataillon in terms of satisfaction at her departure (cf OPS 1:12)].

[7] It seemed that this lady spoke not only for herself but also for a society of ladies with whom she had previously come to an understanding.

[8] This is probably the same project spoken of on page 62 of this volume [cf *A Founder Acts*, Doc 297, Rome, 1983] for Father Colin told us, 'They would not take the religious habit, nor make vows.'

[9] 'In fact', he added, 'their salvation would be in less danger out there than in France.'

Further Sources and Bibliography

Girard, Ch (editor), *Lay Marists: Anthology of Historical Sources* (Rome, 1993).

Lessard, G (editor), *‹Colin sup›: Documents pour l'étude du généralat de Jean-Claude Colin (1836–1854),* volume I, 1836–1842, (Rome, 2007).

Jean-Baptiste-François Pompallier, *Instructions for Mission Work 1841* (Translated from the French with an introduction by Kerry Bernice Girdwood-

Morgan; thesis, Palmerston North: Massey University polycopy, 1985).

Blazy, S and Prudhomme, Cl *et al* (editors), *De Fourvière au bout du Monde: Le Rayonnement du Catholicisme Lyonnais au XIXe siècle* (Lyon: Musée Gadagne, 1996).

Bria, I, Chanson, Ph, Gadille, J, Spindler, M (editors), *Dictionnaire œcuménique de Missiologie: Cent mots pour la Mission* (Paris: Les Editions du Cerf, Geneve: Labor et Fides, Yaounde: Les Editions Clé, 2001).

Comby, J (editor), *Diffusion et Acculturation du Christianisme (XIX - XX siècle) Vingt-cinq ans de Recherches Missiologiques par le CREDIC* (Paris: Editions Karthala, 2005).

Comby, J, *L'appel à la Mission a Travers les Annales de la Propagation de la Foi (1822–1860)* in Jean Comby (editor), *Diffusion et Acculturation du Christianisme (XIX – XX siècle) Vingt-cinq ans de Recherches Missiologiques par le CREDIC* (Paris: Editions Karthala, 2005), 445–456.

Costermans, M, *Les femmes dans la Mission: l'expérience de l'AFI* in Jean Comby (editor), *Diffusion et Acculturation du Christianisme (XIX – XX siècle) Vingt-cinq ans de Recherches Missiologiques par le CREDIC* (Paris: Editions Karthala, 2005), 407–418.

De Mijolla M-C, *Origins in Oceania: Missionary Sisters of the Society of Mary 1845–1931* (Rome, 1984).

Essertel, Y, *L'aventure Missionnaire Lyonnaise 1815 –1962* (Paris: Les Editions du Cerf, 2001).

Foley, SK, *Women in France Since 1789: The Meanings of Difference* (London: Palgrave MacMillan, 2004).

Garrett, J, *To Live Among the Stars: Church Origins in Oceania* (Geneva and Suva: World Council of Churches and University of the South Pacific, 1982).

Graystone, Ph, *A Short History of the Society of Mary 1854 to 1993* (Rome, 1998).

Keys, L, *The Life and Times of Bishop Pompallier* (Christchurch, Pegasus Press, 1957).

Kovesi, C, *Pitch Your Tents on Distant Shores: A History of the Sisters of the Good Shepherd in Australia Aotearoa/New Zealand and Tahiti* (Sydney: Playright Publishing Pty Ltd, 2006).

Missionary Sisters of the Society of Mary, *The Vocation of the Pioneers: at the Origins of the Missionary Sisters of the Society of Mary* (Rome, 2005).

Missionary Sisters of the Society of Mary, *150 years After . . . Reflections on her who gave the initial impulse: Marie Françoise Perroton* (Rome, 1998).

Occorsio, I, *La Figure Juridique de la Congrégation des Sœurs Missionnaires de la Société de Marie, à la Lumière de ses origines et de l'Evolution de son Droit Propre de 1857 à 1931* (thesis, Rome: Pontificiae Universitatis Gregorianae, 1988).

Simmons, E, *Pompallier, Prince of Bishops* (Auckland, CPC, 1984).

The Work of Mary versus the Works of the Devil
The Ecclesiology of the Early Marist Missionaries

Mervyn Duffy SM

A missionary is, by definition, someone sent by one group in one place to another people in another location. The Marists were from rural Catholic France and they were sent by the Catholic Church, acting through the agency of Jean-Claude Colin, to the peoples of Western Oceania. This paper is intended as theological rather than historical, it considers how the Marists understood the Church of which they were a part and, from that perspective, how they saw other Christian missionaries and the religious beliefs of the peoples they were sent to. My title is the short answer to the question.[1]

The Vicariate of Western Oceania was one of the last great mission territories of the Catholic Church. It was literally on the other side of the planet from Rome, access was difficult and expensive, the vast territory involved was mainly ocean, scattered through it were isolated communities and language groups. The Catholic Church was slow off the mark in launching a mission endeavour to the Western Pacific. Explorers, whalers, sealers and traders had arrived well ahead of the Catholic missionaries. Moreover protestant missionaries were the first to spread the gospel to much of the territory involved. The London Missionary Society was formed in 1795 to send missionaries to Tahiti. In 1813 the Methodists formed the Wesleyan Missionary Society.

As the Marists were planning their mission they were conscious of the presence of the earlier missionaries. As Bishop Pompallier wrote in 1837:[2] 'A third obstacle one may meet with on the largest islands is the non-Catholic ministers from a whole crowd of sects who make every effort and use every possible method to paralyse the work of the true and legitimate missionaries.'

Notice the terminology employed by Bishop Pompallier. Non-Catholic ministers are of 'a crowd of sects' in contradistinction to the one, true Church. He is a 'true' and 'legitimate' missionary. They are, by implication, false and

---

1.　I have modified the text in response to remarks made during the Suva Conference, August 2008.

2.　'Un troisième obstacle qu'on peut rencontrer dans plusieurs îles importantes, ce sont des ministres non catholiques d'une foule de sectes qui s'efforcent en toutes manières de paralyser les travaux des vrais et légitimes missionnaires.' 9 August 1837, Jean-Baptiste-François Pompallier to Claude du Campe de Rosamel, Archives of Marist Fathers, Rome, OOc 418.1.

illegitimate. The protestant missionaries were considered as an 'obstacle' to the proposed Marist endeavor, expected to be actively engaged in turning the minds of the peoples of Oceania against the Catholic French. Father Colin wrote, in 1839, of an incident in Tahiti: [3] 'One day the protestant missionaries gathered the people in their [Methodist] temple so as to show then by means of a magic lantern the Pope and Catholic priests boiling Protestants in a cauldron.'

The majority of ships travelling to and through the Pacific were commanded by English-speakers from the United Kingdom and North America. The first 'Protestant obstacle' encountered by Pompallier was an American captain at Valparaiso who 'said expressly that they would be careful not to let on board Catholic missionaries for [New Zealand].'[4]

This first group of missionaries had waited months for their passage from Le Havre. The Marists soon learnt that London was a better point of departure for the Pacific. For those who had not previously travelled from their Catholic homeland their first experience of Protestants was at the start of their journey. Brother Attale sums up the experience: [5]

> The Christian religion is in a very sorry state in London. The kingdom is riddled with sects - you can count more than eighty different ones. All our belongings and cases are on the ship. Nothing has been lost. A Protestant whose wife is a Catholic has been of great service to us; because he vouched for us, we had only a few of our cases opened by the customs officers. We left

3.   'Un jour les Missionnaires protestants réunirent le peuple dans leur temple, pour lui faire voir au moyen d'une lanterne magique le Pape et les Prêtres Catholiques brûlant les protestants dans une chaudière.' 30 November 1839, Colin to SEM le Maréchal, Duc de Dalmatie, Minister of Foreign Affairs and President of the Council of Ministers, in Gaston Lessard (editor), *'Colin sup'. Documents concernant le généralat du père Colin*, volume 1, *De l'élection au voyage à Rome (1836-1842)* (Rome, 2007) (= *Colin sup*), 179.

4.   'D'ailleurs la Nouvelle Zélande dans laquelle je croyois pouvoir immédiatement pénétrer ne nous offre aucune occasion favorable. Point de vaisseaux ni de navires qui soient en partance en ce moment pour cette région. A la vérité, il s'en trouve bien un qui est américain, mais il est commandé par des protestants, qui ont dit expressément qu'ils se garderoient bien d'admettre à bord pour cette grande île des missionnaires catholiques.' 17 July 1837, Pompallier to Colin, APM OOc 418.1.

5.   July 1839 Brother Attale (John-Baptist Grimaud 1809–47) to Champagnat, in *Correspondance Passive du Père Champagnat*, edited by Aureliano Brambila (Rome, 1993) (= CPC) 163-5. English translation by Edward Clisby.

London on 14 June and set sail at 6 o'clock on the evening of
the 15th. There are thirty-six people on board but we are the only
Christians. There are two Jews, two blacks, and I think the rest
are Protestants.

Again Brother Attale's language is revealing. The multiplicity of Protestant
churches is startling for him. It is noteworthy that they receive assistance from a
Protestant, but he does mention that the wife is Catholic, implying that she may
be the source of this charity. He identifies the group of missionaries as the 'only
Christians' on board excluding from that category two Jews, two blacks (were
they Muslims?), and lastly the Protestants.

During his first voyage into the Pacific, Pompallier writes to Colin, 'The
heretics in these islands exceed us in resources and in all kinds of means.'[6] This
is to be a recurring perception by the Catholic missionaries in Western Oceania,
they see themselves as 'the poor relations', as less well-equipped and well-
resourced than their Protestant counterparts. Note, too, that Pompallier identifies
the Protestants as 'heretics'; he is more accurate than Brother Attale—they
are fellow Christians who hold beliefs contrary to what the Catholic Church
teaches.

An attitude that the Protestant and Catholic missionaries shared was that
a nation state should have a single religion. Neither group promoted plurality
of religions. Part of introducing the Christian faith to an island people was to
ensure that another faith community did not establish a foothold. Pompallier did
not go to Hawaii because, when he called at Tahiti, he heard of the legislation
that King Kamehameha III had introduced there:[7]

I, with my chiefs, forbid, by this document that any one should
teach the peculiarities of the Pope's religion, nor shall it be
allowed to any who teaches these doctrines or those peculiarities
to reside in this kingdom; nor shall the ceremonies be exhibited
in our kingdom, nor shall any one teaching its peculiarities or
its faith be permitted to land on these shores; for it is not proper

---

6.   'Les hérétiques dans ces îles nous surpassent en ressources et en toutes sortes de
      moyens.' 28 July 1837, Pompallier to Colin, APM OOc 418–1.

7.   18 December 1837 *An Ordinance Rejecting the Catholic Religion,* Kamehameha
      III, sovereign of the Sandwich Islands, at Lahaina, Maui. (Kamehameha III
      reigned 1825–54) Cited in Ralph M Wiltgen, *The Founding of the Roman Catholic
      Church in Oceania, 1825 to 1850* (Canberra: Australia National University Press,
      1979), 150.

that two religions be found in this small kingdom. Therefore
we utterly refuse to allow any one to teach those peculiarities
in any manner whatsoever. We moreover prohibit all vessels
whatsoever from bringing any teacher of that religion into this
kingdom . . .

Notice that the motivation given for this legislation, 'that it is not proper that
two religions be found in this small kingdom' takes no account of traditional
Hawaiian religion.

An experienced missionary of the Paris Foreign Mission Society, Dubois,
had advised Pompallier to avoid islands where Protestant missionaries were
established.[8] It was hearing of a proposed Methodist mission which inspired
Pompallier to start his first mission on the islands of Futuna and Wallis. He
wanted the Catholics to be the first missionaries there and to pre-empt and
prevent the Protestant mission. As he told Colin they were 'encore intactes.'[9]
It is as if the Pacific Ocean were a giant 'Go' board with island communities as
stones.

Dubois had advised that New Zealand was so big that the Protestants could
not have penetrated all of it. What was played out in the Pacific island by island
was to be replicated on the tighter stage of New Zealand tribe by tribe. The first
things done in a mission may well prove to be a mistake due to inescapable
inexperience or not listening to wise advice. Le Havre was the wrong port to
depart from; they waited months for a ship there while on the other side of
the channel, ships were departing for the Pacific every week. According to Jan
Snijders they sailed the wrong way around the planet.[10] The journey took a very
long time even for that period. In my opinion, they also finished the journey at
a wrong place. They landed and established a mission station on the Hokianga

8.   Dubois to Meynis, 14 September 1836, Archives of the Propagation of the Faith
      (= APFL), 1836, Paris Divers.
9.   'Les îles de Wallis et de Fortuna, encore intactes, étoient sur le point de recevoir
      des ministres hérétiques; je me suis empressé d'y placer les p(ères) Chanel et
      Bataillon pour prendre pied avant ceux-là.' 14 mai 1838, Pompallier to Colin,
      APM OOc 418.1.
10.   Jan Snijders, *A Piety Able to Cope: Jean-Claude Colin and the Marist Missions in
      Oceania* (private publication, 2007), 40-1. 'The contacts in Le Havre confirmed
      what Pastre had already pointed out in September 1835 and what Pompallier
      must have learned from Coudrin in August, 1836, that is, that there were better
      ways to go to Oceania than around Cape Horn and via Valparaiso. A shipping
      agent pointed out that there was more regular and faster shipping from English
      ports directly to the Pacific.'

Harbour. The contemporary Hocken map[11] records sixteen Methodist chapels around the Hokianga. Recognising this, and the problems of access, Pompallier moved his centre of activities to the Bay of Islands. Brother Pierre-Marie was surprised by one town having a mix of religions:[12] 'The place where we live in New Zealand is called the Bay of Islands and the town is called Kororareka. Although small it has a mixture of Catholics, Protestants, and undecided.'

The surviving Marist building at Kororareka is the printery. Even this was motivated, in part, by what Protestants had done:[13]

> I just arranged to buy a small press to copy letters. That is the advice of the [Paris] Foreign Mission Society and of the Picpus [Fathers] that the Society of Mary would do better to train a few people in the old way of printing and to send out a letterpress with the next group of missionaries. We must not forget that a press of that kind is most useful in our countries where the Methodists make use of it to circulate their heretical teachings.

This brings to light a characteristic of the Oceania mission. Many of the people being evangelised were literate. The Maori had embraced reading with great

---

11. *Map of the Hokianga Harbour*, nd (HM 841, Hocken Library, special collections Otago University library). In 1823 the Wesleyan Missionary Society joined the Church Missionary Society in the Northern region of New Zealand. Initially a mission station was established at Whangaroa Harbour, against the advice of Hongi Hika and subsequently this station was abandoned in 1827. The Wesleyans were then re-established in and around the Hokianga Harbour in 1828 under the protection of the Rangatira (Chief) Patuone. This map of the Hokianga Harbour shows the number of Wesleyan Chapels in the Hokianga as well as the extent of cultivations in the area. See this map on http://www.library.otago.ac.nz/exhibitions/he_tirohanga_ki_muri/taitokerau.html

12. 20 May 1842. Brother Pierre-Marie to Brother Francois. Bay of Islands, Kororareka, *Lettres d'Océanie N. 0 1836–1894*, edited by Edward Clisby (=LO) 34.

13. 28 November 1836, Pompallier to Colin, APM OOc 418.1: 'Je n'ai donc fait acheter qu'une petite presse à copier les lettres. On est d'avis aux missions étrangères et aux Picpus que la Société de Marie feroit mieux de former quelques sujets à l'ancienne méthode d'imprimerie et d'emporter au prochain envoi de missionnaires une imprimerie à caractères. N'oublions pas qu'une presse de ce genre est de la plus grande utilité pour nos pays où les méthodistes en font usage pour faire circuler leurs doctrines hérétiques.'

enthusiasm. Jumping ahead in time briefly, here is Brother Luc's (*1813) description of the scene after the establishment of the mission printery:[14]

> Yet they [the Maori] are very good to us and well disposed towards the Catholic religion which they embrace in daily increasing numbers, especially since we have given them books. When we first arrived they were quite cool towards us and told all the priests they were going to give up praying unless they were given books. But, thanks be to God for this, they now leave the 'missionaries' (as they call the Protestants) in great numbers and come to receive instruction and baptism. On their side, the missionaries do all they can to deceive once more these people who had been too ready to believe them, but they are not listening to them any more. Sometimes they confound them with their astonishing replies; even well-instructed Europeans would often find it difficult to come up with the like. It is to be hoped that she who is strong as an army in battle array will crush the demons and their allies and it will not be said that the Marists are weaker than the devil. Mary, our good mother, is at our head and she is supported by the arms of the Almighty. Who then can triumph against such odds?

---

14.   1 November 1843, Brother Luc Macé to Colin, Bay of Islands, APM Z 208: 'Ils sont néanmoins très bons envers nous et bien disposés pour la religion catholique, qu'ils embrassent tous les jours de plus en plus, surtout depuis qu'on leur a donnés des livres: car quand nous arrivâmes ils étoient bien refroidis et disoient à tous les pères qu'ils alloient abandonner la prière puisqu'on ne leur donnoit pas de livres. Mais grâces en soient rendues à Dieu, maintenant ils quittent en grand nombre les mission(nai)res (c'est ainsi qu'on nomme les protestans) et viennent se faire instruire et bathiser. Les miss(ionnaires) de leur côté font ce qu'ils peuvent pour tromper de nouveau ces peuples qui ont été trop crédules à leurs voix; mais ils ne les écoutent pas beaucoup. Quelquefois ils poussent les miss(ionnaires) à bout par des réponses étonnantes que souvent des Européens, même instruits, auraient peine à trouver. Il faut espérer que celle qui est forte comme une armée rangée en bataille terrassera les démons et ses suppôts; et qu'il ne sera pas dit que les Maristes ont été plus faibles que le démon. Marie, notre bonne mère, est à notre tête; elle est soutenue par le bras du tout-puissant; quel est celui qui pourroit vaincre avec de tels combattans.' Translation by Edward Clisby (editor), *Letters from Oceania: Letters of the First Marist Brothers in Oceania 1841–1843* (= LO), 100–1.

Notice that the Marist missionaries arrived to find the word 'missionary' taken. Missionary (*Mihinari* in Maori) meant protestant. They also encountered an intelligent, articulate argumentative people. Maori welcomed new ideas and were prepared to debate them endlessly. They happily played the ideas of the Catholics off against the Protestants and vice-versa. They were not passive recipients of evangelisation; they wanted to test the ideas and character of these foreigners. This letter to Father Colin reveals a very militant analogy. Brother Luc understands himself and his Marist confreres as being engaged in a war against the Devil and his allies, in this context clearly the Protestant ministers. Meanwhile, on their part, the Marists see themselves as fighting in the company of Mary, under her leadership in this combat. It is from this phrase that I have drawn the title of this paper.

This understanding of Mary as leading in battle against Protestants is a thread of Marist spirituality running back to Jean-Claude Courveille's (1787–1866) inspiration at Le Puy. He recounted to Father Gabriel-Claude Mayet (1809–94) the 'words' of Mary from that event including this passage:[15]

> I am like a powerful army, defending and saving souls. When a fearful heresy threatened to convulse the whole of Europe, my Son raised up His servant, Ignatius, to form a Society under His name, calling itself the Society of Jesus, with members called Jesuits, to fight against the hell unleashed against His Church. In the same way in this last age of impiety and unbelief, it is my wish and the wish of my Son, that there be another Society, on consecrated to me, one which will bear my name, which will call itself the Society of Mary and whose members will call themselves Marists, to battle against hell.

This is a foundational image for Marists, one they would have learnt in their novitiate. However it is metaphoric language. Brother Luc is using the image of battle rather than intending to attack the next Protestant he sees. This is a 'war' which is to be fought with images.

---

15. Edwin Keel (editor), *A Book of Texts for the Study of Marist Spirituality* (Rome, 1993), Doc 1, 5 (c December 1853), Mayet/Courveille narrative on the origins of the Society of Mary, based on letters of Dom Courveille of 1852, in Jean Coste and Gaston Lessard (editors), *Origines Maristes*, 4 volumes (Rome, 1960-1967) (= OM), Doc 718, 5. Courveille does go on to say 'I heard no words. It all happened inwardly, in my heart.'

The well-resourced Methodists had their magic lantern show, Pompallier and the Marists brought a visual aid of their own to show the truth of the Catholic Church and the fate of heretics. This was a large printed poster, backed on canvas, of the *True Vine*.[16] It is custom made for them. It would have been an expensive printing plate to have engraved. It is not something done lightly. It is designed for the situation they knew they were going to encounter.[17] It existed in multiple copies. One survives in the archives of the Auckland Diocese. The copy we have has a few alterations, presumably by the hand of Pompallier. It provides a key to understanding the mindset of the first missionaries and how it was changed by what they encountered. This is my Rosetta Stone for understanding the ecclesiology of the Marists and how, for Pompallier at least, it changed in the first few years of Mission.

Before describing it in detail, here is an account of it being used. The incident was a debate between Father Chouvet (*1814) and Reverend Mr JH Awilson, a missionary of the Anglican Church, at Opotiki, in October 1844:[18]

> We unrolled in front of the natives a big chart which has as a title The Tree of the Church. Then we showed them on this chart the establishment of the Church by our Lord Jesus Christ, the choice that the divine master made of Saint Peter as leader or pope, and the uninterrupted government of this same Church by the successors of Saint Peter down to Gregory XVI, who was then reigning. We called this tree the ladder of the Catholics,

---

16.   The poster must date from after 1835 and be produced for Pompallier since it features Western Oceania. Chouvet refers to it being used in New Zealand in 1844, hence it must date from before then and have time to get to New Zealand from France. The most likely scenario is that it was prepared for the first missionary group in 1836, but, even if it is produced later, it reflects the French missionaries' understanding of the Church, prior to their experience of the New Zealand situation.

17.   The imagery of the poster is reflected in several paragraphs of the letter that Pompallier wrote to Colin on 26 November 1840 (LRO, Doc 80) detailing what he had been preaching to the Maori. For example in paragraph 11 'Il n'y a qu'une vraie église, où l'on puisse avoir Dieu pour père et se sauver. C'est l'église appelée catholique romaine, c'est l'église mère instituée de Dieu et non par les hommes, c'est l'église tronc dont les branches sont étendues par toute la terre, et l'ont été dans tous les âges . . . ' and his reference to the other churches as 'comme des branches coupées' in paragraph 13.

18.   *A Marist Missionary in New Zealand 1843–1846* by Father JAM Chouvet, 70–1.

by means of which they could go back to Saint Peter, and consequently, to Jesus Christ, the originator and object of our faith. I read out loud the names of all the popes written on this chart. This reading charmed the natives who are very fond of genealogical recitals, and vie with each other as to who can recite the greatest number of known ancestors' names. This long list of about two hundred and fifty Popes was listened to with unfaltering patience, or rather, with extraordinary curiosity. The natives had never heard such a long, and, in their eyes, such a glorious genealogy, even though it was of the spiritual order.

The poster illustrates the biblical theme of the Church as a vine. Christ is shown crucified at the base with a pastiche of texts from John 15 on a scroll beneath him: 'I am the true vine' (15:1a) 'Whoever remains in me bears fruit in plenty.' (15:5b) 'Those who do not bear fruit will be cut away.' (cf 15:2b)[19] The branches are the various mission territories of the Church; from the places that Jesus visited during his public ministry to the recently founded dioceses of America and finally at the top of the vine the region of Oceania. Pompallier's territory, the Vicariate of Western Oceania, is the last shoot on the vine. The fruits of the vine are saints, often the founding saint of a diocese; Lyon and Saint Irenaeus are conspicuously worn on the surviving example in the Auckland Archives. Clearly, the missionaries had tapped this spot to indicate the church community that they had come from. The vine is growing up towards the Trinity in heaven. Saints on clouds surround the Trinity, with the Virgin Mary being closest to Jesus. Running, like a ladder, up the trunk of the vine is a list of the Popes. The printed list goes from Saint Peter to Gregory XVI. Alongside the trunk are some twenty Councils of the Church from Jerusalem to Trent.

  The list of councils on the *True Vine* is unusual in three respects. Firstly it starts with Jerusalem, which is not usually considered a General Council, however, it is scriptural, and thus hard for the Protestants to deny. Once they accept the existence and authority of one council they would have to explain which others they accepted and if not, why not. The second respect is the presence of three councils that do not fit Roman definitions of a general council: Pisa, Constance and Basel. This is evidence of Gallican Theology, of Conciliarism, the teaching that the authority of a General Council is greater than that of the Pope. This was strong in France, but interestingly, very much opposed by Jean-Claude Colin.

---

19.   The text on the poster is 'JE SUIS LA VRAIE VIGNE / Celui qui demeure en moi porte beaucoup de Fruit. Celui qui ne demeure pas en moi sera retranché.' A third longer line of text beneath those two is now unreadable.

He ensured that later Marists were formed in ultra-montane theology which stressed the supremacy of papal authority. They produce council lists like that in J Gaume's, 1845 *Catéchisme de Persévérance*, which was also brought out to New Zealand by Pompallier.[20] The third difference is the absence of two of the five Lateran Councils, which I signal as odd without being able to provide a motivation.

Down both sides of the poster, branches that have been trimmed away are falling. Each of these has a name on it, some are philosophers like Hobbes, Rousseau and Voltaire, others are Christian movements and their founders like Presbyterians, Calvinists and Calvin, Anglicans and Henry VIII. These severed branches drop towards a depiction of hell where devils with pitchforks await. This is based upon John 15:6 'Anyone who does not remain in me is thrown away like a branch—and withers; those branches are collected and thrown on the fire and are burnt.'

The poster was intended as an illustration to accompany preaching, not a substitute for it. An indication of what would be said in association with the poster is given by Pompallier, in a handwritten book *Instructions for the Works of the Mission.*[21]

The important phrase to use in reply, and to uphold everywhere, is: The Roman Catholic Church is the living tree. *Ko te tahi take ko te rakau ora o te atua* [the one foundation is the staff of God]. The new Churches are the severed branches. *Ko nga manga ruatiia* [the severed branches]. The Roman Catholic Church is the original Church, the trunk Church, the Church of all times and all places. *Te hahi katorika romana ko te hahi tawito, ko te hahi matua, ko te hahi take, ko te hahi o nga tau katoa me nga wahi katea a te wenua:* [The Roman Catholic Church is the old Church, the parent Church, the original Church, the Church of all times and all places].[22]

---

20.   J Gaume, *Catéchisme de Persévérance* (Paris, 1845), 440: 'On compte dix-huit conciles généraux: deux di Nicée, quatre de Constantinople, un d'Ephèse, un de Chalcédoine, cinq de Latran, deux de Lyon, un de Vienne, un de Florence et un de Trente.' This corresponds exactly to modern lists like that given by Norman Tanner, *Decrees of the Ecumenical Councils* (Georgetown, 1990). Pompallier's copy of this catechism is held by the Colin Library at Good Shepherd College in Auckland, New Zealand.

21.   J Pompallier, *Instructions pour les Travaux de la Mission*, 89 handwritten pages, dated 1841, Auckland Diocesan Archive, English citations from the unpublished translation by Kerry Bernice Girdwood-Morgan.

22.   Pompallier, *Instructions*, 51.

So, under the banner of Mary, the Marists arrived in New Zealand ready to do battle with Protestants for the souls of the Maori people. At least in image, they were prepared to consign heretics to hell. There is evidence, however, that their ecclesiology adapted to their new context.

This copy of the poster of the *True Vine* has several emendations: one name, four numbers and two pieces of paper stuck on.

The added name is that of Pius IX at the top of the list of Popes. This is a natural addition to make once the news of his taking up the office in 1846 reached New Zealand. No subsequent pope has been added so the poster was no longer 'in use' by 1878.

Alongside four of the councils there is a hand-written number. These are the traditional numbers of bishops that attended each of the councils concerned. I suggest that this was the hand of Pompallier and he was explaining the importance and number of bishops in the Church. 'I am one Bishop, at this great Council of Nicea there were 318 like me!' This wasn't considered important when the chart was first designed, but realizing the advantage he had as the only bishop in New Zealand, Pompallier presented a view of the Church in which bishops were very important in its governance and teaching. This accords with his *Instructions*, 'The Holy Spirit set the Bishops to rule the Assembly of God. Thus he who fails the apostles' successors fails God Himself.'[23]

The pieces of paper were stuck on to cover over hell, the glue marks and the shadow of where they were is evident on the poster in the Auckland Diocesan Archives. Thus, at some point, it was no longer judged appropriate to imply that Protestants were going to hell. This may have corresponded in time to the 1841 *Instructions* because, for their period of history, they show remarkable ecumenical tolerance:[24]

> Be steadfast in controversy, but gentle and honest in your approach. To be steadfast means you must have at your grasp all the arguments of the Church against the errors of the pretended reformers and especially against their major error, of which we have spoken. To be good in form is to act inwardly with a pure zeal for saving your neighbour's soul. It is to love warmly, in the Lord. It is to have a care to curb one's pride and self-love. It is to avoid engaging in a dispute in anger or too much emotion, and not using hateful terms—in other words, attacking error without wounding the one who errs. You must, through charity,

---

23.   Pompallier, *Instructions*, 34.
24.   Pompallier, *Instructions*, 81–2.

> or at least prudence, suppose that your opponent is in good faith,
> and inwardly recommend yourself and your erring neighbour
> to the Lord. Silently invoke the protection of Mary, the Queen
> of the Church and powerful Virgin, who will one day rejoice at
> the triumph over all the heresies in the whole world. Frequently
> offer Holy Sacrifice as a Memento for the conversion of those
> who err.
> In conversations and social dealings with them, bring up several
> principles which might shed some light and save them. When
> they engage you in conversation on matters of religion, listen
> to them with interest and join in a friendly discussion if you see
> that that is their inclination.

Pompallier wants his missionaries to love warmly their Protestant counterparts, to offer mass for them, to join in friendly discussion with them, and to avoid wounding them in dispute. That would fit with hell being covered over, but also raises the question of what happened between the commissioning of the poster (between 1835 and 1839) and the writing of the *Instructions* (1841)? The most obvious event in the history of New Zealand is the signing of the Treaty of Waitangi (1840), a foundational event for the country, and something perceived as a major event in its own time. Pompallier, being French and Catholic, was perceived by the Maori as independent of the British crown with whom they were negotiating the Treaty. He was widely consulted in the period leading up to the signing. He was concerned about the effect the Treaty might have on the status of the Catholic Church in New Zealand.

At the first signing of the Treaty, Pompallier and William Colenso, an Anglican missionary, recorded a discussion on religious freedom and customary law. In answer to a direct question from Pompallier, Governor Hobson agreed to the following statement. It was read to the meeting in Maori and English before any of the chiefs had signed the Treaty:[25] 'E mea ana te Kawana ko nga whakapono katoa o Ingarani, o nga Weteriana, a Roma, me te ritenga Maori hoki e tiakina ngatahitia e la—The Governor says the several faiths of England, of the Wesleyans, of Rome, and also the Maori custom shall alike be protected by him.'

---

25.   The significance of this statement is disputed. It was recorded by the missionary witnesses but not in Governor Hobson's official despatches. Maori, being an oral culture, gave it greater weight than the European settlers who focussed on the written text of the Treaty.

Conclusion

We are proud of what Pompallier and Servant (1808–60) contributed to the Treaty of Waitangi, but we usually fail to see just how far these Catholic churchmen have come as a result of their dialogue with the chiefs, with Colenso and with Governor Hobson. I suggest that the Treaty dramatically changed their ecclesiology. If the Governor were to guarantee to treat alike the several faiths, then the Catholics have to accept a likeness among those faiths. Well in advance of the second Vatican Council Pompallier had got to the point of recognising virtue in his protestant counterparts.

The Marist missionaries changed New Zealand, but contact with the Maori and with Protestant ministers changed the Marists, too. We now stress Mary as Mother of Mercy rather than as our leader in battle. We are not as quick to send people to hell as we were in our first fervour of leaving France to save the peoples of Oceania. In New Zealand, we have never printed a Catholic Maori Bible, it has always been simpler and more economic to use and supplement the widely available Protestant translation.

We have *The True Vine* and the *Instructions* of Pompallier as an example of a truly Marist missiology.[26] Today we can benefit from the vision expressed there of a Church founded by Jesus Christ which yet recognizes good faith outside its own boundaries, returns courtesy for calumnies, and knows that Catholics have no monopoly of the Holy Spirit.

---

26. It may also be Colinian; Jean Coste (editor), *A Founder Speaks*, Rome, 1975, Doc 134, 1: 'Round about November 1846 Father Colin said on one occasion, 'Missioners, all Marists, must be men who are grafted into Christ, and follow no will but his, just as the shoot springing from the main branch has no life of its own, other than the sap which comes to it from the vine. If it is cut off from that sap, from its vine, it dies, and it is the same with us'. Colin applies the vine and branches image firstly to Missioners.

The Clash of Cultures. French, English, Catholic[1] and Oceanic Cultures Yesterday, Today and Tomorrow

Mikaele Paunga SM

Introduction

Every great venture begins with 'A Certain Idea'. The whole mystery of the Incarnation began to be immanent with a simple 'yes' from Mary 'let it be done to me according to your word.' Christianity began in a very simple but radical way with Jesus of Nazareth, a Jew and a handful of disciples and friends from an insignificant town in Galilee.

During the twenty-first century, three Occidental ideas for good or bad, that of Peace, Democracy and Free Market, proliferated and conquered the world.[2]

'A certain idea' of the Society of Mary began with a revelation to Courveille at Le Puy in 1812 and shared with a hand-full of seminarians during their time at Lyon major seminary. The idea was later developed by Jean-Claude Colin. The research about Colin and Oceania, 1836 to 1854, began with 'a certain idea'. However, an idea is not effective if the following resources are not available:

a) the idea needs the right people to carry it forward (good management);
b) it needs resources—personnel, money and material;
c) it needs perseverance, and a well-structured plan.

The idea of this research is timely.

Why are we now so interested in studying Colin during that period? What has been done during the past 170 years since the foundation of the Society of Mary? Perhaps it was meant that Oceanic Marists should conduct this study! This is then an opportune time. The Marists from Oceania must see this clearly as a symbolic event.

Further, what is the purpose of this study at a time when the numbers of Marists are dwindling in the Northern hemisphere and in the Western countries of the Southern hemisphere?[3] Have we perhaps concentrated too much on

---

1. Christianity in General.
2. Michael Mandelbaum, *The Ideas that Conquered the World* (New York: Public Affairs, 2002).
3. I believe the same challenges had been raised by Felise Tavo in *Forum Novum*, 7/1 (2005): 135–46.

our past and forget about the present and the future? Why are we becoming irrelevant to the wealthy nations?

This paper is written from the viewpoint of those who have been and are still at the receiving end of colonisation, globalisation, Enlightenment culture and the recent 'new global ethic' now spreading like wildfire in the Pacific. It looks at the past but only in so far as it has relevance to the present and the future of Oceania. The letters of the French missionaries echo their understanding and interpretation of Pacific cultures and religions from a French viewpoint. This paper is an insider's attempt to re-interpret that history from the viewpoint of a Tongan, Polynesian and a Pacific Islander. We thank God for those records, but the time is ripe for us to re-interpret our history.

This paper has two parts. Part one begins with a general observation concerning the Pacific context today as well as the ideologies that influenced the westernisation, colonisation and christianisation of the Pacific. I also highlight the current 'global cultural context' with its claim to absolute cultural truths. Part Two will present examples of how Christianity and Western cultures clashed with some of the Pacific values and cultures during the period under study. See the clash of civilisations explained by Walter Kasper in the context of religious pluralism.[4] Four examples are singled out. The paper concludes with some recommendations for reflections on the future of Oceania.

Pacific and global cultural contexts

Pacific context
Central Oceania in 2007 is in crisis due to the effects of colonisation, westernisation and christianisation. Now we have the advent of global culture, political and economic Globalisation with its inherent 'new global ethic'. The consequences of these foreign forces if left unaddressed will uproot completely two important qualities that have characterised Oceania from time immemorial: our cultural identities and our natural affinity to God and to the natural environment.[5]

The damages brought about by the so-called Western civilisation as well as christianisation, have changed us in every way; even our natural affinity to both God and the environment have suffered. Our people are confused and they are not too sure who and where to turn to. The different waves ranging from

---

4.   Walter Kasper, *That They May all be One, the call to Unity Today* (London: Burns & Oates, 2004), 181.
5.   A personal conversation with professor Seu'ula Johannson-Fua, a lecturer at the University of the South Pacific confirmed my ideas.

colonisation to globalisation have destabilised our traditional political systems and replaced it with democracy, the handmaid of globalisation, and with a new global culture that is alien or indifferent to both Christianity and traditional cultural values. We do not have to look too far for examples of this take-over. The recent events in both Tonga and Fiji are adequate. The colonial ideology of 'divide and rule' has been well accomplished.

Recently, there is a general sense of consciousness in the Pacific academic circles that Christianity is no longer easily accepted by our people. Christianity and the Bible, like colonisation and globalisation are all foreign. They have all invaded our land and our cultures. Our young people seem to feel that the best way to make it in the world is to break the rules. Our Pacific becomes a suspicious environment. Modernity has come to mean a disconnection from tradition, the 'white man' and missionaries are seen as the source of the problems, there is also the rejection of modernity and everything becomes permissible. It also marked the end of the 'tribe' and the beginning of urban life. Such a situation creates confusion and anxiety among our people.[6]

This confusion has an anthropological, ideological, political and philosophical history. In order for Pacific peoples to understand what is going on there has to be a systematic analysis and study of that history. We can never forget, deny or by-pass our past and our history. This is not to create a nostalgic longing for the past. In particular, the focus has to be on highlighting the fact that what we are living and experiencing now is in the words of Peter Kanyandago, 'a product of conjugated historical and anthropological processes'.[7] Those historical and anthropological ideologies have to do with the Western claim to superiority and universality. Unfortunately, this is still very much with us today in the Pacific; even after about 170 years of Catholicism. This means that many of the problems that we are facing in Oceania are recent in origin. This is not to say that the pre-European contact periods had no problems. It is trying to say that Oceanic societies before the advent of Europeans may have had resources both culturally and spiritually that were denied or placed aside but can help us now to navigate through this overwhelming sea of cyberspace and modern telecommunications. It is therefore incumbent to study both past and present in

---

6.   Position Paper 'To Whom shall We Go, Charting Hope in the Pacific, A Pacific Theology of Hope Framework', Discussion Paper prepared for the 2007 Pacific Conference of Churches General Assembly, September 2007, American Samoa, 18.

7.   Peter Kanyandago, 'The Experience of Negation of Particularity and Africa's Struggle for Survival', in *Chakana*, 1 (2003): 47.

order to find meaning to help Pacific peoples survive in the current impasse and welcome the future with optimism or hope.

On the other hand, the modern culture needs to be deconstructed at its very roots. Its mechanism that is inherently subtle, the various global systems (especially political and economic cultures) make it so difficult to detect. The consequence is that the people of Oceania are forced to live without their own roots. The new culture acts like the Trojan horse virus quietly eating away our cultures and indeed all aspects of life without people knowing that this is actually happening. It is like people who feel sick but cannot diagnose the cause.

Global context

The world is witnessing a new imperialism in the making since the fall of the Berlin Wall in 1989. With the fall of that wall we experience what perhaps one may call the rise of 'Pax Americana'. This 'American Peace' is an imposition of a 'New World Order', consisting of a Uni-polar political (democracy), economic and cultural system for the whole world. This new American Peace is underpinned by its military might. The current war in the Middle East is the freeing of the world for globalisation or for the 'new world order'. This is not a clash of culture. Rather it is the domination and imposition of one culture on all.

Some describe this as the clash of civilisations. This is the thesis of the author of the best seller, Samuel P Huntington, in his book *The Clash of Civilizations*.[8] He speaks of increasing clashes between the West and Islam, and between the West and the Sinic (China) civilisations.[9] The current invasion and occupation of Iraq as well as the growing tension between the US and Iran are clear examples of this clash of civilisations. The clash, however, is caused and instigated by the *Pax Americana* imperialism. However, according to Professor Johan Galtung, the founder of the Transcend Institute for Peace and Reconciliation:

> It is a complete mistake to talk about this as a civilisational-religious clash only. It's economic, military, political; it's the full house. The more one says the 'clash of civilisations', the more one is inclined to forget the economic, political, military interests hidden underneath. It must be wonderful for Washington to have all this clash-of-civilisation-talk and establish fourteen military

---

8.   This work was first published in Great Britain by Simon & Schuster UK Ltd, 1997.

9.   *Ibid*, see the illustration in his book on page 245.

bases, and then try to put your paw on all the oil. Keep them discussing civilisation.[10]

I think Pope Benedict XVI has the best insights into this crisis of cultures. I agree with him that it is not so much a crisis based on religion. Islam is not necessarily anti-Christian. Fiji is an example at hand. Christianity and Islam live peacefully together. However, this is the deceptive mantle often put out by the media as the cause of the current tension between the West and Islam. It is certainly not a question of Islam challenging Christianity. Rather it is a clash of cultures. He thinks that the greatest clash of cultures now being experienced is the culture of Enlightenment versus Christianity. The culture of Enlightenment and its positivistic philosophy,[11] the material alone is real, represents the biggest threat to Christianity and to all religions for that matter.[12]

The Pope's position can be summed up in the following way. This philosophy, positivism, is anti-metaphysical in character, so that ultimately, there is no place for God in it. The consequence is that people no longer accept any moral authority apart from their own calculations.[13] People's capability determines what they do. If you know how to do something, then you can do it. However, if this human expertise does not find its criterion in a moral norm, it becomes a power for destruction. We already have many examples of this today. People know how to use human beings as 'storerooms' of organs; hence, they do so because their liberty demands it. They know how to build atomic bombs, so they make them. They know how to clone human beings so they do so.[14] According to Pope Benedict, this philosophy and its definition of liberty, that initially seemed capable of expanding without any limits, leads in the end to the self-destruction of humanity and liberty itself.[15] This culture grew out of Christian Europe. Pope Benedict fittingly describes the source of this new culture:[16] 'If, then, it is true to say that Christianity has found its most efficacious form in

---

10. Johan Galtung, 'What Comes After the US Empire?', Introductory speech at the TRANSCEND International Meeting, 6–12 June 2007, Vienna, Austria, 5.
11. August Comte is the source of this positivistic philosophy. See his work *A General View of Positivism*, 6 volumes, 1830–42 (translated by JH Bridges, Robert Speller & Sons, 1957).
12. See Joseph Ratzinger, *Christianity and the Crisis of Cultures* (San Francisco: Ignatius Press, 2006).
13. *Ibid*, 40.
14. *Ibid*, 41–2.
15. *Ibid*, 40.
16. *Ibid*, 31.

Europe, it is also true to say that a culture has developed in Europe that is the most radical contradiction not only of Christianity, but of all the religions and moral traditions of humanity.'

Furthermore, the Pope says that while we can say that Europe once was the Christian continent, we can also say it was also the birthplace of this new scientific rationality, which has given both enormous possibilities and threats. On the one hand, this new culture has led to the geographical unity of the world, meeting of cultures and continents during the age of great discoveries. This same rationality has left its mark over the whole world today, due to the achievement of its scientific technological culture.

On the other hand, this scientific rationality has developed a new culture that was previously unknown to humankind: it alienates God from public awareness; hence, God is irrelevant to public life and cannot be its foundation. It maintains that what is rational is only that which can be demonstrated by scientific experiments. That leaves morality and religion as irrational at best. This culture has attempted to construct a human community in a manner that absolutely excludes God.[17]

This culture claims to be complete without needing any other cultural factors to complement it. It therefore has a claim to universality. The 'rights to liberty' is the core of this culture.[18] Liberty is the fundamental value and criterion for everything else. It claims the freedom of choice in matters of religion, which includes the religious neutrality of the state; the liberty to express one's own opinion, the democratic ordering of the state, and finally the protection of human rights and the prohibition of discrimination.[19] Therefore, there is no higher value than that **human rights, democracy and freedom, be respected everywhere**. These three are the heritage of the Enlightenment and they have Christian roots.[20] They now seem to replace God in public life.

Very recently, there is reference to another new global cultural revolution or a 'new global ethic'. It has imposed itself since the end of the Cold War. The fall of the Berlin Wall accelerated it to become a 'hot war' fuelled by oil and greed. Various new paradigms, norms, values, lifestyles, educational methods and new governmental processes belonging to this new ethic, spread globally. It is post-modern and globally normative. It already rules the world's cultures. This new

---

17.   *Ibid*, 33.
18.   We would do well to note that this notion of liberty is not of Christian origin. It is hedonistic, selfish and individualistic.
19.   *Ibid*, 34.
20.   Martha Zechmeister, 'Crisis of Christianity: Crisis of Europe?', in *Concilium*, 3 (2005): 60.

global ethic has not been carefully analysed or discerned; hence, it has spread like wildfire to the remotest corners of the globe. It has its concepts and a new language.[21] Many of these concepts have become the common language even in Fiji today. No longer can any one deny the predominance of these concepts in contemporary cultures:

> Globalisation with a human face, global citizenship, sustainable development, good governance, consensus building, global ethic, cultural diversity, cultural liberty, dialogue among civilisations, education for all, right to choose, informed choice, gender, equal opportunity, equity principle, empowerment, NGO's, civil society, partnerships, transparency, bottom-up participation, accountability, holism, broad-based consultation, facilitation, inclusion, awareness-raising, clarification of values, capacity building, women's rights, children's rights, reproductive rights, safe abortion, safe motherhood, enabling environment, equal access, life skills education, peer education, bodily integrity, ownership, agents of change, best practices, indicators of progress, culturally sensitive approaches, secular spirituality, Youth Parliament, peace education, the rights of future generations, corporate social responsibility, fair trade, human security, precautionary principle, prevention.[22]

We do not have to condemn or endorse many of these concepts and words altogether. However, after a closer look at this new global language, one is awestruck immediately by the exclusion of terms specifically belonging to the Judeo-Christian tradition, such as:

> Truth, morality, conscience, reason, heart, virginity, chastity, spouse, husband, wife, father, mother, son, daughter, complementarities, service, help, authority, hierarchy, justice, law, commandment, dogma, faith, charity, hope, suffering, sin, friend, enemy, nature, representation.[23]

---

21.   Institute for International Dialogue Dynamics, *The New Global Ethic: Challenges for the Church* (Louvain: Peeters, 2006).
22.   *Ibid*, 1.
23.   *Ibid*, 2.

According to the report, this new global ethic has taken the place of the universal values on which the international order has been founded after World War II in 1945 and the Universal Declaration of Human Rights established in 1948. The supreme value of this new culture is the ***right to choose***, a purely existential and immanent principle.[24] Furthermore, according to the report, 'The global ethic posits itself *above* the authority of parents and educators, even *above* the teachings of world religions. It bypasses every legitimate hierarchy. It establishes a *direct link* between itself and the individual citizen—the proper of a dictatorship.'[25]

We are still trying to rise from the devastation inflicted on us by colonisation and globalisation and now we have new devastating cultural forces at bay. In this context and in view of Oceania I would like to pose the following questions:

- How are we going to face these two new cultures, something that the Society of Mary in Western countries does not know how to handle?
- What hope is there for Oceania if the two cultures have already invaded and conquered the Western minds and hearts?
- How are we going to survive in the new culture that would like to see God eradicated finally, from public life and Oceania in particular, and shut God up in cultural residues from the past?

Imagine the damage and further isolation this is going to inflict on the people of Oceania if people are not aware of them and if they are not subjected to serious scrutiny! We would do well to remember the wisdom of Johan Galtung, this is not just 'a civilisational-religious clash. It's economic, military, and political: it's the full house.'[26]

The clash of cultures in Oceania at the time of Marist arrival

When the first Marists came to the Pacific, being men of their time, it is possible that they may have been influenced by the standard eurocentric and ethnocentric

---

24.   *Ibid*, 15.
25.   *The New Global Ethic*, 18.
26.   *The New Global Ethic*, 8. The more one says the 'clash of civilisations', the more is one inclined to forget the economic, political, military interests hidden underneath.

anthropological view that the 'white man' and his culture were far superior to any other human being or culture. Everything was viewed, interpreted or judged from an eurocentric viewpoint. Hence, it was normal to consider the European religion or Christianity as superior to all pre-Christian Pacific religions. This deliberate orchestrated ideology and flawed anthropology convinced the white man that the black and brown people were lesser human beings. This anthropology was clearly portrayed in the movie *The Mission* (1986). Those tribes were eliminated because they had no souls. If they had no *anima* then they were not fully human beings.

That defective anthropology and superiority ideology were designed to give justification for the blunders and crimes against humanity caused by colonisation, taking by force the sovereignty of countries and the various barbaric European crimes against indigenous peoples throughout the world.[27] The arrival of the white man at that time was considered to be the advent of a superior civilisation. Today, however, we know that it was rather the arrival of dominant barbarism.

In this context, it is hardly true to speak of a clash of cultures since what actually happened was a forced taking over of the weaker culture by the stronger one. The Western culture was imposing itself as the superior of the two cultures. It had superior military capabilities to accompany this claim and to crush any opposition to it. As was in all Pacific Islands, their military capabilities were nothing more than God given human power and strength supported by a strong and fearless will. Unfortunately, bows and arrows, spears and stones, canoes and sheer human power had no chance against superior guns and cannons.

This superior military and technology served to confirm the Western claim that the culture of the white man was stronger, far superior and more civilized than the local ones. The white man was considered superior in matters of knowledge, technology, medicine, religion and that he possessed the God given right to conquer, 'civilise' and Christianise all pagan peoples. This gave the white man therefore the justification beyond doubt to do whatever he thought necessary to advance colonisation without a guilty conscience. The Church was happy to underpin this endeavour as it offered its own contribution to lighten

---

27.　Perhaps we can give some examples here: the enslavement and trading of Africans and their shipment to the USA; the use of Indians as cheap labors in Africa as well as Fiji are examples; the mal-treatment of American native Indians. Much closer to us, we have the sad stories of the Aborigines of Australia and the Maori of New Zealand. All of these were justified because the Africans, Native Indians of America, Aboriginals of Australia and Maori of New Zealand were lesser human beings, hence you can do what you like with them. You can use them and when finished, you can dispose of them.

the God-given 'white man's burden'. Who actually became a burden to whom?
With those words, we can now move to the examples of cultural clashes from
New Zealand, Futuna, Fiji and Tonga.

*Maori culture versus English culture: the clash over the flagpole at
Kororareka*
The flagpole (*Pou Kara*) was re-erected on the same site in early 1858 by the same
people who had cut it down in 1845, naming it *Whakakotahitanga o Nga Iwi e
Rua* /Unity between Two People (unity is not about being the same!), recognised
by Ngapuhi as a symbol of their commitment to the Treaty of Waitangi (1840).
That commitment remains, as does the continued determination for a proper
understanding of its intent—Treaty claims are currently being prepared.[28]

The cause for the first Maori War in New Zealand in 1845 was a clear clash
of cultures. The clash was instigated by the cutting down of a flagpole erected
by the British Government at Kororareka. The events surrounding this story are
both intriguing and fascinatingly colourful. Why did the British put up the flag
in the first place? Was it a sign of ownership? How did the Maori understand
the flag since it was a foreign symbol? Why did they agree to sign the *Treaty of
Waitangi* and later refused to honour it by refusing to recognize the flagpole at
Kororareka?

Once the Treaty was signed, the flagpole became the responsibility of
Governor Hobson. Instead of respecting Maori tradition with such a diplomatic
gift /*taonga*, which if no longer used should go back to its origin it became
the flagpole at Kororareka—with the Union Jack flying on it adding insult to
injury. It became the symbol of the Treaty Partner, the Crown that had not kept
its part of the bargain. It also became a symbol of ownership of the land, it was
a symbol of victory and of conquest.[29] It defied everything that the *Treaty of
Waitangi* stood for.[30]

This was the reason for the cutting down of the government flagpole at
Kororareka by the Maoris. At least this was the view of the Chief Hone Heke, a
nephew of the great warrior Hongi, who had earlier signed the *Treaty*. He was
the leader of the Maori who became rebellious due to widespread dissatisfaction
over the loss of their land.[31] Today we see that the English version of the treaty

---

28.   Letter of Kate Martin to Mikaele Paunga SM, 20 August 2007.
29.   Private conversations with Kate Martin, New Zealand, Suva, Wednesday, 8
      August 2007.
30.   Claudia Orange, *The Treaty of Waitangi* (Wellington: Port Nicholson Press,
      1987).
31.   Lillian G Keys, *Life and Time of Bishop Pompallier* (Christchurch: The Pegasus

was different from the Maori version. The English version understood the treaty to be the ceding of the land and sovereignty of New Zealand to the Queen.[32] The Maori version gave the white man only the use of their land.

It is said that at the actual signing of the treaty in the presence of Anglican, Wesleyan, and Roman Catholic representatives, one of the Maori chiefs who refused to accept the European way and culture of claiming ownership had the following prophetic interpretation of the treaty when he said: 'Do not sign the paper . . . If you do you will be reduced to the condition of slaves and be compelled to break stones on the roads. Your land will be taken from you and your dignity as chiefs will be destroyed.'[33] This is another clear clash of cultures. The Maori and the rest of Polynesian people understand land not as a commercial commodity but as a gift from God for their wellbeing and livelihood. The two cultures clearly clashed in this matter.

The conflict was building up over the flag and three times it had been cut down by Hone Heke's men. Again, the British marine force and infantry put the flagpole up and this time strengthened it with iron. When the news reached the Maori Chief, Hone Heke that the flagpole had been once again erected, the other Maori troops joined Hone Heke and planned to go down to Kororareka and cut the flag down. When Bishop Jean-Baptiste François Pompallier (1801–71) heard this, he set out by boat to meet them. The Maori received him respectfully. They explained to the bishop that they merely wanted to cut down the pole, and then they would return home. The Bishop told them that 'by removing the flagstaff they were attacking in a most harmful manner the colonial authorities and the Queen of England, and declaring war by such an act on a power capable of wiping them out'.[34] So one can conclude from what the Bishop said that the planting of the flag represented the Colonial authority of the Queen of England. The Maori people as represented by Chief Hone Heke were correct in their interpretation about the erection of the flagpole, hence the reason for cutting it down. They finally understood it correctly as is clear

---

Press, 1957), 219.

32.   The Treaty of Waitangi was signed in 1840 by over 500 Maori chiefs, and by William Hobson, representing the British Crown. To the British, it was the means by which they gained sovereignty over New Zealand. But to the Maori people it had a very different significance, and they are still affected by the terms of the treaty, often adversely; see Claudia Orange, *Treaty of Waitangi*, back page.

33.   John Garret, *To Live Among the Stars* (Geneva: WCC Publications, 1982), 65–6.

34.   Keys, *Pompallier*, 225.

from the following conversations between the Bishop and the Maoris before the attack at Kororareka:

> 'We would just as soon die as let the flag fly again,' replied the Maoris. 'But what harm is that flag doing to you? It is planted on land that has been sold.' 'If the flag were only for the whites and the land we have sold them we would not take up arms; but this flag takes away the authority of our chiefs and all our lands.' 'I have never heard of anyone wanting to take away your lands.' 'Epicopo, they are hiding the truth from you, but we know everything.' 'I see that you have been deceived by false reports. It would be better for you and the country if you began by speaking to the Governor, and explaining your claims and your rights to him. Things could thus be settled without bloodshed.' 'Epicopo, speaking and writing are a waste of time; we have been deceived. What we have said and what we intend are well known. Let the flagstaff be cut down and all will be at peace. We have no intention of giving up our authority and our lands to any nation whatever.'[35]

When the Bishop returned, he informed the Magistrate that the Maoris would attack the flag and the town. Kawiti of Ngati Hine, Te Whiti of Kapotai, planned the attack, giving Hone Heke and his people the job of cutting the flagpole while they created a decoy at the other end of the town, next door to the Roman Catholic mission.[36]

Hone Heke and his men attacked Kororareka from different angles and the battle did not last more than a few hours. Heke's men cut down the flag for the fourth time and they captured the town. The English soldiers and guards surrendered and retreated on board their ships. After this retreat, the natives hoisted a white flag of truce so that both parties can look after their dead and wounded.[37]

There are two other important points from the above text that represent further the clash between the two cultures. One is concerned with the selling and buying of land. The Bishop asserted the fact that the flag was hoisted on land that was sold. The selling and buying of land were foreign to the Maori culture.

---

35.   *Ibid*, 225–6.
36.   Personal conversation with Kate Martin.
37.   Keys, *Pompallier*, 227.

The other cultural clash relates to the idea of speaking and making claims to the Governor and having them put down in writing. The Bishop suggested this to Hone Heke on a number of occasions. He told them: 'Make claims before you make war. Speech and written agreements are better than the deadly sword.'[38] In his personal letter to Hone Heke, the Bishop suggested that he may perhaps 'write—both you and the other New Zealand chiefs—to the Colonial Governor and to the Queen of England stating your claims on the subject of your lands and your authority in New Zealand.'[39] The custom of writing was completely foreign to the Maori culture. But at the time the Maori people became familiar with it. They hold records of written negotiation attempts between them and the British. But the traditional way of negotiation - face to face at *hui* or meetings— was also attempted before the final attack on the flagpole—to no avail.[40]

In summary, the planting of the flagpole at Kororareka ended up in a war. On the other hand, the incident revealed also other aspects where two cultures clashed: the concept of selling and buying of land and making claims by writing. The *Treaty of Waitangi* was an example. In these incidences, the ideology of the dominant culture that was considered superior anthropologically, religiously and militaristically, forcefully imposed its culture on the Maori people. Both English and French Church authorities co-operated and witnessed to the signing of the Treaty. The Churches, therefore, took part in an illegal act done in the name of God. The chiefs were correct after all when they told Bishop Pompallier that they saw nothing wrong with cutting down the flag. They did not think that God would condemn them.[41]

French and Catholic versus Futunian culture and religion: the breaking of a cultural taboo

Ever since I studied the history of the death of Saint Peter Chanel (1803–41), I was never fully satisfied with the explanations surrounding his death. The reason given namely the conversion of Meitala, son of Futuna's king Niuliki, as the cause of Chanel's martyrdom was not serious enough for me to accept. I found the account of his death pietistic. It had a theological interpretation written with the death of Christ as a background. It was hagiographical.

---

38.   Keys, *Pompallier*, 224.
39.   Keys, *Pompallier*, 222. Quoted in Keys from Pompallier, *Notice Historique*, 202.
40.   Personal Conversation with Kate Martin.
41.   Keys, *Pompallier*, 226.

I have always suspected that the degree of violence used in killing Peter Chanel[42] meant that he must have offended some cultural taboos. There were no other explanations as far as I was concerned that could justify the brutality of the action on the part of the actors. In fact, there was a clash of cultures involved. Peter Chanel did break a cultural taboo which eventually led to his death.

Most of the Pacific Cultures at the arrival of the Marists Fathers and Christianity had various taboo, *tabu* or *tapu* in the Polynesian language. Certain actions must be avoided, certain food were considered taboo also, hence if violated the spirit world would release harmful effects on either the person, family or a whole group. Certain persons, places and objects were considered holy hence considered taboo for the ordinary person. The persons of the chiefs were considered taboo and certain food belonged to him, therefore forbidden for ordinary people to touch. Great harm can come to persons who violate these cultural taboos.[43]

I am not blaming Chanel. I think he was simply unaware of the seriousness and meaning of the cultural taboo. He was unaware that breaking such a taboo would in the end lead to the death penalty. Of course, it too had to do with Meitala wanting to become a Christian. But it did not explain the real cultural reason. King Niuliki had a family taboo. It went something like this:

> The eldest son should refrain from eating yams until he married
> and had a son, then he was released from the taboo, but it was
> laid on the child, who, under the penalty of death, to be inflicted
> by their gods (and they firmly believed it would be inflicted in
> a manner most fearful), would be compelled to abstain from the
> forbidden root until released by his becoming the father of a
> male child . . . The prohibition usually continued for two or three
> years, and during the term, if any native were to eat the fruit
> of this the vengeance of their gods is sufficiently powerful to
> prevent the natives from violating the taboo.[44]

---

42.   Cf début juin 1841, *Extrait d'une Lettre de Pierre Bataillon à Mgr. Pompallier*, traduite littéralement en anglais dans un article du journal *The Tablet*, New Zealand, du 14 mai 1841. See also Claude Rozier, *S Pierre Chanel d'après Ceux qui l'ont Connu* (Rome, 1991), 121–2.

43.   Lewis M Hopfe, *Religions of the World* (New York: Macmillan Publishing Company, ⁵1976), 30.

44.   John Power Twining, *Adventures in the South Seas* (London, ²1850), quoted in Rozier, *Chanel d'après ceux*, 77–8.

One day Meitala went to Chanel and asked for his opinion concerning the prohibition of the taboo. Meitala wanted to know if he were to violate the taboo, would he really die as a consequence. Chanel told Meitala that it was pure folly and idle superstition.[45] Meitala was convinced by what Chanel told him. Meitala took with him about a dozen young men and cooked a large oven full of yams. They ate their fill. In this act, Meitala committed some very serious offences. First, he violated or ridiculed a long hallowed custom. Secondly, he rendered null the authority and vengeance of their gods. Thirdly, he disobeyed his father and their family taboo; hence, he greatly embarrassed and insulted the king and his god.[46]

The news of this act soon reached the ears of the king. King Niuliki was deeply insulted and maddened by his son's act. His own son had broken their family taboo! He dishonoured his father and relativised the taboo. He brought shame to the family and the whole country. For a Futunian, this was an act of treason of the highest degree, and hence deserved the death punishment. The shame of the son's actions would forever stay with Niuliki's family as a curse. The culture of shame is something that a French priest like Chanel would never have understood. His death was therefore, a consequence of this clash of cultures.

Breaking of a Fijian taboo–touching a chief's hair

Perhaps a word could be added here concerning the same clash of culture that took place in Fiji when the famous Reverend Thomas Baker (1832–67) was clubbed to death with seven of his men. He was stripped, except for his boots, cut up into pieces, cooked in the oven and eaten. Father Lui Raco SM, recollects quite vividly his trip to the village that killed Thomas Baker in 1960. He visited the house of the Chief where Thomas Baker stayed during that fatal visit. The Chief's son was still alive. The son recounted the story to him as follows:

> Reverend Thomas Baker stayed here in my Father's house. Every morning the chief noticed with great interest Thomas Baker's comb and the way he combed his hair. One morning, Mr Baker threw the comb over to the Chief for his inspection after noticing his curiosity. For a Fijian, when you give the comb like

45.   Rozier, *Chanel d'après Ceux*, 78: 'Meitala, après avoir quitté son père, se rendit après du prêtre catholique . . . et il lui demanda si la violation de son tabou serait réellement puni de sa mort. Le bon prêtre lui dit que non, et il s'efforça de convaincre le jeune chef de la folie des vraies superstitions.'

46.   *Ibid.*

that, it meant, you can have it. The Chief after combing left the comb in his hair. When it was time for Mr. Baker and his party to leave, he stood up and took the comb off the Chief's hair. The Chief allegedly told him, 'Sir, nobody has ever touched my hair except my mother.' Mr Baker of course did not understand what he was doing. But the people heard clearly what their Chief voiced. As Mr Baker and his party were on their way, they were clubbed to death. Two of them escaped alive. The captors took Mr. Baker's body down the river, cleaned it and cut it up. They made a big *lovo* (earth oven) and had a big feast. [47]

The customs and taboos in regards to touching a Chief's hair are not unique to the Fijian culture. In Tonga and Samoa, it is considered very disrespectful to touch even the head or hair of your father or mother. The head is considered to be the most sacred part of the body. It is the centre of wisdom and knowledge.

According to Brother Eremondo Eliseo SM, in Fiji, the Chief's hair is sacred for various reasons. It is sacred because he is the highest person and authority in the family and community. He is the point of reference. But he is also sacred in a symbolic way. He represents the highest authority in the *yavusa*, the whole district or province. [48]

In this context, Baker's action carried a whole lot of meaning. He was disrespecting not only the Chief but all the people in the district. In Fiji for instance, even to this day it becomes a strict taboo to touch people's hair or head. It is considered most disrespectful and in the case of a Chief, death penalty is very likely to happen. This was what Mr. Baker and his followers found out in 1867. [49]

Lance Martin, an archivist at the School of Oriental and African Studies in London, which holds an account of the Reverend Baker's death, said: 'The

---

47.   Private interview with Lui Raco SM, Suva, Fiji, 31 July 2007.
48.   Private interview with Eremondo Eliseo SM, Suva, 1 August 2007.
49.   In 1859, Reverend Thomas Baker was appointed to Fiji, and threw himself with more than ordinary enthusiasm into the task. In 1864, he was appointed Missionary to the Interior which was a region utterly savage. He erected a new station at Davuilevu, then on the verge of heathen territory. In 1867 accompanied by a Fijian party of nine, he set out for those sinister and unexplored mountains to the west but Baker was never to return to Davuilevu. He and seven of his companions were struck down with the axe by the savage tribes of Nadrau. Two companions alone escaped to relate the sad story. Baker's last indignity was that his body was cut up, cooked and eaten by his captors.

story about the comb may be a bit of a myth. It seems Baker got caught up in some sort of inter-tribal feuding relating to his right to travel across the island. He was ambushed as he and his companions were leaving a village one morning. He was cut up on a flat rock at the base of a ravine. His body was anointed and then eaten.'[50] Martin's view represents in a nutshell how the white man misunderstands the Pacific cultures. He does not understand its symbolic meanings and hence, does not appreciate the seriousness of touching a Chief's hair.

To the Western mind and perhaps modern way of thinking, the war over a flagpole, the killing of Father Chanel and Reverend Baker, were over some senseless issues and the stories often bring smiles to the faces of the audience. But in comparison, Jesus was killed because of the breaking of a taboo; does that killing bring smiles to our faces? The throwing of Christians to the lions and tigers in the arenas was because of the breaking of a taboo; do those killings bring smiles to our faces? In the Old Testament, II Kings 2:23–25 speaks of an occasion when boys mocked and taunted the prophet Elisha saying 'go away baldhead.' As a result, forty-two children were mauled by two bears. II Samuel 6:6 reports another incident where a man named Uz'zah reached out his hand to the ark of God to prevent it from falling because the oxen shook it. The anger of the Lord was kindled against Uz'zah, and God struck him there beside the ark of God. Were those cultural taboos senseless?

Tonga versus Wesleyanism and Catholicism
Because Tonga was not colonised, the question of the clash of cultures was more subtle. The main clash was more religious in nature. It was Methodist versus Catholic (*Lotu Popi*). To a lesser extent, it was also a clash between these two Christian churches and the Tongan traditional religion. The Marists established themselves some twenty years after the Methodist Church.[51] The Methodist Church did their best to ward off the Catholic penetration. In the process the Christian Methodists and the Christian Catholics both incriminated each other in very un-Christian ways. Yes, division and chaos had landed under the banner of the Cross. I find writing about this matter rather sad. Before Christianity arrived, our people lived in harmony under their various chiefs. There were

---

50. Cf 'Fiji villagers to say sorry for eating British missionary', By Nick Squires in Sydney Last Updated: 6:51pm BST 14/10/2003.

51. 'Lettre de Jérôme Grange à monsieur Nicoud, curé de Saint Clair', in Charles Girard (editor), LRO (Rome, APM, 1999), volume 3, Doc 253.

troubles, but at least they had their religions and gods whom they worshipped and who paved for them ways of reconciling differences.[52]

Christianity arrived in Tonga divided and the wounds of the division were still raw. This division was a creation of Europe and it was transported to the Pacific. The consequence of this division was that the Wesleyans and Catholics competed to win followers from the locals. Christianity added a new division to our people as well as successfully pushing asunder the traditional Tongan religions. They were able to do this even with the firm resistance of the Tui Tonga, Laufilitonga. He clearly told Bishop Bataillon (1810–77) when he asked him again to accept the Marist Fathers in his domain:

> I will not receive your missionary. I have refused the request of the 'misis' (that is, the Wesleyans), and have refused the 'black robes' (as the Marists were called on account of the soutanes they wore). We have no need of the *lotu*[53] of strangers; we wish to live to the end in that of our ancestors.[54]

A brief description of the pre-Christian religion is given by Father Grange (1807–52) in his letter to Father Nicoud.[55] The Wesleyans tried to discredit the Catholics by telling the people that the Catholic Church was not the true religion as the 'black robes' were claiming. They told the people stories that the priests were poor and chased away from their country and that the Catholic Church was destroyed. The only remaining Catholics were those on Wallis and Tonga. These clashes are well documented already and people can consult them if they may so wish.[56] The letters of the missionaries from Tonga during the period under study mention repeatedly the opposition and threats from the Methodists

---

52. 'Lettre de Jérôme Grange à Monsieur Nicoud, Curé de Saint Clair', in LRO, volume 3, 744, 756.
53. The Tongan word for religion.
54. Hugh Laracy, 'The Catholic Mission', in Noel Rutherford (editor), *Friendly Islands: A History of Tonga* (Melbourne: University of Oxford Press, 1977), 136–152, here 142. Laracy quotes from A Monfat, *Les Tonga, ou Archipel des Amis et le RP Joseph Chevron* (Lyon, 1893).
55. LRO, Doc 253, § 11–12, 34.
56. See the work of Monfat, *Tonga*; SS Farmer, *Tonga and the Friendly Islands: With a sketch of their Missionary History* (London, 1855); J Thomas, *History of the Friendly Island* (1876); Sione Latukefu, *Church and State in Tonga* (Canberra, 1974); W Lawry, *Missions in the Tonga and Feejee Islands* (New York, 1852); John E Erskine, *Journal of a Cruise among the Islands of the Western Pacific* (London, 1853) and Laracy, 'The Catholic Mission'.

especially against the neophytes.[57] The Marists and their converts continued to suffer right from the beginning of the mission at Pea in 1842 until the fall of its fort at Pea in 1852. That meant the destruction of the Marist beginnings and the dispersion of the followers and Father Piéplu (1818–57) wounded.

In fact, this was what most people hoped at the time of the destruction of Pea; that it would also destroy Catholicism. This is also clear from Chevron's letter to Colin on 26 June 1852. This letter was written in haste to explain the reason why Father Calinon (1806–77) would leave for Tahiti to seek help. His parish, the famous Fort of Pea was about to be attacked. His chief had warned him that there would be a war. While his chief thought it would only be a temporary one, 'all his people believe that the war is to suppress Catholicism not only in Tonga but also at Wallis and Futuna, Samoa and Fiji.'[58]

There were many other areas where the two cultures clashed. We only have sufficient time and space here to mention them randomly:

- there were the concepts of subsistence vs commercial farming;
- oceanic concept of time, commonly known as Pacific Time versus European understanding of time as money;
- the concepts of borrowing and of ownership;
- the relationship to the land as sacred and having a spiritual value versus land as commodity to be sold and bought;
- the European or Christian God as true and Oceanic ones as idols;
- the Europeans considered the notions of cultural mores and *taboos* as superstitious (King Niuliki's family taboo!). Many of the various traditional dances of Tonga were discarded. They were judged by early Missionaries and Europeans alike as pagan and far too sexual;
- there was also the clash between the Pacific understanding of space and boundaries versus that of the Western;

---

57. 'Lettre de Chevron à Colin, 2 août, 1852', Doc 1098 in LRO, volume 3, 829.
58. 'Lettre de Chevron à Colin, Juin 26, 1852', in LRO, volume 3, 813: 'Son fort de Pea se trouve cerné par une armée qui, à en croire le chef, ne feroit à Pea qu'une guerre temporelle mais qui, à en croire son people tout entière, est une guerre qui tend à étouffer le catholicisme non seulement a Tonga mais encore à Wallis, à Futuna, puis aux Navigateurs et à Fidji.' (translation is mine).

- the Pacific ways of learning, skills for boat and canoe buildings and navigation were taken over by the European ones. Sadly, they slowly disappeared;
- There were also the Pacific concepts of economy, various arts especially that of wood-carving, weaving, cosmology and medicine. They discarded them because they were inferior to that of the Europeans.

There were the allegations made by early missionaries that Pacific Islanders were too proud, rebellious, promiscuous, lazy and intellectually weak. Father Chevron spoke of this also in a letter to his family:

> It is difficult to say which is the predominant vice here: pride, immorality and laziness march together . . . Laziness seems to be a predilection moral failing. The natives are not keen to work . . . besides the feasts, they eat very little. The food for one man in France is abundantly sufficient for ten people here. They are suffering but prefer to be hungry rather than to work.[59]

These evaluations were measured by the European standards of thinking and culture. It was the interpretation of Pacific cultures according to European meter-sticks. The superiority ideology described above allowed these allegations to be made and believed to be true. However, these claims were not necessarily true as John Broadbent rightly pointed out in his study: *Attempts to form an Indigenous Clergy in the Vicariates Apostolic of Central Oceania and the Navigators' Island in the Nineteenth Century.*[60] Missionaries from Europe came with the Western European culture with its own value scale. They evaluated the behaviour of Pacific peoples accordingly. This therefore represents a clash of cultures: the individualistic European culture versus the strong kinship structures that preserve order in the community. The conclusion that the Polynesians lacked

---

59.   'Lettre de Joseph Chevron à sa famille, 24–25 juin 1843', in LRO, volume 2, 715: 'Il seroit difficile de dire quel est ici le vice dominant; l'orgueil, l'immoralité et la pareses marchent de pair . . . La paresse semble être le vice de prédilection; les naturels ne font de travail . . . hors les fêtes, ils mangent très peu. La nourriture d'un homme en France suffiroit abondament à dix ici. Ils souffrent, mais pour eux mieux vaut la faim que le travail' (translation is mine).

60.   A Thesis presented in partial fulfillment of the requirements for the PhD in religious studies (University of Louvain, 1976).

in individual responsibility is a favourite child of this clash of cultures.[61] This was the main clash that destabilised the efforts of Bishop Bataillon to train local clergy.

Fathers Chevron (1808–84) and Grange seemed to have had more balanced views as a consequence of their experiences working with Tongans. While Chevron spoke at will about the many defects Tongans had, he also noted that they did not merit the name savage. In spite of their lack of education, they had a great civility in comparison with France.[62] Father Jérôme Grange spoke in the same manner.[63] Both priests clearly spoke of Tongans as intelligent and highly skilled for a people who have not had formal education. They were accomplished builders of both canoes and houses and they were great navigators. The catechists in defending Catholic faith against Methodist intruders showed great intelligent in answering and explaining the Catholic faith.

A dream and a final word of hope

Can the Christian culture as well as the Oceanic cultures survive the onslaught of globalisation, 'Pax Americana', and the New Global Ethic now spreading like wildfire around the Pacific Rim? Can reference to the transcendence survive or would Oceania follow the crisis of Christianity in the West in its current apostasy and continual pushing out of God and morality from public life? On another level, one may ask together with Pope Benedict when he wrote, 'Indeed, is it possible to imagine anything properly called 'civilisation' that lacks a sense of the sacred?'[64] In that sense, can we speak of a future Oceania with no God, Christianity and devoid of its cultural roots? Can we possibly foresee a future for Oceania without its roots? The answer of course is an emphatic no.

In 2001, the Pacific Conference of Churches in collaboration with the World Council of Churches (WCC) held a Conference in Fiji to study globalisation in all its aspects. It came up with a positive word in its final document, which

---

61. Broadbent, *Indigenous Clergy*, 10–1.
62. 'Lettre de Joseph Chevron à sa famille, 24–25 juin 1843', in LRO, volume 2, Doc 250: 'Je crois que ces peoples sont loin de mériter le nom de sauvages qu'on leur donne. Ils sont d'une civilité plus grande que ne le sont en France les gens qui n'ont pas reçu d'éducation.' See also 'Lettre de Joseph Chevron à Jean-Claude Colin', 11–13 octobre, 1845, *ibid*, Doc 393.
63. 'Lettre de Jérôme Grange à monsieur Nicoud, 1er juillet 1843', in LRO, volume 2, Doc 253: 'Aussi, je crois qu'ils sont loin de mériter sous ce rapport le nom de sauvages qu'on leur donne.'
64. Joseph Ratzinger, *Without Roots, the West, Relativism, Christianity, Islam* (New York: Basic Books, 2006), vii.

since has been published in a book entitled *Island of Hope. A Pacific Alternative to Economic Globalisation*. Why Island of Hope? According to the report, the essence of the vision, 'proposes a way of life that is in complete contrast to the way we live today. It is based on principles that do not exclude nor marginalise, and on values that are commonly found in the various Pacific cultures.'[65] Between 200 to 400 years of subjection to colonisation and now globalisation, the essence of Pacific cultures and their noble values, have survived. Here we refer to the Pacific spirituality, family life, traditional economy in the form of reciprocity, mutual care, respect and above all the strong sense of community living. They prioritise relationship; celebrate the quality of life and value human beings and creation over the production of things.[66]

This trend is particularly true of Polynesian societies. They have survived the onslaught of these different forces and will continue to do so in the future. This is the opinion of Professor Ron Crocombe, a well-known South Pacific expert:

> It is easy to explain the changes that have taken place in the Pacific cultures in the last two hundred years. What is harder to explain is their extraordinary resilience; the extent to which they have retained so much in the face of such vast changes in technology, social organisation, communication and belief. Most culture change in the Pacific has not led to the total adoption of foreign models, but rather to a protective reaction, and a creative adaptation incorporating elements from both.[67]

This is what the focus on a 'Pacific Theology of Hope' attempts to formulate. A group of professors from the University of the South Pacific (USP) and theologians from the Pacific Theological College (PTC), Pacific Regional Seminary (PRS), Pacific Conferences of Churches (PCC), South Pacific Association of Theological Schools (SPATS) and the WCC Pacific Desk have met since March 2006. The original paper was entitled *To Whom Shall We Go?* Its main concerns are to make the Pacific Church communities have a better awareness of the fast changing Pacific. For the churches to be able to discern, articulate, and take action against unjust issues; to strengthen their bonds of solidarity; to explore what it means to be 'Church' in the Pacific today; to

---

65.   See *Island of Hope, A Pacific Alternative to Economic Globalization* (Geneva, WCC Publication, 2002), 7.
66.   *Ibid*, see back page cover.
67.   Broadbent, *Indigenous Clergy*, 8.

strengthen and promote ecumenism; create networks of solidarity in sharing faith experiences and to have one voice on issues of concern.[68]

In fact, this is not a new concern. The Pacific churches since 1985,[69] 1991,[70] 2001,[71] have been engaged in a dialogue to make theology relevant to Pacific contexts. Theology of Celebration, the famous 'Coconut Theology' and Indigenization dominated the 1980s. The contexts of the eighties have changed dramatically. Contextual Theology controlled the 1990s and early 2000. The contexts of the New Millennium have changed also. They need a new approach. In this new context, our group has put together a working paper entitled *To Whom Shall We Go: Framework for a Pacific Theology of Hope* to be presented at the PCC Assembly to be held in Pagopago in September 2007. This paper is a 'deliberate attempt, in the current context, to engage Pacific thinkers, intellectuals and academics from various disciplines on what we mean by hope at the theological, methodological and praxis levels; an attempt to articulate a theology that is as much about praxis as it is about methodology, theory and thinking'.[72]

This work is far from complete but it has put together a framework of hope for some kind of roadmap for future researches:

a) Pacific Context Mapping including analytical methodology and regionalism: ethics in the Pacific, symbolism in the Pacific - epistemology - learning and ways of knowing in the Pacific, hermeneutics - interpretations in the Pacific, ecclesiology (and with it mission) in the Pacific.

b) Pacific Theology Mapping, including sources of Pacific Theology![73]

It is with hope that these studies and their implementation become signs of hope for our people who are facing an increasing maximum of uncertainty with the minimum of resources to protect them against insecurity. Change has become

---

68. *To Whom Shall We Go, A Pacific Theology of Hope*, 3.
69. PCC Conference, Bergengren Theological Consultation.
70. PCC General Assembly in Niue with the theme – Proclaiming a Living Hope.
71. Consultation Island of Hope on how to understand Globalisation, cf, Island of Hope Report.
72. *To Whom Shall We Go, Framework for a Pacific Theology of Hope*, paper to be present at the PCC Assembly (PagoPago, September 2–8, 2007), 3, in the possession of the author.
73. *Ibid*, 5.

systemic. Our people no longer feel a sense of control over their lives. In such a situation, despair may seem the only result. Hence, one can understand the high susceptibility and culpability of our people to new and often extreme right wing religious movements in the Pacific.[74] The churches must search for a way of speaking intelligibly of hope and clarity of the gospel message to our people in this context. The pertinent question is how to do this and be signs of hope to our people in these times of dramatic and traumatic social changes. The churches need to stay engaged with our peoples' struggle for meaning and purpose.[75]

This new trend of retrieving a cultural framework from the past is not a nostalgic return to pre-Christian and pre-Western life. That is an impossible task. It is to recapture the wisdom and values of the past discarded by westernisation and Christianity, in order to help us cope with the present and to affirm once more our God given identities. As Walter Kasper iterated 'nobody wants to perish in an anonymous, faceless, globally uniform civilization. So the question of identity is important and constitutive.'[76] It is neither a new form of delimitation that can result in fundamentalism nor an absolute claim on truth. It is more in line with the wisdom of Mahatma Gandhi when he said:

> I appreciate uncompromising avoidance of all that is evil in the old, but where there is not only no question of anything evil in the old but where an ancient practice may be even desirable, it would be a crime to part with it . . . Conversion must not mean denationalisation. Conversion should mean a definite giving up of the evil of the old, adoption of all the good in the new and a scrupulous avoidance of everything evil in the new.[77]

It is also in the spirit of what Ron Crocombe said: 'a protective reaction, and a creative adaptation incorporating elements from both'.[78] In the words of Professor Konai Helu Thaman, 'it is looking towards the source'[79] that is, our

---

74.   Manfred Ernst, *Winds of Change* (Suva: Pacific Conference of Churches, 1991).
75.   *To Whom Shall We Go*, 5.
76.   Walter Kasper, *That They May All be One*, 181.
77.   Mahatma K Gandhi, *Truth is God* (Ahmedabad, Navajivan Publishing House, reprint 1997), 67.
78.   *To Whom Shall We Go*.
79.   Konai Helu Thaman, 'Looking Towards the Source: A Consideration of (Cultural) Context in Teacher Education', in C Benson and N Taylor (editors), *Pacific Teacher Education Forward Planning Meeting: Proceedings* (Suva: Institute of Education, USP), 98–103.

Pacific cultures to find new understandings and new knowledge that is useful for our context.[80]

Conclusion

The Oceania of 1836–54 had a completely different context from 2007 Oceania. The arrival of Christianity in collaboration with westernisation imposed not only a new religion but also the Western life in its totality: the 'full house'. This was possible due to the ability of the early missionaries and Europeans to convince the locals with the ideology that their religion and culture were far superior to theirs. As noted earlier, it was not so much a clash of cultures. Rather, it was the domination and suppression of the local cultures by the more powerful ones. Soon the superior religion, medicine, military, economic, political and education systems were set up. They systematically conquered the minds and hearts of the local people to believe that it was the way to follow. The locals surrendered everything; their lands included. Little did they know that they were about to be unjustly colonized, of course in the name of Jesus Christ and God.

The four examples given above represent different clashes of cultures. In all four cases, Christianity and westernisation came out as winners. The White man was always right hence he either became a saint or a hero. The local people were always wrong and hence became the bad ones. We hope that the study of history will bring a more balanced view of this whole misinformation.

Today we are becoming more aware of two new cultures namely the Enlightenment culture of scientific rationality that pushes God out from life and the 'new global ethic' fashioned out of recent UN programs and ideologies. Both cultures have one thing in common; the fulfilment of the wish of the German philosopher Friedrich Nietzsche: man has become god. It has threatened to eliminate the God of Jesus Christ as well as Christianity. Both modern cultures are materialistic, hedonistic, individualistic, incomplete and irrational. They lead only to self-indulgence and self-destruction. These two cultures will be more devastating for the people of Oceania if they continue to operate unnoticed and unattended to. The ambivalent identity that we have now as a consequence will eventually push Oceanic peoples further to become rootless, cultureless and without identities.

Will the Society of Mary in Oceania continue to perpetuate the mentality 'that the white people are superior to island people'? I hope not. This mentality has poisoned part of our history, spirituality, mentality, and relationships during

---

80.   Dr Seu'ula Johannson-Fua, 'Looking Towards the Source: Social Justice and Leadership Conceptualizations from Tonga,' Unpublished Paper, 19.

the past 170 years. We need to dismantle completely this false ideology and anthropology from our attitudes, language and our Oceania.

What is the role of the Society of Mary in Oceania in the light of this new clash of cultures? For us Catholic Christians the vision of Pope Benedict XVI may be apt for facing the current cultural forces trying to put God out from our Pacific world. It is appropriate to remember his wisdom when he said, that the Enlightenment philosophy with its related culture of scientific rationality is incomplete, it is not rational, nor universally valid.[81] The Society of Mary in Oceania would do well to take heed of the Pope's words of wisdom when he said:

> Our greatest need in the present historical moment is people who make God credible in this world by means of the enlightened faith they live. The negative testimony of Christians who spoke of God but lived in a manner contrary to him has obscured the image of God and has opened the doors to disbelief. We need men *(& women)* who keep their eyes fixed on God, learning from him what true humanity means. We need men (& *women*) who keep their eyes fixed on God, learning from him what true humanity means. We need men (& *women)* whose intellect is enlightened by the light of God, men (women) whose hearts are opened to God so that their intellect can speak to the intellect of others and their hearts can open to the hearts of others. It is only by means of men (& *women*) who have been touched by God that God can return to be with mankind (*humankind*). [82]

---

81.   Joseph Ratzinger, *Christianity and the Crisis of Cultures*, 41, 43.
82.   *Ibid*, 52.

The Personality of Jean-Claude Colin, Superior General

Timothy J Costello SM

Introduction

Jean-Claude Colin (1790–1875) is a complex and at times contradictory figure. This complexity is reflected, for example, in the well-known difficulties and misunderstandings that still cast a shadow over Colin's relationships with other important figures in the Marist story: with Pompallier (1801–71), with Jeanne-Marie Chavoin (1786–1858), with Julien Favre (1812–85), and with Saint Peter Julian Eymard (1811–68).

In his life-time, Colin evoked strong and diverse reactions from those who knew him. The saintly Bishop Devie (1767–1852), for example, admired Colin greatly and yet on his deathbed took the opportunity to exhort Colin to a greater control of his emotions.[1] Father Gabriel-Claude Mayet (1809–94) lived very close to Colin through the period 1836–1854, and had a unique insight into his character including his human limitations. Despite these limitations, Mayet concluded that 'he is the greatest character I have known . . . you felt he was a saint, and as soon as I had spoken with him for the first time, I had this strong feeling in my heart: That is the man you are looking for. I felt drawn to him by an attraction that came from on high . . .'.[2]

So, who was this man, Jean-Claude Colin, and what was he really like? Understanding the human personality is not a simple matter, even of a living person, let alone a man who has been dead for one hundred and thirty-two years. We cannot speak directly with Colin. We cannot ask him questions, nor observe him in action, nor even talk with others who knew him personally. How then is it possible for us to come to a deeper understanding of the human fabric—the psyche—of this man whom we believe was the human instrument used by God and the Blessed Virgin Mary to bring the Society of Mary into existence and to guide the congregation as its first superior general? Exploring that question is the purpose of this paper which is a small but hopefully useful response to

---

1. Jean Coste (editor), *A Founder Acts: Reminiscences of Jean-Claude Colin* (Rome, 1975), 423. Father Poupinel is the source of this information which is included as a note written in the margin by Father Mayet. See also: Jean Coste, *Lectures on Society of Mary History (Marist Fathers) 1786–1854* (Rome, 1965), 130
2. *A Founder Acts*, 119–120.

invitations to enrich the field of Marist studies with questions and insights from other disciplines including the human sciences.[3]

The paper is divided into three sections: Part One considers the relationship between history, biography and psychology; Part Two is a survey of studies already done on the character and personality of Colin; Part Three proposes an anthropological framework for pursuing a more complete analysis of Colin's personality.

History, biography and psychology

Premises and methodology

The discussion that follows is based on three premises. The first two premises are about the relationship of nature and grace; the third concerns psychology as an empirical science.

The first premise is that Colin's life cannot be understood except within the context of religious faith. Every aspect of the Christian life—including, and especially, founding a religious order—depends in a decisive way on the gratuitous action of divine grace. This was Colin's own conviction; it is also the faith of the Church.[4] This belief does not exclude the contribution of the human sciences in seeking to understand the person who has been called by God, but it does place these sciences within a particular horizon. If this paper emphasizes the human and psychological aspects of Colin's life, this is not intended to minimise in any way the role of divine grace as an influence in his life.

The second premise is the belief that normally God acts through instrumental causes and the laws of nature rather than by direct intervention or a series of miracles. It is true that the spiritual life depends essentially on the mystery of grace and, as such, transcends the mechanisms of the human psyche;[5] but it is also true that divine grace is normally mediated through the structures and

---

3.   Jean Coste, 'General Introduction', in *A Founder Acts*, 20–1; Gaston Lessard, 'Introduction', in *The Study of Marist Spirituality* (Rome, 1984), xi: 'Les membres du colloque estiment que la phase suivante des recherches gagnerait à se présenter de manière différente. Ils souhaiteraient particulièrement . . . que, au delà de l'apport des méthodes historiques, soit intégré à ces recherches celui de nombreuses autres disciplines: psychologie, sociologie, linguistique, anthropologie, etc'.

4.   John Paul II, Apostolic Exhortation *Pastores dabo vobis* (25–III–1992) On the formation of priests in the circumstances of the present day, number 36. Also: *Catechism of the Catholic Church*, number 2022.

5.   Congregation for Catholic Education, *A Guide to Formation in Priestly Celibacy* (Rome, 1974), number 90.

dynamisms of the human personality of which God, the creator, is the author. In other words, God called Jean-Claude Colin to the vocation of founder not in spite of his humanity but through his human personality which, in that sense, is not peripheral but integral to the Marist story.

The third premise is that there does not exist one, but many, approaches to psychology which are based on diverse philosophical assumptions about human nature and which sometimes differ in their basic tenets. Consequently, there is no universal agreement within the world of psychology about fundamental concepts such as personality, maturity, identity, or even what constitutes normal human behaviour.[6] This raises an important methodological question that runs as a subtext through much of this paper: what kind of psychological framework is needed to explore and understand the personality of Jean-Claude Colin? The question of a Christian anthropology is raised explicitly towards the end of this paper and, clearly, is material which needs to be further explored on another occasion.

Terminology

Words can sometimes confuse rather than clarify, especially when the word is part of everyday vocabulary but its precise meaning remains unclear. Three words relevant to the present discussion need to be briefly defined for the sake of clarity: personality, temperament and character.

Personality has been defined as 'a complex pattern of deeply embedded psychological characteristics that are expressed automatically in almost every area of psychological functioning'.[7] My personality is the relatively stable pattern of perceiving, thinking about, and relating to the environment and to myself that is manifested in a wide range of social and personal contexts.

Temperament refers to the biological aspect of personality which is present even before birth, and provides the basis on which personality later develops.[8] Temperament is evident from earliest childhood whereas personality is shaped throughout childhood, adolescence, and into adult life. Temperament theory

---

6. A paper that analyses Colin from the perspective of behavioural psychology, for example, ascribes no scientific validity whatever to the concept of 'personality'. Raymond P Carey, 'Jean-Claude Colin from the Perspective of Behavioural Psychology', in *The Study of Marist Spirituality*, 71–83, here 72–3.

7. Theodore Millon and Randall Davis, *Personality Disorders in Modern Life* (New York, 2004), 2. See also: American Psychiatric Association, *Diagnostic and Statistical Manual (DSM-IV-TR)* (Washington DC, 2000), 686.

8. SC Cloninger, *Personality: description, dynamics and development* (New York, 1996), 403.

has its ancient roots in Greco-Roman medicine, particularly the teaching of Hippocrates (460–370 BC) who believed that certain behaviours were caused by the movement of body fluids called 'humours'.

Character is usually associated with the process of socialization, the acts and imprints of nurture and environment on the human psyche especially during the formative years of infancy, childhood, and adolescence. Character is the sum of a person's acquired qualities, and is often judged according to social, cultural, or religious criteria.

Psychohistory and Psychobiography
The relationship between history and biography has long been a matter of discussion and debate among historians. 'History is the record of an encounter between character and circumstance' writes Donald Creighton, former professor of history at the University of Toronto. Consequently, 'the historian's first task is the elucidation of character'.[9]

In 1957 William Langer, president of the American Historical Association, challenged his colleagues to find a suitable psychological basis for better understanding the motivation and actions of historical subjects.[10] This is considered to be the formal beginning of psychohistory as a professional method of inquiry. The purpose of psychohistory is to study the psychological component of historical events using frames of reference, concepts, and data drawn from the human sciences, especially sociology and psychology. Psychobiography, a subdivision of psychohistory, aims to shed light on the character and motivations of historical persons. More than the random psychological remarks which have long been associated with historical biography, psychobiography is the systematic attempt to reach a deeper understanding of the subject's psyche.

The reaction of academic historians to psychohistory and psychobiography has been at best mixed and at worst hostile. Yet despite the mixed reception to Langer's challenge, the rapidly growing influence of the human sciences during the last fifty years has forced both historians and biographers to develop new forms in an attempt to uncover the personality dynamics of the subject or protagonist.[11] Mazlish points out some of the strengths and limitations of these new forms:

---

9.   Donald W Creighton, *Towards the Discovery of Canada: Selected Essays* (Toronto, 1972), 19.

10.   William L Langer, 'The Next Assignment', in *American Historical Review*, 63 (1958): 283–305.

11.   R Craig Brown, 'Biography in Canadian History', in *Journal of the Canadian Historical Association*, 15 (1980): 1–8.

Because the psychohistorian focuses on aspects of the historical process that are different in nature and quality from the traditional focus of historical interests, his methods, his approach and his concepts are also different. The results should not stand in contradiction to the results of historical investigation; they may complement those findings and understandings, they may cast them in a somewhat different light, they may give rise to a more nuanced and variable interpretation, but they never can contradict established historical facts. Without such facts, the psychohistorical hypotheses are empty vessels without meaning and content.[12]

Psychological studies of Jean-Claude Colin

A survey of the literature on Colin
Two recent surveys of Marist writings by Alois Greiler give a comprehensive list of studies whose focus has been on the person of Jean-Claude Colin.[13] Many of these papers have never been formally published; the vast majority have been historical or spiritual in nature. At least some of these works have begun to raise questions and explore matters relating to Colin's personality.

If the first task of the historian (as Creighton says) is 'the elucidation of character', then to what extent have Marist studies shed light on the character of Jean-Claude Colin? To what extent have these studies been able to identify the critical questions, to explore the paradoxes and seeming contradictions, to analyse the events and experiences that have shaped and formed the complex personality of Colin?

Many of the books and papers about Colin do not focus on his character and personality as their principal interest. For example, the biographies written by

---

12. Bruce Mazlish, 'Group Psychology and the Problems of Contemporary History', in G Cocks and TL Crosby (editors), *Psychohistory: Readings in the Method of Psychology, Psychoanalysis, and History* (New Haven, 1987), 232.
13. Alois Greiler, 'Between History and Spiritual Renewal: A Survey of Recent Marist Studies', in *Forum Novum*, 5/3 (2000): 315–341; 'From Jeantin to Coste. A Survey on Marist Studies in the 20th Century', in *Forum Novum*, 7/1 (2005): 38–71.

Stanley Hosie,[14] Antoine Forissier[15] and Donal Kerr[16] sometimes raise questions relating to character, and make observations about his personality, but these are the random psychological remarks commonly associated with biography rather than a systematic study of Colin's personality. This is not a criticism, since the intended purpose of these authors is not to make such a study. Kerr, in fact, states quite explicitly that 'the title, *A Founder in an Era of Revolution and Restoration* indicates that this volume intends to give prominence to the background of his life and to those people who influenced him and his project'.[17]

There are relatively few works whose explicit purpose is to make an analysis of Colin's character. Some studies form one section of a larger work, for example: Jean Coste, *Lectures on Society of Mary History* (chapter XIII)[18] and Franco Gioannetti, *A Spirituality for Our Time* (chapter 2).[19] Others have been written as stand-alone papers which are specialized in nature and limited in scope such as: G Lessard, *Une crise d'adolescence: Première communion de Jean-Claude Colin*;[20] Raymond Carey, *Jean-Claude Colin from the Perspective of Behavioural Psychology*;[21] Stephen Truscott, *Hello Jean-Claude! An exploration of the personality of Jean-Claude Colin through the Enneagram.*[22]

Finally, the two volumes *A Founder Speaks*[23] and *A Founder Acts* while having general rather than a specifically psychological interest, provide valuable source material for making a psychological portrait of Jean-Claude Colin and, for this reason, have been included for discussion in this study.

14.   Stanley Hosie, *Anonymous Apostle* (New York, 1967).
15.   Antoine Forissier, *For a Marian Church. Marist Founders and Foundresses* (Middlegreen: St Paul's, 1992).
16.   Donal Kerr, *Jean-Claude Colin, Marist: A Founder in an Era of Revolution and Restoration: The Early Years 1790–1836*, (Dublin: Columba Press, 2000).
17.   Kerr, *Jean-Claude Colin, Marist*, 8.
18.   Coste, *Lectures*, 127–143.
19.   Franco Gioannetti, *A Spirituality for our Time. Jean-Claude Colin Founder of the Society of Mary* (Rome, 1989), 63–102.
20.   Gaston Lessard, 'Une crise d'adolescence: Première communion de Jean-Claude Colin' (thesis, Université d'Ottawa, 1976).
21.   Carey, 'Jean-Claude Colin from the Perspective of Behavioural Psychology'.
22.   Stephen Truscott, 'Hello Jean-Claude! An Exploration of the Personality of Jean-Claude Colin Through the Enneagram', typed manuscript (Rome, APM, 1987).
23.   Jean Coste (editor) *A Founder Speaks: Spiritual Talks of Jean-Claude Colin* (Rome, 1975).

Coste's lectures on Society of Mary history: a first attempt at psychobiography
Jean Coste (1926–94) began working on Marist history while a scholastic
at Sainte-Foy, Lyon. From 1945 until 1955 he studied in Lyon and in Rome
specializing in sacred scripture. In 1955 Coste was appointed by the General
Administration to the Society of Mary's historical committee and worked for
the next ten years, collaborating with Gaston Lessard and Seán Fagan, on the
origins of the Society of Mary.[24]

During the scholastic year of 1961–62, Coste gave a series of lectures on
Marist history at the Society's International Scholasticate in Rome.[25] These
lectures treat Colin's personality in a more explicit and systematic way than in
previous studies. Coste develops the material in three stages: Colin's physical
appearance and general health; the complexities of his emotional life; and his
dedication to the mission of the Society of Mary.[26] He captures something central
to Colin's personality with his concluding words: 'Father Colin was a man with
a mission, bent on a single great enterprise, one of those men who personify a
few big guiding ideas'.[27]

In making this portrait of Colin's personality, Coste uses an approach to
character study developed at the University of Groningen by Gerard Heymans
(1857–1930) and popularized in France by René Le Senne (1882–1954) and
Gaston Berger (1896–1960). These academics developed a typology approach
to personality which is based on the idea that personalities can be categorized
according to type—hence the word typology.[28] Le Senne defines character
according to three basic elements: emotionality, action, and retentivity. The
combination of these three elements (or their opposites) yields eight fundamental
character types: nervous, sentimental, choleric, passionate, sanguine, phlegmatic,
amorphous, and apathetic.[29]

---

24.   Greiler, 'From Jeantin to Coste', 51–2.
25.   Coste, *Lectures*.
26.   Coste, *Lectures*, 127–143.
27.   Coste, *Lectures*, 138.
28.   Since the mid-1960's there has been little reference to the Groningen methodology
      in spiritual writing which has tended to favor the Jungian-based Myers-Briggs
      Type Indicator and the Enneagram, both of which are examples of typological
      personality theory. The Enneagram, despite its popularity in some circles, holds
      little interest for scientific psychology because its characterisations are based
      on an arbitrary set of personality dimensions that cannot be verified using the
      scientific method.
29.   René Le Senne, *Traité de Caractérologie* (Paris, 1945). Le Senne was a
      metaphysician and psychologist at the Sorbonne University 1929–31, 1942–52.

Using the Groningen method, and his exceptional knowledge of the subject, Coste classifies Colin as a 'passionate type'. These are people who tend to identify themselves with their work and whose energies are very concentrated on their life mission. 'Such certainly was Father Colin,' writes Coste, 'who lived only for the Society. We can discern in him features of all the great men who can be classified as 'passionate': the ambition to achieve . . . the natural authority which commands respect and obedience . . . the permanent state of tension . . . impatience . . . the tendency to make use of others in the furtherance of his projects . . . the capacity for work, indifference to sensible pleasures . . . the absence of vanity and ostentation'.[30] Coste also notes that there are elements of Colin's behaviour that do not fit neatly into this typology.

Why does Coste, in these lectures, show such an interest in Colin's character and personality? This may be related to the fact that during this time he was also assistant to the postulator for the cause of Colin's beatification. This work meant addressing a number of obstacles that had been raised by the officials of the Congregation of Rites and which needed to be answered before the canonical process could continue. The obstacles related to Colin's truthfulness with regard to Courveille's signature on letters written to Rome; his difficult relations with the vicars apostolic in the Pacific; his tense relationship with Julien Favre, the second superior general; and his slowness in completing the Constitutions.[31] Coste was thus faced with some concrete and specific questions relating not simply to historical data but to the complexity of human behaviour.

A Founder Speaks (1975) and A Founder Acts (1981)
A Founder Speaks was published in 1975.[32] Jean Coste, the editor, explains that the purpose of the book is 'to present in as objective way as possible the fundamental themes of a man to whom a good number of men and women look as their spiritual master'.[33] The body of the book consists of talks given by Father Colin at the annual retreats, during informal gatherings, and to certain individual persons. The material comes from the Memoirs of Father Gabriel-Claude Mayet, and is presented in chronological order covering the period November 1837 to September 1854 which corresponds almost exactly with the period that Colin was superior general. This collection of talks gives no analysis

---

30.   Coste, *Lectures*, 132–133.
31.   Jean Coste, 'Brief History of the Cause of Father Colin', in *Forum Novum*, 5/3 (2000): 311–314.
32.   The French original and the English translation were published in the same year, 1975.
33.   Jean Coste, 'General Introduction', in *A Founder Speaks*, 3.

of Colin's personality, but does provide an important resource for understanding Colin's thinking. Theories of cognitive development, part of the field of human development, shed light on a person's way of thinking, their central ideas, their recurring themes and images, personal values and religious ideals. The documents presented in *A Founder Speaks* open the door to the world of Colin's thought.

A Founder Acts was published in 1981[34] as the companion volume to *A Founder Speaks*. An important difference between these books is already indicated in the title. Whereas the first book allows us to hear the voice of Jean-Claude Colin, the sequel shows Colin in action, translating his spiritual insights into concrete decisions, and dealing with problems during the period when he was superior general. *A Founder Acts* covers the same period of time as the previous volume.

Six years after the first publication, Coste's interest in Colin's psychology is even more evident. This may be related to developments in the wider ecclesial environment during the 1970's and 1980's, especially the growing emphasis given to the human sciences as a result of the Second Vatican Council. Coste returns several times to the paradoxical aspects of Colin's personality. He contrasts, for example, Colin's profound spiritual intuitions with a personality 'marked by both light and shade'.[35] Coste suggests that Mayet himself, from 1842, was gathering material not only as a chronicle of events but also for the purpose of making a portrait of Colin's character. Mayet, writes Coste, wanted 'to hand on to future generations of Marists as nuanced a picture as possible of their Founder, just as in everyday life he appeared to those who lived with him, with all his successive changes of mood, his faults and his genius, his obvious limitations and the impact of his astonishing personality'.[36]

What kind of things can we learn about Colin's personality from this material? Coste draws attention to a long article on Father Colin's failings (Doc 235) 'where Father Mayet combines in ingenuous fashion both a profound admiration for his subject and an acuteness of observation in a way that makes the article essential for any psychological study of the Founder'.[37] The following extract from a document titled 'ulterior motives' (*vues ultérieures*), dated 1845, illustrates the skill with which Mayet portrays the paradoxes in Colin's character:

---

34. The French original was published in 1981; the English translation in 1983.
35. Jean Coste, 'General Introduction', in *A Founder Acts*, 18.
36. Coste, *A Founder Acts*, 19.
37. Coste, *A Founder Acts*, 89. See also 30. 85. 88.

When he went to Rome, he knew that the Jesuits were very powerful there, and had they wished, could have blocked his enterprise. He went to see Cardinal Castracane and Cardinal de Bonald, who was in Rome at the time. To Cardinal Castracane he said: 'Your Eminence, whom would you advise me to present my rules to for examination? . . .' and he engineered the Cardinal into recommending Reverend Father Rosaven, Assistant General of the Jesuits. He added: 'Eminence, would you allow me to say that I have come at your behest to submit our rules to him?' The Cardinal agreed. He then went along to Cardinal de Bonald and put the same question to him. The Cardinal replied, 'But you know that Father Rosaven is against you'. 'Indeed, Your Eminence, that is precisely why I would like to call on him'. The Cardinal agreed to Father Colin presenting himself under cover of his name. So off he went to this Reverend Father. Father Rosaven excused himself on grounds of lack of time. Father Colin answered: 'I know it is true that your every moment is most precious, but it is said that you do very easily what another would take such a long time to do'. Then he added that it was Cardinals Castracane and de Bonald who had advised him to call on him. 'At these words,' said Father Colin, 'a faint smile of satisfaction appeared on Father Rosaven's lips and he accepted my manuscript.' [. . .] 'Messieurs,' he said, 'let us act with the spirit of God. The good Lord has told us that we must act with the simplicity of a dove and prudence of a serpent.' As Father Colin did not subsequently present his rules to the Roman Curia to have them approved, Cardinal Castracane asked him, 'What was the use of having your rules examined if you did not want to have them approved?' Father Colin's reply was: 'Eminence, I want to rework them and test them against experience.' To that the Cardinal found no reply and Father Colin had reached the objectives he set himself. He went on: 'Moreover, on my return, I found a great difference in our relations with the French Jesuits, and I knew that they had been instructed from Rome to show an interest in us. Since then these Fathers have been full of kindness and gone so far as to render with great readiness any services we have asked of them.'[38]

---

38.   Coste, *A Founder Acts*, 313–5 (Doc 335).

Mayet uses the expression 'ulterior motives' to capture what is going on in the back of Colin's mind. As with many saints, founders and foundresses, Colin reveals a measure of shrewdness without which great works would never get beyond the realm of pious dreams. Mother Teresa of Calcutta possessed the same quality in the single-minded pursuit of her mission. Colin's rural background helps explain that mixture of affability and astuteness that is often found in country people.[39] But Mayet concludes his reflections with this warning: 'If the words that I am writing here should fall into the hands of the worldly, God forbid, they would interpret them in a merely human fashion, and separating the letter which kills from the spirit which gives life, they would see nothing but cunning and craft in the conduct of the man of God. But it is not for them that I am making these notes.'[40]

Coste's increasing desire to penetrate the mystery of Colin's personality eventually resulted in his 'Portrait of Father Colin' at the end of *A Founder Acts*.[41] Coste himself does not attempt a psychological analysis of Colin but he compiles an extensive index (61 pages) in which he gathers and classifies the elements that might provide the basis for such an attempt.[42]

In this index, Coste has bequeathed to future generations of researchers and biographers a treasury of material, carefully verified and systematically organised. He explains his goal in creating this working instrument:

> Far from wanting to foster in the reader the illusion that henceforth he knows the whole Colin, [*A Founder Acts*] intends merely to document his everyday conduct, his typical approaches as noted by a reliable witness, and by so doing to focus attention not on the man's ideas, but on the person himself and so stimulate renewed studies on his personality. It is possible to envisage monographs, theses, and eventually a thorough-going biography, all of which alone would serve to bring out the true stature of the man whom we aim only to grow a little more familiar with here.[43]

---

39. A dramatisation of these rural qualities is seen in *Jean de Florette* and *Manon des Source* (based on original works by Marcel Pagnol) set in the Provence during the 1920's.
40. Coste, *A Founder Acts*, 313.
41. Coste, 'Portrait of Father Colin', in *A Founder Acts*, 456f.
42. Coste, 'Portrait of Father Colin', in *A Founder Acts*, 456.
43. Coste, 'General Introduction', in *A Founder Acts*, 20–21.

Gioannetti, A Spirituality for our Time (1989)

A Spirituality for our Time was written by Marist Franco Gioannetti during a sabbatical year at the Centre for Marist Studies in Rome. The book consists of five chapters dealing with the history, spirituality, and charism of the Society of Mary. The second chapter of the book is devoted to the personality of Jean-Claude Colin.

The author's intention is to move beyond the historical, social and religious events surrounding Colin's life in order 'to capture the thrust of his personality and to gain a view of him as he lives through his own times and lives once again in ours'.[44] To reach this goal, says Gioannetti, 'we must investigate, reconstruct and relate to one another the links of a chain of deeds and events and lay bare their subtle undertones'.[45]

Gioannetti analyses the impact of Colin's family situation on the development of his character. 'Absence of father and mother always creates a sense of abandonment even though the child's reactions differ according to age, and will be intimately bound up with the experience of the substitute parent. Whatever was the case with Jean-Claude, it is certain that he experienced an enduring affective deprivation, inclining him to introversion, renunciation, flight from reality, and to reliance on compensatory dreams and fantasies'.[46] The author then identifies other manifestations of the inner conflict which deeply marks Colin's personal life and which shapes, in different ways, his attitudes and actions.

Perhaps Gioannetti's most helpful contribution is to bring a developmental perspective to the discussion of Colin's personality, even though he does not explore it very fully. Nevertheless, the second chapter of this book concludes with a succinct explanation of the interplay of the dynamic forces out of which Colin's personality is forged: 'It can be said that on a foundation of insecurity, due to an unhappy childhood deprived of love, and to a youth full of scruples and interior struggles, to a maturity in which he lived out a role of exceeding importance without wanting to, a spiritual superiority got the upper hand and enabled him to encounter and overcome, encompass or overturn situations with a persistency and self-denial that bear the hallmark of faith, humility, gentleness and firmness typical of those of whom the Scriptures say: 'Blessed are the poor in spirit, for theirs is the kingdom of heaven'.[47]

---

44.   Gioannetti, *A Spirituality for our Time*, 65.
45.   Gioannetti, *A Spirituality for our Time*, 65.
46.   Gioannetti, *A Spirituality for our Time*, 68.
47.   Gioannetti, *A Spirituality for our Time*, 102.

A behavioral approach

At the 1984 Colloquium held in Rome, Raymond Carey delivered a paper titled 'Jean-Claude Colin from the perspective of behavioural psychology'.[48] This twelve page study is divided into three sections. The first section situates behavioural theory among other major schools of psychology with regard to the question of personality. The second section examines several specific episodes from the life of Colin from the perspective of reinforcement theory. The third section raises theoretical and methodological questions and makes suggestions regarding further behavioural research on Jean-Claude Colin.

The paper identifies some important methodological questions, and analyses the principles used by Colin in his leadership and pastoral ministry. The author's stance is deliberately restrictive by denying the validity of other psychological viewpoints; however, behavioural theory, per se, does not provide the comprehensive framework necessary for understanding the whole human person, not only in his natural and earthly dimensions, but also in his supernatural and eternal dimension.[49] Furthermore, advances made in the field of Christian anthropology during the last thirty years, some of which have been absorbed into the Church's magisterium, favour approaches that are dynamic, integrative and holistic rather than limited to the externals of human behaviour.[50]

A framework for psychological analysis

A Christian anthropology

What kind of framework is needed to bring about a deeper understanding of the character of Father Colin? The survey of the literature presented in the previous section of this paper acknowledges the achievements but also the limitations encountered during the past fifty years. Recent studies identify three distinct but converging perspectives regarding the human person: theological, philosophical, and scientific.[51]

---

48. Carey, 'Jean-Claude Colin from the Perspective of Behavioural Psychology', 71–83.
49. Paul VI, Encyclical Letter *Humanae vitae* (25–VII–1968) On the Regulation of Human Life, number 7.
50. John Paul II, 'Allocutio ad Rotae Romanae Auditores coram admissos, die 5 februarii 1987' in *Acta Apostolicae Sedis*, 79 (1987):1453–1459, numbers 2–4; 'Allocutio ad Romanae Rotae Auditores simul cum officialibus et advocatis coram admissos, anno forensi ineunte, die 25 ianuarii 1988', in *Acta Apostolicae Sedis*, 80 (1988) 1178–1185, numbers 2–4.
51. Luigi M Rulla, *Anthropology of the Christian Vocation*, volume 1: *Interdisciplinary Bases* (Rome, 1986), 31–68.

The theological perspective considers the human person in the light of revealed faith and the ultimate destiny to which we are called by God. The philosophical perspective seeks to identify those capacities inherent in the human person that favour the possibility of a dialogue between man and God. The scientific perspective endeavours to explain the concrete structures within society (sociology) and the human psyche (psychology) through which this dialogue is actualised. These three perspectives—taken together, and in mutual dialogue—provide the foundations for an interdisciplinary approach to the human person and the basis for an authentic Christian anthropology which overcomes the tendency of any one science to make an absolute and exclusive datum of its particular contribution.[52]

An interdisciplinary dialogue, by its very nature, is a complex undertaking. The experience of other fields where this has been attempted has highlighted the need to establish a correct method in approaching such a dialogue, since 'collaboration among the different sciences evidently could not come about by means of a simple addition or juxtaposition of the conclusions coming from different disciplines, nor from the external agreement of results obtained autonomously and compared.'[53] Future studies on the personality of Jean-Claude Colin may make considerable progress by adopting the lines suggested here—although this, clearly, requires further explanation and development.

A developmental perspective

Conventional wisdom once believed that human development took place during infancy and childhood and, once the fundamental building blocks were set in place, that adult life stretched out like a long uninterrupted plateau lasting until death. The study of adult life is a relatively recent field of psychological research whose findings show that significant development also takes place during adult life.

Daniel J Levinson, author of *The Seasons of a Man's Life* (1979) captures the dynamic quality of adult life by using two images: the life cycle and seasons. The first image, the life-cycle, conveys the idea of a journey that has a starting point (birth) and an ending point (death). The image also implies that the journey from birth to death is governed by an underlying pattern or a basic sequence. The second image is that of seasons; or alternatively, the acts of a play or the major divisions of a novel. Adult life is not appropriately understood, then,

---

52.   Giuseppe Versaldi, 'The contribution of psychology to canon law', in Franco Imoda (editor), *A Journey to Freedom: An Interdisciplinary Approach to the Anthropology of Formation* (Leuven, 2000): 307–326.

53.   Versaldi, 'The Contribution of Psychology to Canon Law', 308.

as continuous and unchanging block of time but is marked by qualitatively different periods each with its own character. Based on his research, Levinson shows that the human life span passes through a sequence of four periods each lasting approximately twenty to twenty-five years: childhood and adolescence, early adulthood, middle adulthood, and late adulthood. These periods (called 'eras') are partially overlapping so that as one is ending a new one is getting under way. Each era has its distinctive qualities which give a sense of unity and cohesion to the person's life.[54]

The historical studies show that Colin's life falls naturally into four broad periods: his early years (1790–1816), the foundation of the Society (1816–36), the generalate (1836–54), and his last years (1854-75).[55] These broad periods have a duration of twenty-six years, twenty years, eighteen years, and twenty-one years respectively, to give a life span of 85 years. Even though Levinson's research took place in a social context vastly different from that of nineteenth century France, remarkably, the major events that punctuate Colin's life correspond almost exactly to the major life transitions delineated by Levinson.

Adopting a developmental framework thus enables us to explore not just the historical events but also the inner processes at work as Colin's life moves forward: from seminarian to priest, from priest to founder, from founder to superior general, from superior general to wisdom figure.

Continuity and change

A developmental perspective emphasizes the interplay of two elements, continuity and change, that characterise the different stages of a person's life. Colin's psychic life is marked by a dialectical tension which is experienced as an inner struggle between the defensive tendency for self-protection on the one hand, and the profound personal realization that comes from transcendence of the self on the other. As Colin is compelled to respond to the demands that confront him at the different turning-points of his life, the man grows humanly and spiritually—yet he is never totally free from the influence of the deep wounds that are rooted in his early experiences and which have been amply identified by his biographers.

---

54.   Daniel J Levinson, *The Seasons of a Man's Life*, 18–39.
55.   Jean Coste, 'Getting to Know a Founder', in *Forum Novum*, 3/2 (1996): 117–25. Coste has subdivided the third period, the generalate, into six periods demarcated by the 1839 move from Belley to Lyon, the 1842 visit to Rome, the 1845 General Chapter, the 1851 letter of resignation, and acceptance of his resignation by the 1854 General Chapter. See Jean Coste, 'General Introduction', in *A Founder Speaks*, 6–9.

By way of illustrating this developmental dynamic during his adult life, we can examine the events impacting on Colin's development as founder. A brief consideration of five events shows that he assumes the role of founder only through a gradual process over a period of many years. Or, to say the same thing in psychodynamic terminology, the vocation of founder becomes part of Colin's self-identity slowly and progressively.

What are some of the elements in this developmental process? First, the vow to go to Rome, which Lessard dates to the summer of 1819, is a significant element in the process by which leadership of the Marist project becomes associated more with Colin and less with Courveille.[56] Second, his appointment as superior of the College of Belley by Bishop Devie in 1829 weighed heavily upon Colin yet, at the same time, this new role enabled him to receive into the house candidates aspiring to join the Society. Third, his election as the central superior in 1830 shows that Colin is seen also by others as the natural leader and the point of unity between the 'Belley group' and the 'Lyon group'. Fourth, Colin's journey to Rome in August 1833 to make an official presentation to the Holy See of the project is a clear indication of his undisputed role as founder. The fifth event is Colin's election as superior general three years later, 1836. For the next 18 years it will be the role of general that dominates his life, yet Colin uniquely remains the Father Founder—a role that takes on renewed significance during the last period of his life as the growing congregation struggles with the question of the Constitutions.

These historical events, seen in a psychodynamic perspective, point to an inner transformation in Colin's self-concept; from the shy and reclusive youth; from the pious and scrupulous seminarian; from the priest with a rather wooden pastoral style; slowly to embrace—largely against his natural inclinations—the call from God and the Blessed Virgin Mary to be founder of an ambitious religious project. Colin's own testimony reveals that this transformation came about only by struggling with, and eventually transcending, many of his natural instincts and inclinations for the sake of the mission to which he was called. Speaking about his election as superior general three years later, Colin confessed: 'If I could have foreseen that I would be elected superior general, I would be a Trappist today.'[57] And again: 'This blow overwhelmed me, and I have not yet recovered from the stunning effect it had on me.'[58]

---

56. Gaston Lessard, 'Jean-Claude Colin Makes a Vow to go to Rome', in *Forum Novum*, 2/2 (1993): 276–288.

57. Jean Coste and Gaston Lessard (editors), *Origines Maristes* (Rome, 1960–67), Doc 504.

58. *Origines Maristes*, Doc 502.

The developmental approach—located within the context of a Christian anthropology—highlights the interplay of two great existential realities: the first is the call to self-transcendent love; the second is the experience of human limitation. In the person of Jean-Claude Colin we see both realities written large. This gives us a framework that makes it possible to understand how the complexities, paradoxes and apparent contradictions in Colin's character (human limitation) can coexist with many signs of competence, maturity, and holiness (self-transcendence).

A big vision

'Father Colin was a man with a mission, bent on a single great enterprise, one of those men who personify a few big guiding ideas.'[59] The Marist project, from its inception, embodied a big vision. This is its great strength; it is also its great weakness. Colin's willingness to accept responsibility for the evangelisation of Western Oceania reflects the great breadth, and even daring, of the vision. The original plan for a Society with four branches, under one superior general, and aimed at bringing all the faithful under the protection of Mary—a plan rightly questioned and eventually rejected by the Holy See—points to the weakness of a great vision that too easily becomes impractical and unmanageable.

Colin was the personification of this vision although, of course, the other founding figures and indeed many of the first generation of Marists shared and lived the same vision. Father Mayet, for example, had no doubts about this. 'He did things on the grand scale; he took big strides, not mincing steps, and though at times he splashed the man next to him he covered quite a distance before those who worried themselves over details had hardly started; they were still looking where to put their feet!'[60]

Father Coste, like Mayet before him, had an unparalleled insight and understanding into the complexity of Colin's personality. Just months before his own death, Coste declared to the members of the 1993 Marist General Chapter: 'Forty years of studying Colin have shown me, more than to many others, the foibles and important defects of the man. But in spite of that, my affection for him and indeed, let me say, my devotion to him, have never ceased to grow . . . I am convinced that few men in his time served God better than he, and I do think that, whatever happens, I shall keep that conviction to my dying day.'[61]

---

59.   Coste, *Lectures*, 138.
60.   Coste, *Lectures*, 140, citing Mayet, *Mémoires*, volume 6, 421–30.
61.   Coste, 'Brief History of the Cause of Father Colin', 314.

Conclusion

This paper began with a question. How is it possible for us to come to a deeper understanding of the human fabric—the psyche—of a man whom we believe was the human instrument used by God and the Blessed Virgin Mary to bring the Society of Mary into existence and to guide the congregation as its first superior general? That question was followed by two others. If the task of the historian is the elucidation of character, then to what extent have Marist studies shed light on the character of Jean-Claude Colin? To what extent have these studies been able to identify the critical questions, to explore the paradoxes and seeming contradictions, to analyse the events and experiences that have shaped and formed the complex personality of Colin?

By surveying some of the relevant studies, we have seen the slow development of interest in questions relating to Colin's character together with initial attempts to identify and explore critical questions. A key person in formulating these questions has been Jean Coste but now, of course, the questions and further research need to be taken up by others. Any worthwhile presentation should raise as many questions as it seeks to answer. Why, for example, does a paper with the title 'The personality of Jean-Claude Colin' never really get to the point of telling us what kind of person Colin was? Why no psychoanalytic analysis of his defence mechanisms, his relationships with women, his preference to be hidden and unknown? Why no detailed exploration of the many apparent contradictions, or even flaws, in the man's personal relationships.

The short answer to those questions is very simple. I don't think it can be done, at least, not at this point in time. Anyone, of course, can give a psychological viewpoint about some aspect of Colin's personality—but to construct a systematic and balanced analysis which neither minimises what is important nor emphasises what is peripheral, that is quite another matter. For this reason, the underlying thread throughout this paper has been the effort to explain why the question of methodology—which, at base, is a question of anthropology—is absolutely crucial. This, it seems to me, needs to be discussed and clarified as a necessary condition for making the next step forward in seeking to understand the personality of Jean-Claude Colin, Founder and Superior General of the Society of Mary.

Marist Approaches to Mission: Then and Now

Gerard Hall SM[1]

Marist approaches to mission inevitably reflect the prevailing ideologies and theologies of their time. It will come as little surprise, then, that the Marist mission to the Pacific in the mid-nineteenth century looks very different to contemporary Marist missionary approaches. Our task, however, is not simply to contrast these approaches, but to ask the question: is there a specific Marist way of being missionary that expresses continuity as well as transformation? While this same question could be asked of the other congregations and the Church itself, our focus on the Society of Mary provides a case-study with wider applicability.

Marist mission then—nineteenth century

Roman Catholic mission model
The nineteenth century Roman Catholic mission model was as much a child of modernity as it was a reaction to the liberal ideas modernity had spawned. The reactive side was perhaps strongest in France where the upheavals of the French Revolution were most pronounced. It was also the centre of the Ultramontane movement which gave new impetus to papal authority and the universal church in both the theology and politics of the day.[2] The Catholic Church saw itself as the bulwark defending the 'true faith' not only against liberalism and rationalism, but also against Protestantism. If not official theology, the dictum of 'outside the church, no salvation' was firmly entrenched in Catholic missionary theology and praxis. For Catholics, 'the Church' meant Roman Catholic Church. Consequently, the goal of mission was seen in terms of establishing local churches under the authority of Rome and the Pope.[3]

---

1. *Note by the editor*: Gerard Hall was present at the conference from which many of the papers in this volume originate (Suva, 2007). This chapter, however, was written after the event.
2. The 'romanisation of the clergy' was a general movement throughout France. Jean-Claude Colin's own Ultramontane leanings are well known. I have argued elsewhere that Colin's Ultramontanism is linked to his preference for Ligourian moral theology in opposition to the Jansenist rigorism of the Gallican Church. Gerard Hall, 'The Political Dimension of Colinian Eschatology and Praxis', in *Forum Novum* (= FN), 1/2 (1990): 213–40.
3. The Roman Catholic approach to mission in the 'Age of Progress (1792–1914)'

In some ways, this represented a return to the 'Christendom ideal' whereby the Church saw itself as the essential 'civilising' force in the world.[4] However, there are also significant differences indicative of the Church's adaptation to new political realities, especially the rise of the nation-state. As we have seen, the Church distanced itself from a too close identification with national interests. In this, there was an at least implicit acceptance of the Enlightenment principle of separation of Church and state. On the other hand, the Church continued to ride on the bandwagon of colonial expansion; and it shared with colonial powers a belief in the superiority of western culture. As well, both Catholic and Protestant missionaries continued their post-Reformation struggle accounting for their competitive—at times aggressive—approaches towards one another. This was nowhere more evident than in the Pacific where French Catholic missionaries and English Protestant missionaries saw themselves in opposition. This was further compounded by nationalistic agendas in which France and Britain competed for territorial gains across the Pacific.

Theologically, nineteenth century Roman Catholicism was at a low ebb. There was, at the time, no developed theology of mission—or even what we would call today a theology of Church. If 'saving souls' was the prime motivation for mission, the main strategy was one of bringing these 'souls' into the Church through baptism. The approach has been linked to Augustine, medieval theology and a particular reading of Luke 14:23: 'Compel them to come in'.[5] Here, the empirical, institutional Roman Catholic Church is understood as the 'kingdom of God' on earth. The notion of salvation, for which the Church was considered necessary, was both other-worldly and individualistic. This translated into an eschatology focusing on individual judgment and hope of heaven at the end of time. Although stronger in Protestant than Catholic theology, there is also

---

is outlined by Stephen Bevans and Roger Schroeder, *Constants in Context: A Theology of Mission for Today* (Maryknoll NY: Orbis, 2004), 221–7. Also see David Bosch, 'The Medieval Roman Catholic Missionary Paradigm', in *Transforming Mission: Paradigm Shifts in Theology of Mission* (Maryknoll NY: Orbis, 1991), 214–38.

4.   Alois Greiler notes the influence of the 28 volume work of René-François Rohrbacher (1789–1856), *Histoire Universelle de l'Église Catholique* which pictures the Catholic Church's role as beacon of salvation and regeneration of the human race. The work was apparently studied by the Marist missionaries after 1845; information to the author.

5.   Bosch identifies this text for 'missionary purposes' in Augustine and later in the Middle Ages, *The Medieval Paradigm*, 236.

a connection between Christian mission and millennial expectation of the approaching 'end time'—something we also note in Jean-Claude Colin.[6]

Despite what has been said about assumed western superiority, Roman Catholic missionary theology and praxis, even in the nineteenth century, often displayed a degree of cultural acceptance and adaptation that should be acknowledged. One expression of this was the early training and use of indigenous catechists throughout the Pacific. Still, it would be fair to say that the overarching Catholic mission model followed the *tabula rasa* approach which identified the Gospel in predominantly European cultural terms—even though some accommodation to local cultures was admitted. In time, this accommodation transformed missionaries' own experience and praxis.

Colin's Marist mission model

As people of their time, the Marist missionaries to the Pacific operated predominantly out of this Roman Catholic model. It could hardly be otherwise. However, beyond these broad strokes and motivations, we need to explore ways in which Marists understood and expressed their own sense of mission. Such a task, of course, is too huge to cover in a single paper or colloquium—and beyond my competence. My approach here is simply to identify major themes in the missionary spirituality of Jean-Claude Colin, founder and first Superior General (1836–54) of the Society of Mary. This reveals an outline of a particular mission model which puts him at odds with ecclesiastical authorities who favour a different approach. The results of this are particularly significant in relation to the Society's mission in founding the Church in Western Oceania.

Colin himself had a profound sense of mission which related, first and foremost, to the call of the Society to be a catalyst for transformation so that 'there would be seen at the end of time what had been seen at the beginning: *cor unum et anima una*' (one heart and one soul).[7] This idea, often repeated by Colin, sheds light on a number of factors. First, the role is ascribed not only to the priests' branch of the Society: the Marist call included laity, sisters, brothers;[8] and it was further inspired by the utopian vision of 'the whole world Marist'.[9] Second, it refers to the reinvigoration of the Church according to the model of

---

6. Multiple references in Jean Coste (editor), *A Founder Speaks* (Rome, 1975; FS). I have elsewhere reflected on the importance of 'end of time' for Colin in *The Political Dimension*, 213–40.

7. OM 2, Doc. 247, 2; '*cor unum et anima una*' Acts 4: 32.

8. In the original vision, the Society was to be a 'many branched tree', something that Colin, Champagnat, Chavoin and the early Marists all worked to achieve.

9. Often repeated by Colin. See, for example, FS, Doc 1, 1.

the first Jerusalem community: 'we must begin a new Church'.[10] Third, it clearly identifies Colin's missionary call in universal rather than particular terms: it is not confined to Oceania, other 'mission districts' or specific 'apostolic works'. In a word, with reference to Mary's role in the beginning and now at the end of time, he says: 'Let us march at the head of the faithful: this is your mission'.[11] How, though, does such a universal missionary vision translate into Colin's acceptance and administration of the mission to the Western Pacific?

Colin's missionary theology is based on the sense of divine calling that comes from God the Father to share in the mission of the Son who, in turn, confides his mission to the Church represented by the Pope and the Congregation of Propaganda Fide.[12] The papal mandate given to the Society for the missions of western Oceania confirms, for Colin, its place in the eternal mind of God. He never questions this. Equally, Colin understands this call in relation to Mary, mother of God, from whom the Society takes its name: it is she who is true founder, perpetual superior and only model. For Colin, there is no opposition here: 'On the one hand, it is the Son who sends; on the other, it is the Mother'.[13] On other occasions, Colin tells his departing missionaries that while the superior (namely himself) sends them forth, it is actually the Holy Father (the pope) who entrusts them with this mission. Through these multiple mediations of God's will, Colin understands the missionary call to the Pacific as a special grace for the Society; yet he also knows it is God alone who brings people to faith. This is sound Catholic missionary theology for any age.

As Colin accepts the specific mandate for the Society's missionary role in Oceania, he also has particular views about the manner in which that mission is to be carried out. While making due allowances for the special situation in the Pacific (although he never left Europe), he nonetheless reads the Pacific mission in terms of the Society's universal mission. Being concerned to spread the faith according to the model of the first Jerusalem community, Colin's first concern is with the spiritual formation of the Marists themselves. His insistence on prayer, the need to 'taste God', the interior life, 'hidden and unknown', the spirit of Nazareth, sacrifice, self-denial, community, the sacraments and 'the rule' are correctly interpreted today as apostolic principles of mission.[14] Rather

---

10.   Also often repeated by Colin. For example, FS, Doc 120, 1.
11.   Jean Coste (editor), *A Founder Acts: Reminiscences of Jean-Claude Colin by Gabriel-Claude Mayet* (Rome, 1983, FA), Doc 396, 5.
12.   Colin's missionary theology is investigated by Pierre Allard, *Le Père Colin et les Missions* (Ottawa: Université Saint Paul, 1966; MA Diss).
13.   Mayet *Mémoires*, in Allard, *Colin et les missions*, 10.
14.   The work of Jean Coste in this important reinterpretation of Colin, especially

than being opposed to the work of the true Marist missionary, Colin understands these as its very foundation.

Consequently, for Colin, the geographical, cultural and political complexity of Oceania cannot compromise the heart and soul of what it means to be a Marist missionary. This comes to a crisis point and ongoing ache for Colin in his dealing with Bishop Pompallier who wants to separate the missionaries, to send them out one by one in order to cover the geographical dispersal of the Pacific islands.[15] Colin was interested in establishing Marist communities on the model of Mary and the apostles. This has sometimes been incorrectly interpreted as Colin not founding a missionary congregation.[16] The Society itself, as we have seen, was founded for mission; and its very approbation coincided with its mandate for the Oceanian mission.

What was at stake here was the manner of such missionary endeavour. Colin emphasised community because he saw it as the power-base for apostolic mission. Once this principle was established, he was realistic and adaptable. For example, he foregoes his insistence on communities having a minimum of four—but, at least 'there should always be two together on the foreign missions'.[17] Moreover, 'the Rule that we give to our missionaries, Messieurs, will be broad in scope, so that it can be kept'.[18] On another occasion Colin says Marists have 'the vocation of the apostles: a spirit of prayer and action',

---

in regard to *ignoti et occulti* as a principle of apostolic mission, is recounted by Patrick Bearsley, 'From *Ascesis* to *Kenosis*: The Evolution of the Marist Understanding of the 'Hidden and Unknown', in *Forum Novum*, 5/1 (2000): 69–94.

15. See Ralph Wiltgen, 'Tension Mounts between the Marists and Pompallier' in his *The Founding of the Roman Catholic Church in Oceania 1825–1850* (Canberra: Australian National University Press, 1979), 246–66.

16. Wiltgen states that the 'Society of Mary was not founded as a foreign mission society' (522). This is true in the sense that the Society was not founded exclusively for foreign missionary work in the manner of congregations such as the Columbans or Divine Word Missionaries. Nonetheless, Wiltgen makes the judgment that the 'Society of Mary went on to become one of the greatest missionary orders in the Roman Catholic Church, with Oceania as its field of specialization' (548).

17. Colin reports the words of Father Forest on what he (Colin) required. FS, Doc 66, 2. In his official request to Cardinal Fransoni in 1842, Colin asks that 'missionaries ordinarily be not isolated, as they have been for entire years in the past'; rather they should be 'in a group of at least two or three'; cf Wiltgen, *Founding of the Roman Catholic Church*, 248.

18. FS, Doc 141, 15.

adding that he wishes the Society 'to have less time devoted to vocal prayer so as to have more time to devote to souls'.[19] Clearly, though, Colin's model for Marist mission gave priority to the religious quality of life as the catalyst for missionary endeavour.[20] This has been called the 'intensive' versus 'extensive' model of mission.[21]

Colin does not perceive his insistence on personal holiness and community-life as undermining the apostolic, missionary vocation.[22] To the contrary, by focusing on the hidden presence of Mary with the apostles in the early Church, he believes he has uncovered the most effective way for spreading the Gospel in his time—whether in Europe or the foreign missions. He never divorces the idea of Marist spirituality from missionary effectiveness: 'Let those who are leaving for Oceania imitate the apostles; let those who are staying in Europe imitate the early Church'.[23] This is an entirely missionary spirituality requiring great faith and perseverance especially for those assigned to Oceania: 'You are going to leave your homeland, your relatives, your friends, everything, to save souls and suffer martyrdom'.[24] However, to paraphrase, you are not being sent as ones, but at a minimum as twos, so the effectiveness of your mission is safeguarded and enhanced.

We know that Colin selected his best men for Oceania; and that he put much effort into their spiritual direction and formation. We also know that twenty-one of the 117 Marists sent during his time as General died from disease, hunger or more violent means. His personal contribution to the work of the Oceania mission—such as administration, finance and letter-writing—are documented elsewhere; his limitations are also noted.[25] The point I wish to emphasise

19.   FS, Doc. 132, 15.
20.   Hugh Laracy claims that Colin 'expected the Marists, members of a religious order, to have as their primary concern not the active apostolate but the seeking of personal holiness according to the Marist Rule, for which the maintenance of community life and a semi-monastic routine were deemed necessary'. *Marists and Melanesians: A History of Catholic Missions in the Solomon Islands* (Canberra: Australian National University Press, 1976), 13.
21.   These models are developed by David Bosch. See Alois Greiler in this volume.
22.   Stephen Bevans mentions that the original Constitutions for the Society of the Divine Word also named the salvation of its own members as its primary purpose. 'Learning to Flee from Bishops: Formation for the Charism of Priesthood within Religious Life', in *Australian eJournal of Theology*, 10 (Pentecost 2007).
23.   Father Mayet's annotation of Colin's words, 2 September 1848, cf FS, Doc 159.
24.   FS, Doc 143, 4.
25.   For example: Jan Snijders, *A Piety Able to Cope* (private paper, 2007) and other presentations such as Alois Greiler.

is that Colin consistently, if not fully coherently, articulated a missionary spirituality that gave priority to community, witness and presence *for the sake* of the Church's mission. In Marist-speak, Nazareth and Pentecost are co-joined symbols of authentic missionary praxis. This was often not appreciated, nor always followed, in the first century and a half of Marist involvement in the Pacific or elsewhere. However, neither was it ignored but remained in creative tension with the so-called extensive missionary model. Today its power as an effective mission model for Marists (and others) in the Pacific and elsewhere is more clearly recognized.

Marist mission now — twenty-first century

The Catholic Church's renewed call to mission
Nobody doubts the immense changes that have occurred in both the world and the Church in the past century. Two world wars, the rise and fall of communist and fascist states, post-colonial independence and liberation movements, technological and communication revolutions, advances of globalism and secularization, the population explosion and the greatest migration of people in human history, cultural and religious resurgence of indigenous traditions and 'non-Christian' religions together signalled the end of assumed European cultural and religious supremacy. There is also the post-modern challenge that provides an intellectual rationale for deconstructing all universal claims to truth or validity, whether cultural, religious or otherwise. Catholic and Protestant Churches alike have been challenged to deep soul-searching of their missionary motivations and strategies in light of these wider agendas.

The response of the Catholic Church is epitomized by Pope John XXIII's convocation of the Second Vatican Council in 1962 where over a third of the twenty-three hundred bishops attending came from Africa, Asia and Oceania. The Council affirms the missionary character of the Church by locating it in the mystery of the Trinity: 'It is from the mission of the Son and the mission of the Holy Spirit that she draws her origin, in accordance with the decree of God the Father' (*Ad Gentes* 2). Since the Trinity is the source, origin and goal of Christian mission, what then is the role of the Church? In the Council's view, the Church is called to be universal sacrament of God's saving presence in the world. The goal of mission then is not the Church itself, but God's reign in the world, a reign which cannot be restricted to membership of the Church. We are reminded it is Christ, not the Church, who is 'light of the world'. The Church's mission is to be sign and instrument of Christ's illuminating presence (*Lumen Gentium* 1) — both within and beyond the visible Church.

The Council also enriches the Church's theology of mission by acknowledging the importance of local churches, diverse cultures, interreligious dialogue, liturgical inculturation and integral human development. There is new emphasis on people's freedom in view of the Church's aim to bring Christ's freedom and peace to people. Missionary activity is now described in terms of witness, solidarity, mutual encounter and enrichment (*Ad Gentes* 26). The conquest model of mission is replaced by the model of reciprocity in which we 'learn of the riches which a generous God has distributed among the nations' (*Ad Gentes* 11). This also means the Church's missionary agenda is set by listening to the 'hopes, joys, griefs and anxieties' of all people (*Gaudium et Spes* 1). In particular, it is through dialogue we learn to speak the Gospel in ways the modern world will understand.

Post-conciliar thinking about mission is focused on the complex interaction between gospel, Church and culture. Paul VI's 1975 apostolic exhortation, *Evangelii Nuntiandi* (EN), describes mission as 'evangelisation': the aim is to bring 'the Good News into all the strata of humanity' (EN 18) through direct proclamation, authentic witness and profound dialogue with culture. Importantly, the Church begins the process of evangelisation by 'being evangelized herself' (EN 15) so as to be formed into the community of Jesus' disciples. We have seen that this is also central to Colin's missionary model: Nazareth and Pentecost belong together as symbols of authentic missionary praxis. However, today it is more clearly recognised that the evangelization of cultures includes the work of justice, peace and liberation. This document also gives prominence to the roles of local churches and popular piety in the Church's evangelising mission. Finally, we are reminded that 'the Holy Spirit is the principle agent of evangelisation' (EN 75).

The diverse situations in which the Church is called to live out its evangelising mission are enunciated in John Paul II's 1990 missionary encyclical, *Redemptoris Missio* (RM). He distinguishes three distinct types of mission: 'mission *ad gentes*', for those who have not heard the gospel; 'pastoral care', for established communities of faith who always require ongoing evangelisation; and 're-evangelization', for those who have lost contact with their Christian roots (RM 33). More specifically, he calls for new methods and expressions of evangelisation directed to particular groups—the urban poor, youth, immigrants, refugees, women and children—as well as cultural sectors—communications, peace, development, rights of minorities, liberation of peoples, scientific research and international relations. Ecumenism and interreligious dialogue are integral to the Church's evangelizing mission; base Christian communities are also seen as a force for evangelisation.

There are three metaphors which help us draw together these various threads for the Catholic Church's renewed call to mission.[26] The first is the 'sending out' image of mission highlighted by classical missionary approaches. It is based on solid biblical foundations: 'As the Father sent me, so I send you' (John 20:21). This gives priority to evangelisation through direct proclamation of the Gospel. It most clearly resembles the 'extensive' model of mission most prominent at the time of the Society's foundation.

The second is the 'gathering in' image epitomised in the life of the first Jerusalem community, later monastic communities and the newer charismatic-type movements. The emphasis is on evangelisation through witness, worship and fellowship. This is most closely aligned to the 'intensive' mission model which, in broad terms, has been identified with Colin's own approach to Marist mission.

The third image is one of solidarity or 'walking with' people, especially with those on the margins of society, something at the heart of Jesus' own life and mission. Today, solidarity manifests itself in dialogue with cultures and religions, option for the poor, work for peace and reconciliation, respect for creation and care for the earth. I will call this the 'tensive' or 'dialogue' model of mission which has taken on a new urgency in light of the massive humanitarian and ecological challenges confronting the world today.

Whether we speak in terms of metaphors, images or models of mission, these are not necessarily oppositional. Models, for example, can and often do overlap.[27] Recent Church teaching makes it clear that all three approaches—which we are naming proclamation, witness and dialogue—are considered essential for the Church's single, evangelizing mission. Moreover, it is clearer today than in the nineteenth century that all Christians are called to mission. However, in this new world, the challenge is to develop strategies for mission in response to one's particular gifts, charisms and opportunities. The very complexity of the Church's missionary agenda, as well as the diverse situations in which we are called to live the gospel, demand of us deep discernment and courageous decision-making in regard to setting and enacting our Christian missionary vocation. This is also our task as Marists at the start of the twenty-first century.

---

26.   See Donal Dorr, *Mission in Today's World* (Dublin: The Columba Press, 2000), 186–192.

27.   In this regard, I would argue that while Colin gives priority to the 'intensive' model of mission, he is also aware of the need to include aspects of the 'extensive' model, especially in regard to Oceania. The purer 'intensive' model is more properly applied to monastic communities which were never the vision of Colin.

Marist mission today

Demographically, the Society of Mary today, in terms of numbers and age-profile, is dominant in the 'south'. Its missionary outreach to Oceania is now reversed: the periphery has become the centre so that Oceania is becoming the major source of missionaries to other lands. In terms of the Society's original mission, the Catholic Church is now well established in those parts of the Pacific for which it bore responsibility as founding missionaries. Elsewhere, in Asia, Africa and South America, there is evidence of small growth in the Society which is contrasted to declining numbers and aging members in Europe and North America as well as Australia and New Zealand. However, with the Church itself, the missionary focus of the Society of Mary is undergoing significant change in response to the kind of culture shock and mission reevaluation identified by Robert Schreiter as ferment, crisis and re-birth.[28]

The 2001 Marist General Chapter produced a document entitled 'Declaration on the Mission at the Beginning of the Twenty-First Century'. Earlier Society documents, such as the 1988 Constitutions, recognize that Marists are called to form a 'communion for mission' (36–56), to be a Marian presence in the Church (15–21) as Mary has been since the days of Pentecost (5). They are called to be 'truly missionary' (12), to 'establish the Church where it does not exist and to renew existing communities' (14). Marists are to be 'fired with apostolic zeal for the Kingdom' (23). They have special concern for the sick, imprisoned, neglected and those who suffer injustice (12). By being 'hidden and unknown in the world' Marists are able to hear the longings of God's people and discern the signs of hope in today's world (22–25). The importance of the hidden virtues, the vows, prayer, humility, learning and unity in the Society is given emphasis (26–29; 93–113). Any Marist meditating on the Constitutions will surely be inspired by the return to Colinian themes of a profound spirituality for mission today.

However, it is only in the 2001 Declaration that mission is enunciated in terms of deep dialogue with cultures, peoples and religions. Here we learn that 'Marists wish to listen to and understand other Christian Churches and other religions' (7). Further, 'we want to enter into dialogue with them and all persons of good will in order to work together for mercy, reconciliation, justice and

---

28.   Schreiter identifies four periods of Catholic missionary approaches which he names: certainty (1919–1962); ferment (1962–65); crisis (1965–75); and rebirth (1975–). Robert Schreiter, 'Changes in Roman Catholic Attitudes toward Proselytism and Mission', in James Scherer & Stephen Bevans (editors), *New Directions in Mission and Evangelization 2* (Maryknoll NY: Orbis, 1994), 113–25.

peace' (7). Moreover, Marists are committed to work for 'full participation of the laity in the mission of the Church' (16) and especially for the 'dignity of women and their participation in the Church and in all walks of life' (15). With the rest of the human family, Marists are also committed to work for 'human rights' and 'the integrity of creation' (14). Here, we find the Society beginning to articulate its mission with a closer eye on conciliar and papal documents, including those of the two Pontifical Councils for Interreligious Dialogue and the Evangelisation of Peoples.[29]

Some of these themes, especially the importance of dialogue, are further developed at the 2005 General Council of the Marists in Mexico. In fact, we are told our 'ministry of evangelisation . . . should follow a path of dialogue' at all levels of life, action, exchange and religious experience.[30] The Society is called to 'increase its contribution to evangelisation among non-Christians' (3) and to consider the feasibility of 'implantation in a predominantly non-Christian area' (15). Prominence is also given to developing 'partnership with the laity as missionaries and as active collaborators in its evangelizing task' (4). This is a vision for Marist laity that is genuinely Colinian.[31]

Unless I am mistaken, a point of omission in all three documents is specific mention of the Church's and Marist responsibilities in relation to indigenous people. At any rate, there seems little reflection in official Society documents in this regard.[32] This is something that needs to be rectified in future articulations of the Marist mission of evangelisation—not least on account of our history in Oceania and the significant commitment of many provinces and districts to this most Marist of works.[33]

---

29.   These two Pontifical Councils produced an important joint document, *Dialogue and Proclamation*, in 1991.

30.   Council of the Society of Mary, 2005, Policy Document on Mission, No. 2. These levels of dialogue reflect the document of the Secretariat for Non-Christians [later elevated to the Pontifical Council for Inter-religious Dialogue] on *Dialogue and Mission* (1981), no 42.

31.   See Frank McKay's *The Marist Laity: Finding the Way Envisaged by Father Colin* (Rome, 1991). Two more radical expressions of laity involvement in the Society's evangelising mission are: Marist Mission Ranong on the Thai-Burma border where two of the six members of the community are Lay Marists; and Australian Marist John Hopkinson's community of Lay Marists in Bolivia, South America.

32.   Of course, the importance of Oceania in the mission of the Society is acknowledged (for example, Council of the Society 2005, 7–9); I am here referring mainly to indigenous people who are minorities in their own countries.

33.   In this regard, the ground-breaking missionary work of former Marist Superior

From this brief survey of recent Society documents, two movements can be recognised. The first is the reclaiming of Colinian themes that re-establish the essential missionary charism of the Society. We have seen here significant emphasis on an 'intensive' approach that sees personal conversion and community life as primary instruments of apostolic mission. Marists are asked to be missionary not just by doing 'works of mercy', but by inculcating Mary's own virtues and attitudes in order to bring the new Church to birth. The second movement is one which responds to the wider Church's agenda and renewed call for mission. This requires deep dialogue with other churches, religions and peoples. It also calls for specific commitment to inculturation, liberation, reconciliation and the ecology. This 'tensive' or 'dialogue' approach to mission is now recognised as central to the Church's and the Society's own evangelising mission.

Conclusion: continuity *and* transformation

It is clear that the Church's understanding of and approach to its mission have undergone enormous change since the nineteenth century. The weight of this change is particularly strong in the Catholic Church since the Second Vatican Council. An outsider looking in might suggest we now have a different Church. In some ways this is true. The Church has made many transformations since the days of the apostles. Without agreeing that every change has been good, the fact is that unless the Church changes and adapts to the emergent world it finds itself in, its life and relevance will have little meaning beyond the remnant who wish to keep things in some kind of time capsule.

Still, if it is also true that the Church continues to have a mission to this emergent twenty-first century world in which we live, this is because its unchanging message of proclaiming and witnessing to God's reign has, if anything, even more relevance today. However, proclamation and witness are not enough. We have a new call to dialogue and engagement with people of all cultures, traditions and religions. We might be spooked by the challenges this brings. Here, though, we will do well to remind ourselves that we are not the bringers of the kingdom: only God can do that since it is 'the Holy Spirit who

---

General, Bernard Ryan, in working with Australian Aboriginal people, a mission now supported by the three Pacific provinces, needs to be acknowledged. The New Zealand province has a long and distinguished record of mission work with Maori people which stretches back to the original Marist mission under Bishop Pompallier. See the presentation of Mervyn Duffy in this volume. There are other examples such as Marist missions in Brazil, the Philippines and North America.

is the principal source of evangelization' (EN 75). Equally, it is the Holy Spirit who is the principal source of continuity and transformation in the Church.

This, at least, I take to be the central inspiration of Marist mission in our world. Some things are essential and, to that extent, unchanging. Marists are called to 'see, think, judge and act as Mary in all things', especially in their evangelising mission. This requires a deep commitment to the interior life, epitomised for Colin in the home of Nazareth and the first Jerusalem community, where Marists discover their true missionary calling. It is here their hearts are set on fire with apostolic zeal for spreading the Gospel and where they learn from Mary the 'hidden and unknown' way of responding to the challenges of their times. To this extent, the 'intensive' model of mission will always have a certain priority in Marist missionary praxis.

However, like the Church itself, Marists are also called to transformative missionary praxis identified by the 'tensive' mission model's emphasis on dialogue and engagement with others. In the words of the Constitutions:[34]

> The Society is no longer true to its calling whenever it becomes so caught up in particular works as to cease to be available for more urgent needs to which it may be called by its mission.

Those 'more urgent needs' are currently knocking at the Society's door in a manner equivalent to the urgency to go to Oceania and the Bugey region of France in the nineteenth century. As the Church called us then, the Church calls us today, not to a particular region or country, but to a new manner of mission in solidarity with the poor, the marginal, refugees and other victims of violence and oppression. It calls us to this mission in dialogue with people of every race, tradition and language. Moreover, it is this model which most requires of us conversion of mind, heart and spirit; and it may well provide the avenue whereby the laity feel themselves called to be active collaborators with us in the Church's evangelising mission.

The Society of Mary has never existed for itself. Since its foundation, the Society has only ever seen itself as a catalyst for the mission of the Church. Today, it is challenged as never before to reincarnate its original vision in a manner that responds to the urgent but very different needs of our time and world. We should not get too caught up with models, but return with fresh eyes to interpret our mission anew in light of Mary's role at Nazareth, Pentecost and the 'end of time'. That is the deep continuity that Marists today share with Jean-Claude Colin and the first Marist missionaries. To keep the vision alive, it needs

---

34. Constitutions of the Society of Mary, 1988, no 14.

to be transformed according to the newly articulated mission of the Church and the very different challenges that confront us in the twenty-first century.

Catholic Beginnings in Oceania

Declan Marmion SM and Alois Greiler SM

Three key elements, ritual, event and content (introduced by reflections on the method and historiography) can summarise the reflection on 'Catholic Beginnings in Oceania'.[1]

The Ritual Dimension

The program of the conference reflected the theme and the place by means of a ceremony following local custom and protocol. The inaugural address by Father Rafaele Qalovi called on Oceania Marists to reflect on the past in view of the missionary élan in the present. The *sevusevu* entailed a welcome to all the participants, with the bowl of kava offered to the representatives of the guests. The *veiqaravi* in the presence of one of the major Fijian chiefs, Ratu Filimone Ralogaivau, in effect linked the group with the wider Oceanian context. The final Eucharist with the archbishop complemented this link. These ceremonies expressed in ritual and speech the relevance of the colloquium for the local churches and particularly for our Fijian hosts. Celebrating the liturgy together also strengthened the bond between the participants themselves and added a spiritual dimension to the event.

Engaging with the colloquium as event

This coming together of experts and listeners, religious and laity from around the world was marked by renewing of old contacts and the making of new ones. In a relational culture as is found in the Pacific this aspect was not just a matter of courtesy but was crucial for the event. The format of the week aimed to facilitate sharing and personal reflection. Space was allowed for interaction including question and answer sessions and group sharing. The many young faces of different colours reflecting various Pacific cultures made a big impression on the participants from Europe. Yet, whether student or expert, old or young, all shared the common concern to re-discover the story of the early missionaries. All were listeners, yet each could find his or her own voice.

---

1. Text based on the summary by Declan Marmion SM at Suva 2007.

On the content of the colloquium

Method and historiography

The theme focussed on the years of generalate of the Marist founder, Jean-Claude Colin, from 1836 to 1854. This demarcation is necessary for any evaluation. In short, the question was: What can we learn about Colin's and the first missionaries role in the origin and development of Catholic Christianity in Western Oceania? The development of Catholicism and the Marist experience in Oceania are strongly intertwined and thus the conference was both Marist and Pacific in its orientation. Not all pertinent themes could be explored.

A variety of methods were used with history as the starting point. The story element in history linked in with the narrative culture of the Pacific. Heretofore much Marist work in this area had been intended for spiritual edification and personal reflection.[2]

Research on Catholic beginnings in the Pacific is now on a much firmer basis thanks to the editorial work of Charles Girard (LRO), the source material edited by Edward Clisby for the Marist Brothers, and Gaston Lessard's 'Colin sup'.[3] However, the letters (LRO) also have their limitations: letters to superiors—originally not intended for a wider audience—tend to focus on difficulties and needs rather than on positive aspects. Nevertheless, they do present us with an insider's view of missionary life. Also, the missionaries were no homogenous group.

Pacific history and Pacific Church history reveal certain trends.[4] As Michael King pointed out in the case of New Zealand, the Catholic contribution was often undervalued. Similarly, Margaret Knox stressed the broader impact of the Catholic Church particularly in education and health services.[5] Also, the

---

2.	See the survey Alois Greiler, *Zwischen Geschichte und geistlicher Erneuerung. Umschau zu neueren maristischen Studien*, in *Marianum*, 52 (1997): 571–600.

3.	Edward Clisby (editor), *Letters from Oceania. Letters of the First Marist Brothers in Oceania 1836-1875*, ten parts (Auckland, 1993–2005); Gaston Lessard (editor), *'Colin sup'. Documents concernant le généralat du père Colin*, volume 1, *De l'élection au voyage à Rome (1836–1842)* (Rome, 2007); Charles Girard (editor), *Lettres reçues d'Océanie par l'administration générale des pères maristes pendant le généralat de Jean-Claude Colin*, 10 volumes, 2009.

4.	Examples in Dough Munro – Brij V Lal (editors), *Texts and Contexts. Reflections in Pacific Islands Historiography* (Honolulu: University of Hawai'i Press, 2006).

5.	Michael King, *God's Farthest Outpost: A History of Catholics in New Zealand* (Penguin Books, 1997); Margaret Knox, *Voyage of Faith. The Story of the First 100 Years of Catholic Missionary Endeavour in Fiji and Rotuma* (Suva:

specific French contribution is sometimes overlooked—Patrick O'Reilly was a pioneer in bringing this to the fore.[6] John Hosie and Hugh Laracy pointed out the sometimes untapped Marist sources.[7] The Marist contribution highlights faith as the driving force for the missionaries. A second element came out less clearly. Colin and the first Marists were religious and gave priority to a spiritual life in common according to their rule or constitutions.

Introducing Colin and the theme

Alois Greiler emphasised a point that recurs with others, namely, Colin's desire *to safeguard the spiritual dimension of Marist religious life*. The Marist retreat house at La Neylière testifies to this as does the rule that a Marist community is to have no fewer than four priests and a number of brothers as well.

This stress on the Marist spirit, or on what used to be called the 'interior life,' impinges directly on Colin's *model of mission*: to live as a religious community following the Marist rule, to evangelise by presence, witness and catechesis. It was not a question of occupying as many virgin missionary territories as possible before the Protestant 'sects' could get there ahead of Catholic missionaries. Still less did he envision Marists living as isolated individuals as he thought this would undermine their identity as religious. Greiler referred to the first Marist chapter in New Zealand in 1841 which discussed not mission policy, but the daily rule. Of course we might feel today that Colin's view of salvation and spirituality is an overly individualistic one. Nevertheless, his point holds good: without a sound spiritual foundation our particular way of life makes little sense and our apostolate is unlikely to bear lasting fruit.

Archdiocese of Suva, 1997); Philip Turner, 'The Politics of Neutrality. The Catholic Mission and the Maori 1838–1870' (thesis, University of Auckland, 1986).

6. Mary C Goulter, *Sons of France: A Forgotten Influence on New Zealand History* (Wellington: Whitcombe and Tombs Ltd, 1958); John Dunmore (editor), *New Zealand and the French. Two Centuries of Contact* (Waikane: The Heritage Press Lt, 1990); John Dunmore, *Visions and Realities: France in the Pacific, 1695–1995* (Waikanae, Heritage Press, New Zealand, 1997); Hugh Laracy, 'Patrick O'Reilly: Bibliographer of the Pacific', in Gl Cropp, Noel R Watts, Roger DJ Collins, Kerry R Howe (editors), *Pacific Journeys. Essays in Honour of John Dunmore* (Wellington: Victoria University Press, 2005), 97–106, here 104.

7. John Hosie, *Challenge: the Marists in Colonial Australia* (Sydney: Allen & Unwin, 1987; on Bishop Polding and the Marists in Sydney); Hugh Laracy, 'The Archives of the Marist Fathers - An Untapped Source of Material on the History of the Pacific', in *Journal for Pacific History* 3 (1968): 165–71; *Id.*, 'The Archives of the Marist Fathers. Addenda', in JPH 5 (1970): 158–9.

These Colinian convictions were amplified by Carlo Maria Schianchi. Firstly, the Marists in the vicariates of Oceania are *members of a religious family*. They are not diocesan priests. They are not directed by bishops. They depend on a religious superior. Secondly, the Marists are *called to community life*. They are not to be dispersed, isolated, or alone. Colin stressed this from the outset. The apostles, whom Jesus sent out in pairs, are to be their only model for evangelisation. The Marists are to be *at least two together*. Thirdly, while it might be necessary in exceptional circumstances, the isolation of missionaries is not to be accepted as the norm. The Society of Mary is a religious congregation and the essentials of religious life were not to be lost from sight. Colin wanted his men to be able live out what he saw as the core of their vocation, namely their personal sanctification and the salvation of their souls.

Major issues around Colin and Oceania

John Broadbent has offered in this volume a nunanced response to the crucial question of Colin, Marists and their relationships with political powers.[8] Aside from his personal inclinations for the monarchy, Colin operated mainly in France and in a pragmatic rather than opportunistic way. His interest was *the spiritual and material welfare of his men* and the spiritual benefit of spreading the gospel, not the expansion of a nation state or even the numerical growth of souls. Broadbent contends that Colin was a major player in the founding and development of the Catholic Church in the Pacific. Though he laboured in France his influence was felt in Oceania albeit in an indirect way. This influence is reflected in his choice of missionaries and bishops, the spirituality into which he inducted his men, and the general guidelines he gave them in order to resist the temptations of political success. All this had a lasting influence on the various Marist founders of local churches and their *modus operandi*. This was a style of Church marked by Colin's Marian approach, yet also a style that reflected the values of the French Revolution. France supported Marists in their identity as French citizens rather than as missionaries and permitted missionary activity in as much as this indirectly supported French colonial and military interests. Of course, these mutual interests overlapped in many ways. Politically Colin was pragmatic and astute. He did not want his missionaries perceived as agents of the French government. His initiatives had a lasting and positive effect in

---

8.   Broadbent speaks of France as the only European power Colin dealt with. We could add in a certain sense the Papal States, a power at the time, even if seen by Colin spiritually. Douarre proposed the Pope to take on New Caledonia as a colony.

what was a pluralistic religious situation. France was not the only power in the Pacific; in fact, no one power had hegemony.

Likewise, Jessie Munro has dealt with a specifically problematic issue, namely, *the fractious nature of the relationship between Colin and Pompallier*. It ultimately forced the issue of the demarcation of authority: to define clearly the respective powers of a vicar apostolic or bishop and the superior general or provincial. Clearly Colin felt let down by Pompallier to whom he had entrusted his men. His reservations about Pompallier's suitability to take on such a role seem to go back a long way. In essence, he believed his men were not in good hands while with Pompallier. He felt Pompallier did not understand or take seriously the role of the religious superior as the 'soul of the Society'. Munro sensed that Colin was justified in his uneasy feelings about Pompallier. Pompallier was, in effect, annexing his Marist confreres and placing them solely under his own authority believing that he was answerable only to the Holy See. For Colin, this subordinated the Marist vocation. And, given that the Society was still in its infancy and had no body of knowledge from which to draw, it is not surprising that problems arose.

Colin, in contrast to Pompallier's rather exalted and autocratic style, advocated a spirit of simplicity. As he wrote to Pompallier in 1836: 'Remember the poverty and simplicity of the apostles; they too were bishops and yet they often worked with their hands to provide the basic necessities of life. Simplicity, poverty and zeal must always be the companions of the missionaries of Mary . . .' For Colin, a bishop in the mission was to be more a missionary than a bishop. It seems Pompallier had a deep-seated need to control and he consistently alienated his priests. It is not as if he was dealing with a group of radicals; indeed, the Marists were initially reluctant to raise a critical voice against their superior and bishop. It is to Colin's credit that his men were willing to unburden themselves to him and that he took a firm stance on the issue even if it left him feeling rather disillusioned.

Not that Pompallier was without his achievements. His rapid success with the Maori and the high esteem in which he was personally held all testify to a charismatic character who knew how to exploit his Episcopal status to the full in his missionary task. Even Colin had to acknowledge as much. Further, as Jessie Munro points out, 'His name will always be linked to the Treaty of Waitangi's "Fourth Article" on freedom of religion for European and indigenous peoples, and to a gradualist and tolerant approach in Christian witness. His 1841 "Instructions for the works of the mission" stands as a historical mission document of careful reasoning and insight, which helped form Marist mission perspective.'

Colin shaped Catholic life, the notion of 'Church,' and local churches by the spirit he imbued in his men. While Pompallier and Colin differed on many points of internal affairs, not very unusual for strong personalities and pioneers, Colin's stance would ultimately be vindicated.[9]

The theme of rifts and failure resurfaces in Hugh Laracy's 'Colin and Melanesia'. Not that failure was the final word. It was rather that the early missionaries expected too much too soon. They were ill-prepared for what awaited them and we read of complaints to Colin of the mission being poorly managed and having a lack of direction. These problems were only compounded by *interpersonal rivalries and squabbles*, a real Achilles' heel of the early missions. Not all the problems that led to an initial failure were internal however. As Laracy puts it, 'Melanesia was characterized by diversity, fragmentation and multiplicity . . . a region that contained many large islands; and was inhabited by people speaking a multitude of different languages.' Add to this endemic malaria and the reigning mutual hostility between the various local tribes and it is not hard to see the vulnerable position in which the early Marists found themselves. Even if Bishop Epalle went as part of the largest single group Colin ever sent to Oceania, they had little to go on by way of prior knowledge and preparation. Laracy narrates their sad fate, with Epalle mortally wounded less than three months after the group left Sydney in October 1845. It was, in Laracy's words, a quixotic, visionary and faith-driven enterprise. Epalle and others were not afraid to 'think big'. While some might regard the venture as foolhardy, the early missionaries were willing to take the risk of being killed for the sake of planting the seeds of the gospel.

Even so, Colin had decided not to send any more missionaries to Oceania after 1849 and instead to consolidate the Society in Europe. Some missionaries were redeployed elsewhere in the Society, for example in New Caledonia and in the newly-opened Marist house in London. There was a positive institutional legacy in a new ecclesiastical configuration of the region and the arrival of other missionary orders. When the Marists returned to the Solomons in 1898 a pattern of European contact had been established and security was less problematical. The risk to 'think big' was ultimately successful.

---

9.   Munro herself pointed this out in an answer to a question from the audience. See also the story Colin–Polding, in John Hosie, *Challenge*, and Jessie Munro, 'Jean-Marie Grange, Clerc de Saint Viateur in New Zealand', in Gl Cropp, Noel R Watts, Roger DJ Collins, Kerry R Howe (editors), *Pacific Journeys: Essays in Honour of John Dunmore* (Wellington: Victoria University Press, 2005), 107–123.

Here hindsight reveals achievements hidden by the initial lack of outward success. This links in with the faith and religious motivation of the early Marists. Only their faith enabled them to endure so many difficulties and setbacks without giving up. The Marist spirit, their religious zeal, and fidelity to the rule, even to the point of martyrdom, needs to be acknowledged in order to do these missionaries justice. Here again the contribution of Colin is evident both indirectly and over the long term.

Relations within the Marist family and with other Christian denominations in Oceania

The Society of Mary, in its original inspiration at least, is wider than the branch of the Fathers. Edward Clisby treatment of *the invisible men of the missions*, that is to say, the contribution of the Marist teaching brothers and the Marist coadjutor brothers in Oceania during the generalate of Father Colin. He explored their relationship with one another and with the Fathers in the context of the missionary project. At this stage, the term 'Society of Mary' applied to all the branches of the Marist project. When Colin suggested a separate group of 'Joseph' brothers to be primarily at the service of the priests, it did not meet with support from Champagnat. When Colin asked him to release a brother for sacristy work and when Champagnat was not forthcoming, Colin accused him of being 'too fixed on certain points'. The reverse is probably the case. The separation was approved however in 1839. Nevertheless, good relationships between the Hermitage and the Fathers continued.

The same was true for the overseas mission where the separation did not have much impact. The little Brothers of Mary continued to work alongside the Fathers. Clisby concludes that 'the Oceania missions can be seen as part of a common or shared history and [why] the Society of Mary can justifiably include these men in its necrology.'

If the Brothers were seen in official circles at least as 'catechists', this is not how they were remembered. Rather, it is in their various trades—as builders, blacksmiths, and particularly in the area of printing—that they made a decisive impact on the work of evangelization. Many of the Pacific peoples were initially more attracted to the material benefits offered by a European tradesman than they were to his spiritual message. It led one Father to conclude that in the beginning 'a brother in the islands . . . is more useful than a father, and if Wallis is converted, it is rather to Brother Joseph than to Father Bataillon that we owe it.' Success in Oceania came at a great cost to the Brothers however, with a sizable proportion either leaving, dying, or being killed.

While, on the whole, the story is one of good working relationships, there is a negative side and it has to do with how some of the Fathers treated the Brothers as little more than domestic servants. Many Brothers also suffered difficulties similar to the Fathers, *isolation and difficulty accessing the sacraments.* Pompallier liked to draw clear distinctions between Fathers and Brothers to impress the status-conscious Maori, while the Church at the time was perceived in a very hierarchical manner. None of this helped the Brothers despite Colin's comments regarding the Brothers as 'members of the same body.'

Another aspect of our story is Colin's attitude to *women missionaries* or better the possibility of women missionaries. Catherine Jones in her case studies of four significant women traced how Colin received mixed messages about whether to send women missionaries. Pompallier initially asked Colin to send some sisters but it was not long before he too had reservations. It seems these have to do with problems we have met before, *the dangers of isolation and loneliness.* Colin's own attitude appears to be one of reticence. This had partly to do with the contradictory information he received from Oceania and Rome about whether or not to send women out at an early stage to the missions. He would neither encourage nor discourage and did not feel God had entrusted this particular task to him. Not that any of this prevented a woman like Marie Françoise Perroton from going; she simply went, and Colin was informed afterwards. There seems to be a certain ambiguity regarding women missionaries, captured in Bishop Bataillon's understated comment: 'I was not really annoyed to see Mademoiselle Perroton arrive in Wallis.' The bias seems to be that women are more liable to be fanatical and unreliable but Perroton punctured that particular stereotype. Women like Pauline Jaricot gave essential support to the missions and her organisation financed many of Colin's missionaries.

In terms of today, an important point Jones makes is the value of undertaking projects as a *Marist family* rather than always thinking in terms of our own particular branch. Her case studies reveal the missionary and *collaborative* nature of Marist spirituality.

What was the *ecclesiology* of these early Marist missionaries? The title of Mervyn Duffy's 'The Work of Mary against the Devil' clearly indicates to us that the early Marists, whatever they were, were not pioneers in ecumenism! They learned the ecclesiology of their time which restricted salvation to Catholics. They were, in Pompallier's words, the only 'true and legitimate missionaries' over and against the Protestant sects and were fighting a battle for souls under the banner of Mary. Of course this rather sectarian mentality was not confined to Catholic missionaries. What is interesting is how Pompallier and others were able to adapt this 'official line' in certain circumstances so as not to jeopardize the success of the mission. Thus that part of the 'true vine' canvas (used by Pompallier and other missionaries as a catechetical tool in New Zealand) pointing to hell, was glossed over—possibly in view of the impending *Treaty of Waitangi* and its emphasis on freedom of religious expression (rather than giving a privileged place to Catholicism). Also, in his 'Instructions for the work of the mission', Pompallier urges his men to 'Be steadfast in controversy, but gentle and honest in your approach' (to non Catholics). There is evidence even at an early stage of recognizing good faith outside the Church.

All this does away with stereotypes. Not all brothers were treated badly by the priests. That Colin did not send women does not imply that he was opposed to such an idea. He was simply not in a position to make an informed decision. And finally, if Marist missionaries set out with a defensive ecclesiology, they were nonetheless capable of developing their teaching in a more open direction.

Cultural and psychological perspectives

From the historical background discussions we move to modern perspectives on 'Colin and Catholic beginnings in Oceania'. The rituals, venue and the various inputs helped to see the multicultural nature of the missionary presence.

Mikaele Paunga's talk confronted the hagiographic reading of the martyrdom of Saint Peter Chanel and other Europeans with a reading of aspects of missionary behaviour as culturally offensive and demanding compensation. Paunga offered four quite graphic examples of how the early missionaries were often unaware of various *cultural taboos,* with dire consequences in some cases, and how they operated with rather patronizing conceptions of the natives to whom they had come not only to bring the gospel but also to civilise. Certain Pacific values, for example the importance placed on community and on respect for elders, the affinity to the divine and to the natural environment, concepts of work and time, etc. were thrown aside. The early Marists were *influenced by a mentality similar to that of the colonizers.* He also sees the process of Westernisation accelerating today with a growing sense of confusion among Pacific people. God and morality are relegated to the private sphere and the supreme value is the right to choose. This is the context in which the Gospel will need to be preached not only in Europe but also in the Pacific. Such an interpretation can only be further developed through ongoing dialogue by all concerned. The process and outcome of such dialogue will determine to what extent the colloquium can be deemed to have been a success.

Costello directed us to the person of Colin, in many ways the focus. He presented the complexities of Colin's character and the difficulties associated with any psychological assessment of him. By any standards Colin is a complex, contradictory and an elusive figure. Despite his natural inclination to be in the background, he was conscious of being a human instrument used by God to bring the Society into existence and to guide it as its first superior general. In that sense, as Jean Coste has pointed out, Colin was 'a man with a mission, bent on a single great enterprise . . .' He was a passionate type who lived only for the Society. He had difficult relationships with many of the other key players in the development of the Society. Yet despite this, those closest to him, like Mayet, felt that they were in the presence not only of a great man but of a saint. Costello provided an outline of psychobiography, the interplay between character and circumstances as a model to read the role of a personality like Colin, a personality we need to see from a faith dimension. Earlier attempts at a psychological reading followed topical models. We already have a lot of data and with additional material we will be in a position to pursue a rigorous psychological study of Colin. For now we can point to some traits of Colin that reveal a leader capable of transcending personal weaknesses for his one passion, the Society of Mary. Although Costello left the audience without the psychological portrait they probably expected, he was still able to bring Colin the leader alive while at the same time underlining the importance of an exact and serious methodology.

The final paper by Gerard Hall discussed Marist approaches in missiology. The initial Marist mission to the Pacific reflected the nineteenth century Catholic mission model which stands in stark contrast to the renewed missionary focus of the Church today. Recent Marist documents reflect this change by reclaiming the essential missionary charism of the Society and responding to the Church's new missionary agenda. While this represents a transformative missionary praxis, there is deep continuity with the Marian symbols of Nazareth, Pentecost and the 'end of time'. For Marists, this means re-emphasising the 'intensive' approach to mission favoured by Colin as well as commitment to 'dialogue' as equally crucial dimensions of Marist mission today.

Questions for further research

As we have aleady mentioned, many topics related to the theme cannot be explored here. Work remains to be done — and this is possible given the extensive documentation now to hand.

The papers bring to light some invisible actors, lay people and local people who deserve our attention and merit further research. Their names are not always recorded, their role not always mentioned. The Poyntons in Hokianga, the Cliffords in Wellington, the Irish Catholics in Sydney, Peter Dillon and his voyages, and the settlers in the present-day Hamilton diocese in New Zealand[10]

10.　　Hugh Laracy, 'The Settler Church', in D O'Sullivan–Cynthia Piper (editors), *Turanga Ngatahi. Standing Together. The Catholic Diocese of Hamilton 1840–2005* (Palmerston North: Dunmore Press, 2005), 37–45 (names of the first

all facilitated the arrival of the Marists. Added to that, local catechists, Protestant and Catholic, inculcated the faith in the various villages and islands, helped the priests and translated for them.[11] Examples include Mosese Monatavai in Fiji, isolated for years but who persevered in his faith. Catechists from Fiji went to Vanuatu to begin the process of evangelization. The women of Wallis invited French women to come and Perroton discerned this as her call. We admire Léopold Verguet's drawings of nineteenth century Oceanians but do we know their names? Is it now opportune to write on 'Catholic beginnings' in the Pacific from their perspective? Even whalers, traders and beachcombers deserve a closer examination concerning their role in the acceptance of missionaries on the islands and the consequent cultural changes that took place. Thomas Boag facilitated the landing on Futuna.[12] The missionaries cooperated with the traders and sometimes offered an alternative to their often negative example as Europeans. The Marists started a 'reduction' (settlement for Catholics) in New Caledonia to protect local people from the negative influence of other Europeans.

Thus Marists were not operating in a *tabula rasa* situation. The islands themselves were marked by internal warfare, were undergoing varying degrees of cultural change and shifting political alliances. In New Zealand the Maori had come to adapt to European business practices prior to the economic crash

---

settlers); John Hosie, *Challenge*; Owen O'Sullivan OFMCap, *Apostle in Aotearoa. A Biography of Father Jeremiah Joseph Purcell O'Reily, OFM Cap. Wellington's first Catholic Pastor* (Auckland: The Word Publishers, 1977); Lillian G Keys, *Philip Viard: Bishop of Wellington* (Christchurch, 1968), 26.

11.   Hugh Laracy, 'Roman Catholic 'Martyrs', 190: Adviser who counsels Niuliki to accept Chanel and Marie-Nizier on the island, and 193, catechist Sam Keletaona, and the former catechumens of Chanel contribute to rapid conversion of Futuna after 1841; Hugh Laracy, 'The Missionary Position: Messengers of Grace and The Works of Ta'unga', in Dough Munro–Brij V Lal (editors), *Texts and Contexts: Reflections in Pacific Islands Historiography* (Honolulu: University of Hawai'i Press, 2006), 127–139 (Works on indigenous missionaries in the Pacific, mainly Protestant); *One Hundred Years of Mission: The Catholic in Vanuatu, 1887–1987*, nd; JMR Owens, 'Maori as Missionary: A Whanganui Case Study', in Gl Cropp, Noel R Watts, Roger DJ Collins, Kerry R Howe (editors), *Pacific Journeys*, 124–134.

12.   Stressed by Munro and by Jack Lee, *The Bay of Islands* (Auckland: Reed Books, ³2006); For Boag see books on Peter Chanel. See now Susan Williams Milcairns, *Native Strangers: Beachcombers, Renegades and Castaways in the South Seas* (Auckland: Penguin Group, 2006).

(due to the change of capital from Russel to Auckland)—a crash that partly explains Pompallier's financial difficulties at the time.

Key players like Colin and Pompallier were responding to, and living in, a complex and difficult situation. Their relationship went through different stages over many years and one or other incident should not be singled out as typical of their relationship without examining the broader picture.

As far as Colin is concerned, we need to move away from the childhood image of the timid orphan and gain a greater appreciation of the person elected into leadership, engaged in a world-wide missionary work, politics, church affairs, material concerns and the nitty gritty of human relationships. For Pompallier, we would need an edition of his writings to get a more rounded picture of the man and his legacy.

Concluding remarks

The Great Australian Clock in the Queen Victoria Building in Sydney is the world's largest hanging clock. It tells the story of Australia from the perspective of both Aboriginal and European settlers. Something similar is now possible for 'Catholic Beginnings in Oceania' thanks to the new source editions. This will change Pacific studies not only in the religious but also in many other fields.

What emerges is the new importance of Oceania in the founding story of the Society of Mary. Is it time to include 'Oceania' with 'Fourvière, Cerdon, Bugey' as a fourth foundational symbol? Oceania illustrates the founding vision: the involvement of the wider Marist family, the missionary thrust, meeting the real needs of people, the Church as international, the Marist charism not confined to France but relevant to other cultures—all these factors seem to point to a fourth founding symbol. It is from Oceania that the provinces of England and Germany were founded.[13]

Future work will bring even more to the fore the 'invisible men and women' associated with the beginnings of the faith in Oceania. The Brothers, the Sisters, and the local catechists played a much greater role than is generally appreciated. Their work in schools, in the areas of health, trades, in developing local contacts, all point to a social model of evangelization. In part this is reflected in Colin's emphasis on the importance of Brothers for Oceania.

---

13.   Chaurain and Bernin returned from Oceania to start a Marist house in London (1850), and Karl Flaus (1865–1920) from the North Solomons who started a Marist house in Germany; *Festschrift 1900–2000: 100 Jahre Maristen in Deutschland* (Passau, 2000), 24–35.

A key to understand Colin in his myriad responsibilities is the word 'pragmatic'. Colin was not opportunistic nor given to colonial enthusiasm. Here he could refer to the words of the Gospel about using the wisdom of this world for the upbuilding of the kingdom. However, he saw a clear limit to this practice. The religious vocation of the Society of Mary was his primary criterion. His support for the missions was only in jeopardy when this criterion, namely, Marist religious and common life, was at risk. This criterion is reflected in the tremendous fidelity of the first missionaries in the face of immense difficulties. It was their spiritual life, the training they received from Colin, and their fidelity to the Marist rule of life and their congregation which enabled most to persevere despite illness, persecution, internal tensions, and martyrdom. In this sense Colin's emphasis on Marists as men of God proved prophetic.

Though never having been to Oceania, Colin was soon regarded as an expert on this region. Propaganda Fide accepted him as a consultor and took note of the men he recommended to be bishops in the missions. His humanity shines out as he struggles to cope from afar with ongoing and seemingly insurmountable problems. Not having been to Oceania made it difficult for him to acknowledge that the European way of doing things might not work in Oceania. This places his role as founder of the Catholic Church into perspective. To evaluate his role we need to see his position and standing in France, his indirect influence via his men, and his ongoing influence beyond the period of his generalate and lifetime. The more data and facts we have, the more likely we are to avoid polemic and prejudice in our assesement of his decisions and of how he handled his many responsibilities. All in all, Colin emerges as a different personality, much stronger and more signficant than even his own congregation might have imagined. Oceania in many ways highlights his achievements rather than his limitations.

There is no doubt that Colin retained an abiding interest in Oceania alongside a real concern for his men working there. Charles Girard's monumental work of nine volumes of letters of missionaries to Colin only amplifies this. One image that persists is that of Colin's room in La Neylière at the end of his life where on his desk there is *a map of Oceania with his glasses on it*. Perhaps we should leave the final word to Father Colin himself:[14]

> Here my humble effort of my care for the missions comes to
> an end. I loved the missions. Nobody has desired more their
> success and prospering than I did. On our part, we made all the
> sacrifices we could make. It has not been the cannibalism of

---

14.   Quoted by Carlo-Maria Schianchi in this volume.

the locals that has halted our zeal and the number of vocations for the missions. The problems had a different reason. God has allowed this to happen. No doubt, he reserved for the missions abundant blessings in the future. I will not cease to ask this from him in my humble prayers.

Main historical persons and main authors

A

Allard, Pierre, 42n, 61, 204n
Angleviel, Frédérick, 135
Anliard, Jean-Baptiste, 24
Anliard, Michel, 24
Aristide (Brun, Jean), 98
Attale (Grimaud, Jean-Baptiste), 144, 145
Aubert, Suzanne (Mother Aubert), 77n, 134n, 135
Avit (Billon, Henri), 106n, 107, 109, 117n
Awilson, JH, 150

B

Baker, Thomas, 171, 172, 173
Ballara, Angela, 73, 79n
Barnabò, Alessandro, 50
Basile (Monchanin, Michel), 85
Bataillon, Pierre, 11n, 31, 60, 81n, 93, 101n, 113, 118, 119, 126, 128, 130, 131, 140, 170n, 174, 222
Baty, Claude, 81
Beaglehole, John Cawte, 95n
Belich, James, 65n, 72n, 78n
Berger, Gaston, 189
Bernin, Claude-Marie, 16
Bertrand, Claude-Marie (Claude-Marie), 114, 118
Bevans, Stephen, 202n, 206n, 210n
Binney, Judith, 79n
Boag, Thomas, 225
Borne, Raymond, 106
Bosch, David, 10, 202n, 206n
Bourjon, Michel, 24
Bourtot, Bernard, 19n, 67n, 107n, 108n, 116n
Brasseur, Paule, 11n
Bréhéret, Jean-Baptiste, 4, 120
Broadbent, John Vincent, 19n, 176, 177n, 178n, 218
Browning, Robert, 94
Broughton, William, 79n

The Contributors

John Vincent Broadbent, Catholic priest of Wellington diocese, New Zealand; after parish work he obtained a doctorate in 1976 (Leuven); lectured church history in New Zealand and Fiji.

Edward Clisby FMS, Marist brother, New Zealand, engaged in historical research for his congregation. He translated the letters of the first Marist brothers in Oceania.

Timothy Costello SM, New Zealand Marist, involved in formation of religious and priests. Since 2002 he teaches at the Institute of Psychology at the Pontifical Gregorian University in Rome. He also teaches in Melbourne and Auckland.

Mervyn Duffy SM, Marist priest from New Zealand. After teaching in secondary schools, he has obtained a doctorate from the Gregorian University in Rome. He lectures in theology at Good Shepherd College, Auckland.

Ratu Filimone Ralogaivau, Fiji, a chief from the island of Vanua Levu, Bua province, and member of the council of chiefs of Fiji.

Charles Girard SM, Marist from the USA. He holds a doctorate in French literature. After pastoral work and teaching, he edited the documents on the history of the Third Order of Mary (1993) and 1300 letters of the Marist missionaries from Oceania, 1836 to 1854.

Alois Greiler SM, German Marist. After pastoral work he obtained a doctorate from Louvain (Belgium) in 1998 on Vatican II. At present he works as Marist historian in Rome.

Gerard Hall SM, Associate Professor of Theology at Australian Catholic University, Brisbane, Qld, is editor of the Australian *eJournal of Theology*. He specializes in interreligious dialogue.

Catherine Jones SMSM, Missionary Sisters of the Society of Mary. She holds a degree in education (USP, Fiji) and a Masters degree in Church History (CUA, Washington DC).

Hugh Laracy is Associate Professor in the History Department of the University of Auckland, New Zealand. In 2005, he won the John Dunmore Medal for 30 years of research (with a special focus on the Society of Mary in Oceania). He published widely in this field.

Declan Marmion SM, Marist priest from Ireland with a doctorate in theology from the Catholic University of Louvain (Belgium). He is lecturing in the Milltown Institute of Philosophy and Theology, Dublin, Ireland. He published on Karl Rahner SJ.

Jessie Munro, New Zealand, where she teaches French and researches religious history. In 1997 her biography of Mother Aubert won the Montana New Zealand Book Award.

Mikaele Paunga SM, Marist priest from Tonga. He worked in parishes and formation. After his doctorate (Greogriana, Rome) he is now teaching at the Pacific Regional Seminary, Suva, Fiji. He published on local theologies and Vatican II.

Rafaele Qalovi SM, Fiji/Rome, assistant general of the Society of Mary.

Carlo-Maria Schianchi SM, Italian Marist. He did pastoral work in Italy and Venezuela. He is the archivist of his congregation in Rome and gives retreats in Italy and abroad.

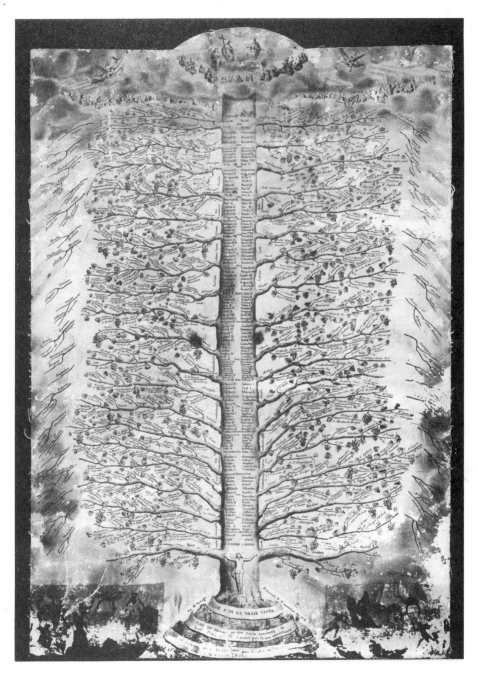

'The true vine', catechetical tool used by Pompallier and early Marists in New Zealand (Catholic diocese, Auckland)

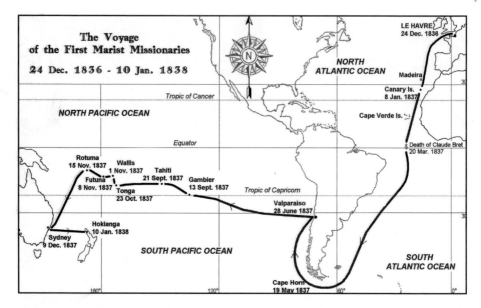

Voyage of Bishop Pompallier and the first Marist Missionaries (copy in APM)

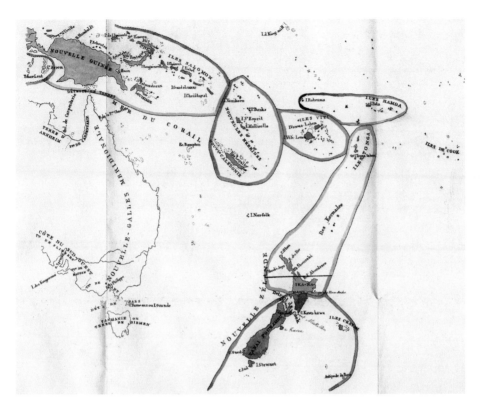

Planned vicariates in 1847, from a report by Bishop Pompallier for Propaganda Fide in Rome (copy in APM): Nouvelle Guinée (Papua New Guinea), Iles Salomon (Solomon Islands with Santa Isabella), Nouvelle Hébrides (Vanuatu) and Nouvelle Calédonie (New Caledonia), Iles Viti (Fiji), Iles Hamoa (Samoa), Iles Tonga, the northern part of New Zealand with Shouki-Anga (Hokianga) and Bai des Iles (Bay of Islands), and the eastern part of Australia (Nouvelle-Galles Meridionale) with Port Philipps (Melbourne)

Jean-Claude Colin (1790-1875), Marist founder, Pompallier's pro-vicar in Europe, and consultor for Rome for the Oceania mission (APM)

Jean-Baptiste-François Pompallier (1801-71), first vicar apostolic Western Oceania, founding bishop in New Zealand (copy in APM)

Pope Gregory XVI (1831-46) who entrusted the Marists with the apostolic vicariate of Western Oceania (APM)

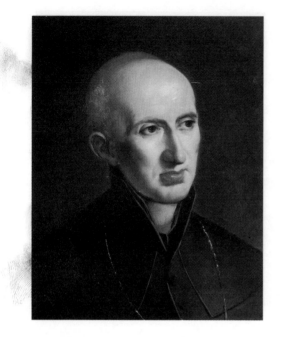

Giacomo Filippo Cardinal Fransoni (1775-1856), Cardinal prefect of Propaganda Fide, Rome (copy in APM)

Pierre Chanel (1803-28 April 1841), among the first Marist missionaries, called 'the man with the good heart'. Canonized in 1954 and declared patron saint of Oceania (APM)

Pierre-Marie-Louis CHANEL
Prêtre de la Société de Marie
missionnaire et provicaire apostolique en Océanie.
Né le 12 Juillet 1803 a Cuet Ain, et mis à mort en haine de
la foi le 28 Avril 1841 par les Insulaires de Futuna

Jeanne-Marie Chavoin (1786-1858),
foundress of the Marist sisters

Marcellin Champagnat (1789-
1840), Marist priest, Saint,
founder of the Marist Brothers

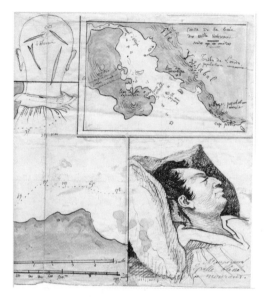

Martyrdom of Bishop Jean-Baptiste Epalle (1808-45) in Melanesia (by Léopold Verguet, missionary, eye-witness; APM)

Bishop Guillaume Douarre (1810-53) opened a Catholic mission in New Caledonia three times. This group left in 1848 (APM)

Marie Françoise Perroton (1796-1873), Marist
lay woman from Lyon, first woman missionary,
began the movement which led to the Missionary
Sisters of the Society of Mary (SMSM)

Léopold Verguet, 2 Maoris from New Zealand (APM)

Léopold Verguet, design of an Oceanian (Museum of La Neylière).

Léopold Verguet, Martyrdom of Brother Blaise Marmoiton, Balade, New Caledonia, July 1847 (APM)

Léopold Verguet, Villa Maria, Marist office Sydney, logistic base for the Marist missions (APM)

Pauline Jaricot (1799-1862), inspired the Propagation de la Foi, fund raising organisation for foreign missions in Lyon, which financed also the Marist missions.

Palazzo Propaganda Fide, where Colin and the bishops negotiated with Cardinal Fransoni (reproduced from Origines Maristes 1, p. xl).

Chief Filimone Ralogaivau receives gifts of welcome at the opening ceremony, Suva, 2007 (photo: private)

Colloquium Suva 2007 (photo: private) – young and old church – participants from various continents

Colin desk (for the insert) (photo: private)